# THE WAY THINGS WORK BOOK OF THE COMPUTER

*An Illustrated Encylopedia of*
*Information Science, Cybernetics*
*and Data Processing*

SIMON AND SCHUSTER ● NEW YORK

Original German language edition entitled *Wie funktioniert das? Information*
© 1969 Bibliographisches Institut AG Mannheim. This translation and adaptation by C. van Amerongen, M.Sc., A.M.I.C.E., copyright © 1974 George Allen & Unwin Ltd. All rights reserved, including the right of reproduction, in whole or in part in any form.

The periodic table on page 57 is reproduced by permission of Doubleday & Company, Inc., and William Heinemann Ltd. from *Moseley and the Numbering of the Elements* by Bernard Jaffe, copyright (c) 1971 by Doubleday & Company, Inc.

Published by Simon and Schuster
Rockefeller Center, 630 Fifth Avenue
New York, New York 10020

SBN 671-21900-6
Library of Congress Catalog Card Number 74-11702
Designed by Helen Barrow
Manufactured in the United States of America
Printed by The Murray Printing Company, Forge Village, Massachusetts
Bound by The Book Press, Brattleboro, Vermont

1 2 3 4 5 6 7 8 9 10

# A FOREWORD FROM THE PUBLISHERS

*The Way Things Work Book of the Computer* explores and explains the history and development of information science — a broad field that is summed up in the popular imagination by the word "computer."

Readers of *The Way Things Work* Volume Two may recall that in the Foreword to that book, we mentioned being at work on the preparation of *The Way Things Work Book of the Computer* — which you now see before you. Whether familiar with Volume One*, Volume Two or both volumes in this best-selling series, the reader will recognize in this new book the same very helpful format.

In part this book is concerned with the science underlying the development of the machines: the problem of finding a suitable theoretical set of concepts associated with the interlinking of information, communication and documentation. The numbered equations that run through the book will illustrate various mathematical interrelationships for the sophisticated reader. The 2-color drawings facing the text will help readers at every level of sophistication follow the discussion.

In part this book describes the practical applications that have grown out of the theoretical principles. We view the computer as the central technological innovation of our time. Even those of us least informed about modern technology recognize that our lives are touched by one or another of the many machines of the computer family. The records of our charge accounts, our gas and electricity consumption, our telephone use — all are kept in data banks, and once a month "the computer" sends us a bill. The records of many businesses, including publishing houses, are now kept by computers. The typesetting of this book was done by a method of film typesetting similar to those described on page 210. But there are many more applications of computer science, and among those described in this book are applications in the fields of biology, economics, linguistics, physiology, sociology and teaching.

---

* British title, *The Universal Encyclopedia of Machines;* American title, *The Way Things Work.*

A popular notion is that computers are thinking machines, or mechanical brains. As we learn from the article on artificial intelligence (see page 234), there is a vital aspect of human thinking that has yet to be captured in a computer: the irrational element. "Heuristic" or trial-and-error programming has been introduced. (Chess-playing computers are in this category.) "Adaptive heuristic" programming—enabling a computer to alter its own circuitry—is an intriguing possibility. While the "thinking machines" fall short of duplicating the marvels of the human brain, they do serve as instructive models, suggesting theories to explain the still little-understood way in which the brain functions.

Pierre Bertaux has formulated the fundamental difference between human intelligence and the intelligence of the "thinking machine" as follows: "There is hardly any human activity that could not be done by machines—except for one: asking questions." If your questions have to do with computers, with information science, with cybernetics, with data processing—*The Way Things Work Book of the Computer* will prove a rich source of information.

# CONTENTS

# THE WAY THINGS WORK BOOK OF THE COMPUTER

# INFORMATION AND DOCUMENTATION

Because of the way we use it in everyday speech, the word "information" produces a number of specific mental associations. Bound up with its use in the sense of "communication" or "report" are such derived words as the verb "to inform," that is, to communicate knowledge about events or facts, and the adjective "informative," meaning that a communication has a high information content, while "informant" is a term describing a person who supplies information. The word "information" itself is derived from the Latin "informare," meaning literally "to give form to" or, metaphorically, "to give expression to" something. When information is given, an event or a set of facts is described in a form that can be communicated from one person to another.

The term "information" has, in present-day usage, come to denote a comprehensive concept – a whole complex of concepts. Closely linked to it are the concepts of "communication" and "documentation" (Fig. 1). Communication comprises methods and procedures for the transmission of information, while documentation refers to the methods of storing information and making it accessible as speedily as possible whenever it is required. The original means of communication and documentation are human speech and memory. Speech can, however, transmit information only as far as its sounds will reach and as far as the human being who utters the speech can travel. Also, it depends on the extent to which the brain is capable of receiving, comprehending and storing the information. Thus speech offers only relatively limited scope for the propagation of information. When recalled to the conscious mind, the information stored in the memory may, moreover, be found to contain errors which are due to limitations of the human memory itself – for example, such errors as wholly or partly forgetting certain items of information, or confusing them with others. For this reason, at an early stage in the history of the human species man already looked for other ways and means of communication and documentation in an effort to supplement and extend the capabilities of speech and memory.

Among the earliest aids to the transmission of messages are smoke and fire signals, or the beating of drums. In these methods we already find applications of what is now generally referred to as coding, that is, the linking of speech concepts to particular signs or symbols – whether they be long and short puffs of smoke, or flashes of light, or different drum notes whose meanings vary according to their rhythm (Figs. 2a-c).

To aid his memory, and to store information reliably and free from error, man discovered and developed the art of writing; he used particular signs or symbols to represent the sounds of the spoken language, another example of coding. In the Babylonian empire these signs were pressed into soft clay tablets as cuneiform writing (Fig. 3a), while the Egyptians used hieroglyphs which they drew on papyrus (Fig. 3b). Great libraries, such as the famous one that flourished in Alexandria, were established in ancient times and became veritable storehouses of the accumulated knowledge of many centuries. During the Middle Ages Arab and Christian scholars collected and disseminated the knowledge of antiquity through the medium of writing inscribed on parchment, a material prepared from the skins of sheep and other animals. How great an advance was achieved in this respect, particularly for Western civilization, by the invention of printing, probably by Gutenberg around the middle of the 15th century, can well be imagined (Fig. 3c).

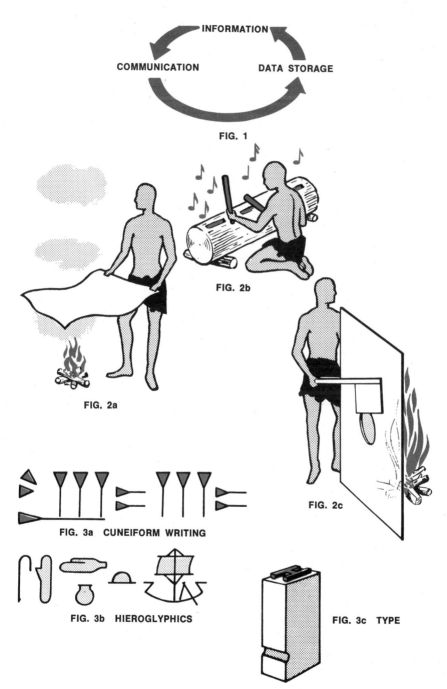

INFORMATION

COMMUNICATION

DATA STORAGE

FIG. 1

FIG. 2b

FIG. 2a

FIG. 2c

FIG. 3a  CUNEIFORM WRITING

FIG. 3b  HIEROGLYPHICS

FIG. 3c  TYPE

Meanwhile the art of paper-making had become widely known, providing a cheap and plentiful material to receive the printed word. As a result, the amount of information stored in books and other documents in libraries increased greatly. Catalogues, and indexes of names and subjects, enabled the seeker of information to find the documents he required. But the sheer volume of information continued to grow apace.

According to recent estimates, the sum total of human knowledge was doubled in the first half of the 20th century. It took only another ten years, from 1950 to 1960, for it to be doubled again. By 1969 it had doubled yet again (Fig. 4). The flow of information is increasing exponentially; it can be disciplined and kept under control only by means of new methods and techniques. It has now become impossible for any one individual to keep track, even of the literature that appears in his own specialized professional field of work or research. New methods of communication and documentation have been evolved, and continue to be evolved and elaborated, in order to achieve the speediest and widest possible dissemination and storage of information and to ensure that those who wish to use this stored information can have access to it quickly and conveniently (Fig. 5).

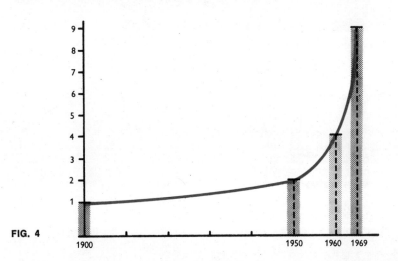

FIG. 4

Every new problem requires new ways and means of solution — which, though they be based on existing conceptions and methods, improve these and raise them to a higher level of effectiveness as a result of new insight — so emerged a new procedure for solving the problem of ordering, sifting, storing and communicating the vast spate of information: cybernetics. This word was introduced in 1948 by Norbert Wiener, to denote a science of communication which is concerned with the transmission and control of information in the widest sense. It is derived from the Greek "kubernētēs," meaning "steersman," which is also the root of a number of other words, as for example the Latin "gubernator," the English "governor," and the French "gouverneur." Wiener did not originate the term "cybernetics" (it was coined by Ampère, the 19th century French physicist), but he revived it and used it to denote a theory concerned with patterns of information, communication, and control systems. An alternative designation, which is coming into widespread use, is "general information theory" — possibly because the first applications of cybernetics proved to be of great value in developing a theory of the communication of

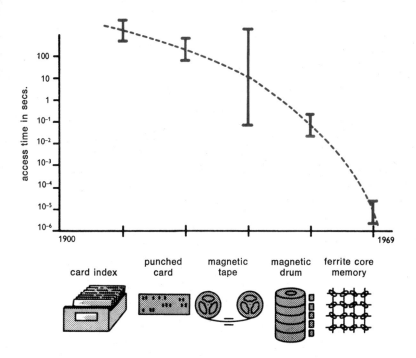

**FIG. 5 ACCESS TIME FOR VARIOUS STORAGE DEVICES**

information, but perhaps also because the term "information" is more deeply rooted in the language and has a more familiar ring.

We know that the problems associated with the interlinking of information, communication and documentation present two main aspects: first, to find the most suitable theoretical set of concepts, together with their mathematical interrelationships; and second, to give practical technical effect to these relationships. Accordingly, the following treatment of the subject will comprise two fundamentally different parts: on the one hand will be discussed the conceptual considerations on which the theoretical principles are based and, on the other, the technical ways and means of carrying these principles into practical effect (Fig. 6). The latter aspect of the subject comes within the meaning of the term "computer science."

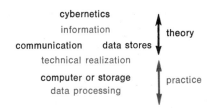

**FIG. 6 SUBDIVISION OF THE SUBJECT**

# INFORMATION AND CYBERNETICS

In order to obtain a clearer picture of the scope and content of general information theory, or cybernetics, we must consider what kinds of thought patterns we normally employ for understanding and describing events, and furthermore, for forming theoretical conceptions that possess heuristic value, which are, in other words, capable of leading us on to fresh knowledge and insight.

Basically, two conceptual patterns are applied. One of these conceives of the phenomena as continuous processes, whereas the other treats them as being of a corpuscular character, that is, composed of a succession of separate elements. These two different views can be illustrated with reference to a familiar example: When we look out of the window early on a drizzly foggy morning, we observe a continuum, namely, a multitude of minute water droplets forming a grey mass that fills the entire field of vision; but when we go outside, we become aware of another manifestation of the same substance (water), namely, the raindrops as separate entities, which undoubtedly constitute a discontinuum, a succession of separate elements. These two manifestations of the foggy drizzle correspond, respectively, to the two above-mentioned patterns.

This correspondence between observation and conceptual pattern can be further illustrated by many other examples. Consider, for instance, a distant field of corn swaying in the wind. This statement in itself indicates that we are not concerned with the individual cornstalks, and that instead we wish to consider the innumerable stalks collectively, as a totality in continuous motion (Fig. 2). Thus the individual "cornstalk" has become submerged in the waving of the "cornfield" conceived as a whole. Only when we look at the cornfield more closely, for instance, through a telescope, which gives an enlarged picture of the phenomenon (but at the same time narrows down the field of vision), does the overall picture of the totality, or "collective," become resolved into a discontinuum in which the stalks are seen as distinct individuals (Fig. 3). This example teaches us a very important fact, namely, that one and the same phenomenon may appear as a continuous process when observed as a whole or, alternatively, as discontinuous, "corpuscular," process when examined in closer detail.

These two conceptual patterns, the continuous and the discontinuous, are encountered in every sphere of knowledge. Arguments as to which of them is the more realistic extend far back into the history of human thought. A well known example is the controversy between Newton and Huygens about the nature of light: Newton supported the corpuscular theory, whereas his opponent favored the wave theory (Fig. 4). Although it subsequently appeared that, in terms of conventional physics, Huygens was "right," the controversy continued until the mid-nineteen-twenties. Modern research has shown that, in this case, the two descriptions are two different ways of viewing one and the same reality: light, in fact, has both continuous (wave-like) properties, and discontinuous (corpuscular) properties.

On closer consideration, it becomes apparent that these two different ways of considering any particular phenomenon are mutually contradictory in terms of logic; they are antitheses. For the concept of the continuum implies that a medium is continuously distributed throughout space, so that a certain density must exist at every point in space. On the other hand, a discontinuum requires that the medium be concentrated in certain regions in the form of "corpuscles," or "particles," while other regions are completely empty, or void (Fig. 5). This has already been exemplified in the case of raindrops and fog, and of cornstalks and cornfield. But common sense tells us that a medium cannot, at one and the

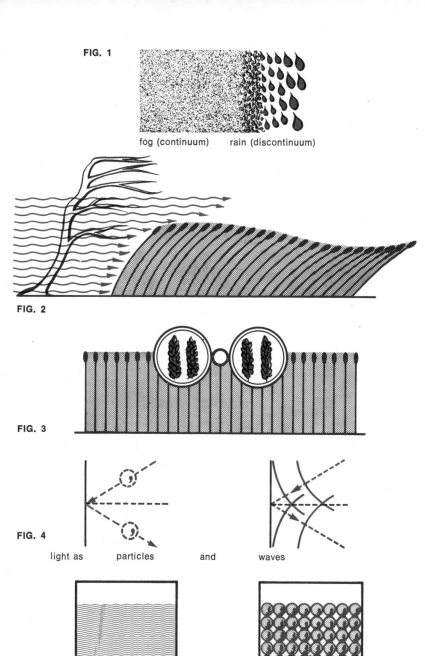

FIG. 1

fog (continuum)    rain (discontinuum)

FIG. 2

FIG. 3

FIG. 4

light as    particles    and    waves

continuum    discontinuum

FIG. 5  DISTRIBUTION IN SPACE

7

same time, be continuously distributed in space and yet be discontinuously concentrated in certain regions.

In the case of light and other electromagnetic waves the resolution of this dilemma was achieved only by interpreting both hypotheses on a higher plane of thought, to the exclusion of conventional reasoning at the level of antithetic contradictions. Indeed, this is the intellectual step to which modern physicists have inescapably been compelled by the results that their experiments have yielded. These results lend equal support to the continuum theory of light (so-called wave mechanics) and to the discontinuum theory (so-called quantum mechanics). The intellectual step involved consists in regarding both outlooks as of equal value and in conceiving the different pictures that emerge from them as different aspects of one and the same underlying but transcendental reality (Figs. 6a and b). Although we can thus achieve a closer and closer approximation to that reality, it will never be possible to penetrate to its transcendental core.

These considerations seem far removed from our present subject. Yet actually they form the background and the foundation on which general information theory — cybernetics — is based. In the eighteen-twenties, the mathematician J. B. Fourier showed that the mathematical description of any discontinuous phenomenon can, for purposes of analysis, be transformed by a rigorous procedure into a mathematical description of a continuous phenomenon (Fourier's theorem). This process has already been presented here, in a visualizable form, in the example of the cornfield (Fig. 2). In our consideration of plausibility we have, however, also envisaged the inverse process: that of resolving a phenomenon into the individual sub-phenomena of which it is the overall manifestation. It was not until 1948, however, that the mathematically rigorous — and therefore general — validity of this inverse process was demonstrated. It was then that Norbert Wiener furnished the required proof and established his theorem as the inverse counterpart of Fourier's theorem (Fig. 7a). He showed conclusively that any continuous progression can be resolved into discontinuous sequences (Fig. 7b).

Wiener's theorem constitutes the basis for general information theory. Its importance, in the purely formal sense, is first and foremost that all processes which we have hitherto (for good reasons or simply from habit) regarded as continuous, and have therefore described in terms of wave phenomena, can now, alternatively, be validly conceived as the totality, or overall manifestation, of individual — discontinuous — pulse-like phenomena. The indefiniteness of the continuum thus gives place to the countable precision of the discontinuum. Countable processes are, however, susceptible to statistical interpretation; approached through cybernetics, then, the whole field of phenomena that had previously been described only in terms of continuity at once became accessible to statistical analysis.

Another simple example may serve to clarify these abstract points. When we look from a distance at a flock of sheep guarded by sheepdogs (Fig. 8a), we cannot distinguish the individual sheep, but merely see a "collective," a totality of individuals, which is in motion, the shape and course of which is controlled by the dogs. On approaching the flock and obtaining a close-range view of the individuals and their behavior, we perceive how the dogs exercise control over them. The animals at the edge of the flock are methodically chased inwards by the dogs and bump into their neighbors; these sheep, in turn, pass the "message" (the directed push) to other sheep in their immediate vicinity, so that eventually the whole flock is brought under a controlling influence, exercised by an external agency (Fig. 8b).

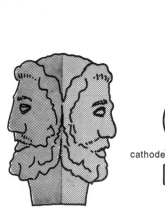

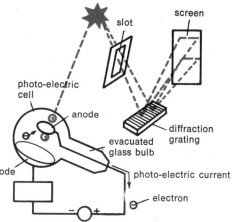

FIG. 6a
THE GOD JANUS SYMBOLIZING
THE EQUIVALENCY OF TWO
DIFFERENT WAYS OF VIEWING
THE SAME PROBLEM

FIG. 6b
LIGHT CONCEIVED AS PARTICLES
WHEN MEASURED WITH A PHOTO-ELECTRIC
CELL AND AS WAVES WHEN REFLECTED
BY A DIFFRACTION GRATING

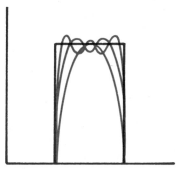

FIG. 7a REPRESENTATION OF A
FUNCTION BASED ON
FOURIER'S THEOREM

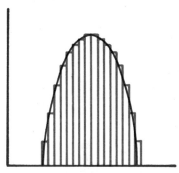

FIG. 7b BREAKDOWN OF A
CONTINUOUS FUNCTION INTO STEPS
ACCORDING TO NORBERT WIENER

FIG. 8a

FIG. 8b

The theory evolved by Norbert Wiener derived its name — cybernetics — from the combination of random behavior and methodical control. As already stated, the cybernetic approach can also be applied to branches of science which had previously not been regarded as amenable to statistical treatment. It was especially advantageous that Wiener had, from the outset, made his theory of such wide and universal scope that it provided a promising new scientific tool, ready and waiting to be used by any one of a number of sciences.

There is, however, always a problem to be faced whenever cybernetics is to be applied to any particular set of phenomena. If we are to employ statistical methods, we shall require a so-called statistical element. Examples of such a statistical element are provided by a number thrown with dice, or the individual set of numbers drawn in the game of lotto (Fig. 9a). The fundamental property of a statistical element is that it is interchangeable with any other such element; it is largely devoid of any individual content. This process of de-individualization in establishing the basic element for statistical treatment (for the purposes of information theory) constitutes the primary function of cybernetics (Fig. 9b). It is interesting to note that, in fact, we have already introduced this principle in the example of the flock of sheep in that we referred merely to "sheep," without considering that there are large, small, fat, thin, shorn and unshorn sheep in the flock. All these individual characteristics are ignored: there remains only the schematized standard individual: "the sheep." Thus, whenever cybernetics is to be applied, we must first extract from the mass of observations and variable parameters, by a process of abstraction, the group that can be utilized as the statistical element. Solving this fundamental problem of cybernetics always remains a matter for our creative human intuition. There are as yet no devices, however sophisticated, that can perform this task for us.

A classic example of the application of cybernetics is afforded by communication theory, or special information theory. C. E. Shannon managed to make the concept of "message" so devoid of any individual content that finally the only information element it retained was the decision between a "yes" and a "no" statement — a binary decision. This brings us to an important definition — that of the "binary digit" (commonly abbreviated as "bit"): the term is applied to each of the two digits (L and O) used in binary notation, which will be explained further on in this book. These two digits L and O (also known as "on" and "off") are the kind of number that computers use internally for performing their computations. In electrical operations, the bit may consist of a single pulse or a group of pulses. In a more general sense, the bit constitutes a unit of information. Sequences of pulses (pulse trains) are represented in Figs. 10a and 10b. The period during which the current is flowing represents the one, while the period of zero current represents the other of the two "yes-no" alternatives. By this means, fresh possibilities for the processing of information — transmitting, storing, and documenting — are opened up.

In a general way, the terms "information," and "data," may be employed as synonyms. "Data" is used more particularly to denote the basic elements of information as received into, operated upon, and put out by a computer or other data processing machine (a machine for handling information), while "information" is said to be the result of processing the data, in other words, the assembly, analysis, or summarization of data, into a meaningful form. Sometimes data are considered to be expressible only in numerical form, whereas information is not so limited.

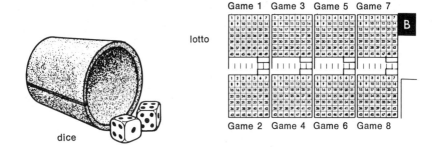

Game 1  Game 3  Game 5  Game 7

lotto

dice

**FIG. 9a**

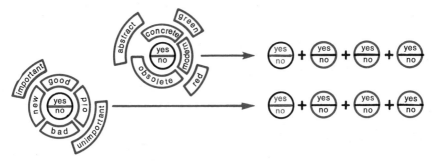

**FIG. 9b  DE-INDIVIDUALIZATION OF INFORMATION INTO A
SERIES OF BINARY DIGITS**

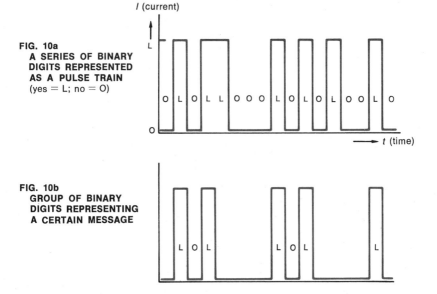

**FIG. 10a
A SERIES OF BINARY
DIGITS REPRESENTED
AS A PULSE TRAIN**
(yes = L; no = O)

**FIG. 10b
GROUP OF BINARY
DIGITS REPRESENTING
A CERTAIN MESSAGE**

# COMMUNICATION AND DOCUMENTATION

As has already been explained, it is now possible to break down a continuous flow, or continuum, of communication or information "material," into a discontinuum, or sequence of discrete communication or information units. In practical terms, we are faced with the difficult task of so resolving a message into a succession of individual questions that each of these questions need be answered only by a "yes" or a "no." In attempting this, we very soon find how lax and imprecise our ordinary habits of speech are in this respect and how seldom a question is formulated with such precision as to rule out an indefinite answer such as "perhaps."

The process of passing on or transmitting a message, a piece of information, can be presented as a flow of information elements once the message has been suitably broken down into a series of bits. To compare this process with certain phenomena envisaged in the theory of fluid flow (hydrodynamics), particularly the flow of water, which can likewise be conceived as a succession of particles (water molecules), seems obvious. And just as the water flow can be said to start from a source, so we can speak of a source of information in our analogy of a "bit flow" or "bit stream" (Figs. 1–3). During each unit of time, a certain quantity of information flows from its source. This information is transmitted through channels, which are referred to as information transmission channels, in analogy with water channels. Through these channels, the information is supplied to the consumer. When a water supply system is installed we consider it obvious that, for economic reasons, the bore of the pipelines should be suited to the required rate of flow of the water. For example, it would be pointless and wasteful to install pipes of unnecessarily large bore, in order to convey a relatively small flow of water. Before the advent of Shannon's information theory, however, such considerations played little part in the communication engineer's approach to this subject. He designed his transmission or information channels according to other principles, these principles being more specifically aimed at achieving the most faithful possible true-in-form transmission of information. At the same time, the engineer conceived of "information" as a continuous "material" — more particularly, a superposition of continuous oscillatory processes, whose frequencies had to be faithfully reproduced.

With the new outlook that has come with information theory, which is well illustrated by the pipe flow analogy, this traditional "fidelity" conception of the problem has been largely superseded by the view that it is more economical so to design an electrical transmission channel that it is just able to utilize the full output of the information source and transmit the bit stream flowing from it. The information capacity of the channel, the number of bits per second with which it can cope, must therefore be suited to the output of the source. In that case optimum — and most economical — utilization of the transmission channel will be achieved. To the optimum diameter of the water pipe or channel then, there corresponds, by analogy, a particular electrical quantity associated with the information channel: the so-called double band width (see page 36).

Over-dimensioning a water pipeline, or channel, is uneconomical because only a portion of the internal volume of the pipeline is then actually utilized (Fig. 1). Similar considerations apply to an information channel. On the other hand, if a water pipeline is under-dimensioned (Fig. 2), congestion and build-up of pressure will occur, and only a limited proportion of the desired rate of flow through the pipeline will be achieved. In the case of an information channel, the congestion causes a distortion of the bits, which are transmitted along it in the form of pulses, that is, short bursts of electric current.

This simple analogy between information flow and water flow, or more

12

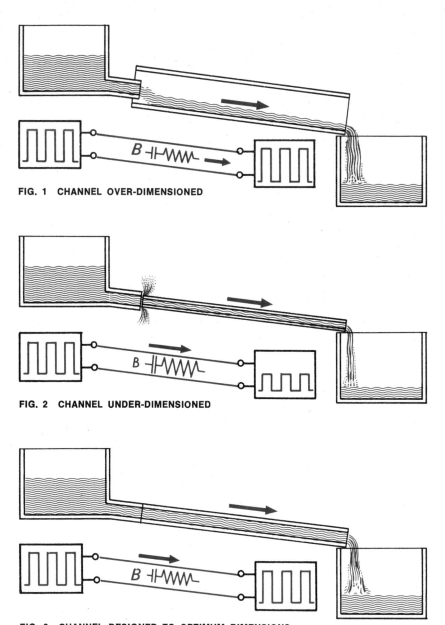

**FIG. 1 CHANNEL OVER-DIMENSIONED**

**FIG. 2 CHANNEL UNDER-DIMENSIONED**

**FIG. 3 CHANNEL DESIGNED TO OPTIMUM DIMENSIONS**

Comparison between a source supplying water
and an information source: transmission through
variously dimensioned channels

$\dashv\vdash\!\!\text{WW}$ = symbol for different magnitude of capacitance $\dashv\vdash$ and self-inductance $\text{WW}$ of the
electric channel

B = symbol for differently dimensioned band width (B) of the electric channel

specifically, between the bit stream and the stream of water molecules, has illuminated a number of valuable concepts, namely: information source, information flow rate, information capacity, information channel, and information element.

Because of the large number of information elements (bits) involved, it may not be possible, or even desirable, to describe and keep track of the behavior of an individual element, and instead it is necessary to adopt a statistical approach, that is, to consider the overall behavior of the aggregate of information elements. Thus information theory, as a statistical theory, yields a number of properties relating to the state of order of the aggregate, properties which the individual element as such does not possess (Figs. 4 and 5). With reference to a single bit, or element, it is indeed not possible to speak of "order" at all. Only when considering the interrelationship of a large number of elements collectively does the term "order" acquire real meaning.

Here again the meaning can usefully be clarified by an analogy: a desk with books on it can rightly be described as tidy only if a substantial number of the books are arranged in a definite and regular manner. If there is only one book on the desk, it is ambiguous, and implausible, to refer to the desk as either "tidy" (well-ordered) or "untidy" (disordered). This example already tells us something that is of major significance with regard to statistical evaluation. When a desk on which, initially, a number of books are arranged in an orderly manner, has been in use for some length of time, a state of disorder will in all probability have developed. We all know that such a state of disorder will develop, even if the desk is not in intensive use, provided we wait long enough. To preserve an ordered state it is necessary to continually apply an ordering force. To remain with our example of the desk: anyone who adds more books to those already on it must make these books fit in with the existing ordered state; for example, he must place the additional books neatly against a row, or on top of a pile, of books he finds already there. If he fails to do this, and simply lays the books down just anyhow, the ordered state will disappear in the course of time and become a disordered state (Fig. 6). In this sense, the meaningful information-bearing transmission of a bit stream from an information source represents a process characterized by a certain state of order. A completely disordered emission of bits by the source would not communicate meaningful information.

From these considerations of the subject, it is evident that the state of order of an information flow is of decisive importance to the information content of the flow. Because of this importance, it appears an obvious choice; to introduce the concept of order as a measure of the information content, and so to choose this measure that it is larger, according as the information flow has a higher information content.

As already noted, the concept of order is a property appertaining to a collective — in our case, the collective consisting of the large number of bits comprising the information. Since the statistical method of investigation is not something that was devised specifically for the purposes of information theory, of cybernetics, but is a familiar mathematical tool of long standing, it is of interest to see in what form this discipline, which constitutes the measure of the state of order of an aggregate of statistical elements, has been formulated in general mathematical theory. This is all the more appropriate because an application of the principles of mathematical statistics to certain problems in physics, especially thermodynamics, has yielded some conceptions that can be

disordered state

linear ordered state

plane ordered state

spatial ordered state

FIG. 4  COLLECTIVE COMPRISING 30 STATISTICAL ELEMENTS

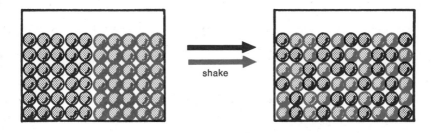

shake

FIG. 5  TRANSITION OF A COLLECTIVE OF STATISTICAL ELEMENTS
FROM AN ORDERED TO A DISORDERED STATE AS A RESULT OF SHAKING

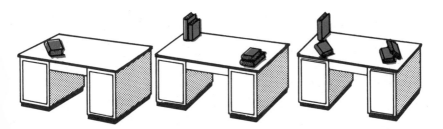

FIG. 6  VARIOUS STATES OF ORDER OF A DESK WITH BOOKS

presented visually (Fig. 7). As will be explained further later (see page 20 et seq.), in thermodynamics the concept of entropy has been introduced as a measure of order, though in a manner not quite suitable for our present purpose. Entropy in its conventional meaning relates to the order of a system: as a characteristic of thermal phenomena, the entropy increases according as the degree of disorder (not order) increases (Fig. 7). The measure of order in thermodynamics has been chosen in this manner because systems, when left to themselves, will always tend toward states of greater disorder, as already noted with reference to the example of the books on the desk. For the state of order of an aggregate composed of bits (elements of information) it is, however, preferable to adopt a measure having the opposite algebraic sign. The general term "entropy" is used to denote this measure, or criterion, of order (not disorder). Thermodynamically speaking, the entropy of information theory is therefore a negative entropy (Fig. 9). The way in which these two entropy concepts are interrelated will be explained more fully later on (see page 44). With the entropy of information theory, which provides a measure of information content, we can now define a new concept of efficiency: the information-theoretical efficiency. It is possible to make the following statement: if we feed a certain information content into an information channel, and if this information content undergoes losses in consequence of the properties of the channel, then the information content at the outlet of the channel will be diminished, relative to that at the entrance of the channel. The information channel efficiency can thus be expressed as the quotient of the information content at the outlet, divided by the information content at the inlet. However, on the basis of our present considerations, this is equal to the quotient of the corresponding information entropies. The losses of information, for example, in a specific case, may be caused by the information channel not being optimally matched to the output of the information source. In the case of electrical transmission, this would mean that the capacitance and self-inductance of the channel (the electrical circuit) do not possess the optimum values. This deficiency manifests itself in a distortion of the pulses that represent the bits stored in the information source. In consequence, the information content of the bit stream passing through the channel becomes inaccurate to a greater or lesser extent, that is to say, the information content at the outlet or receiving end is less than it was at the inlet or input end (Fig. 8).

We see that the cybernetic approach, which in the present case has led us to draw logical inferences for information theory from hydrodynamics and thermodynamics, yields some very useful concepts, which reveal the communication of information by data transmission in a new light. These inferences based on analogy are also very helpful in another field with which information is closely associated, namely, documentation.

The term "documentation" is to be understood as comprising all those methods and techniques for the storage of information that are independent of the human brain and its shortcomings. In documentation, the techniques of electronics play not nearly so dominant a part as they do in the field of communication. This is because the user who desires the information generally demands that the document from which he wishes to obtain the information shall be made available to him in a form that he can easily read. Hence it follows that on output of the documentation, the electrical signals will have to be converted into written characters. Special devices are employed for this purpose (see page 168 et seq.).

Here it will be shown that the hydrodynamic analogies are also of value with regard to documentation. The essential character of documentation lies in the storage of information. For reasons of economy it is important that it be possible to store material quickly, and that stored material take up as little

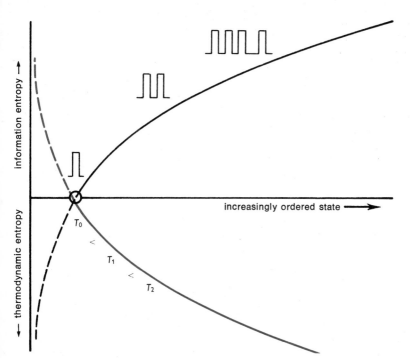

**FIG. 7 INFORMATION ENTROPY AND THERMODYNAMIC ENTROPY (*T*) AS FUNCTIONS OF THE ORDERED STATE**

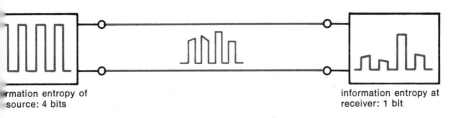

information entropy of
source: 4 bits

information entropy at
receiver: 1 bit

**FIG. 8 BECAUSE OF EXCESSIVE DEFORMATION OF THE PULSE TRAIN, THE INFORMATION TRANSMISSION EFFICIENCY OF THE CHANNEL IS ONLY ¼ (25% of the information is recognizable at the receiving station)**

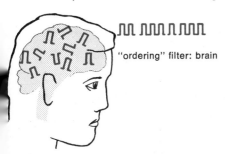

"ordering" filter: brain

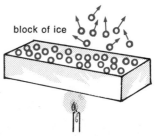

block of ice

with rising temperature, expenditure of
thermal energy produces an increasingly
disordered state (high energy → disorder)

**FIG. 9 INFORMATION ENTROPY AND THERMODYNAMIC ENTROPY CONCEPTS: expenditure of mental energy produces an increasingly ordered state (high energy → order)**

space as possible, and finally, that access to the desired information in the store can be accomplished in minimal time.

In its function, the documentation store is comparable to a water storage tank (Fig. 10). The material to be stored comes flowing in continuously from one or more sources: in the case of the documentation store, the inflow of information comes from the innumerable scientific publications that appear in the form of books and journals. At the same time, users tap off some of the contents of the store. In the case of the water tank, the required quantities are delivered to the consumers through a network of pipes. The material extracted from the documentation store corresponds to the literature research that a documentation center carries out at the request of its clients. The access time — the time required to retrieve specific information from the store — should obviously be as short as possible.

The main difference between the information storage center and the water storage tank is that information, when extracted from the center, is, as a rule, subsequently returned and thus remains available for re-use (Fig. 11). In the long run, of course, the information store must thus become filled to capacity as more and more fresh information is added. Because of this, and to avoid having to make the store excessively large and expensive, it is necessary to constantly discharge some of its contents — let information run to waste, as it were. This procedure consists of eliminating those items of information which have become obsolescent and which, therefore, need not be so quickly accessible as more up-to-date information. Such obsolescent information is removed from the store after a certain length of time and is stored elsewhere (under less readily accessible conditions), or perhaps destroyed. Simple comparisons with the water tank show that any information store can be maintained at a certain constant size if the inflow and outflow of information are kept in balance with each other. Unfortunately, given the present rate of expansion of the volume of information, it is not possible to do this. As already mentioned, knowledge is increasing exponentially, whereas obsolescence merely proceeds linearly (Fig. 12). This means that, in the course of time, larger and larger documentation storage centers will be needed.

To sum up, it can be said that hydrodynamic analogies are helpful in describing the concepts of communication and documentation from the cybernetic point of view and that, more particularly, they yield a set of concepts which, with rigorous mathematical formulation, enable us to come to grips with a whole complex of phenomena — especially the problems associated with communications engineering.

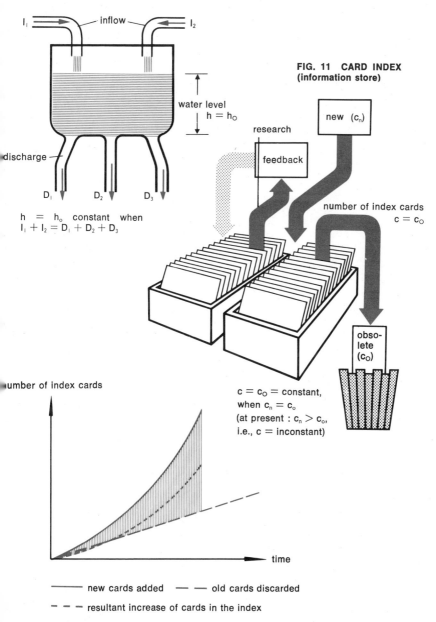

FIG. 10  WATER STORAGE TANK

$I_1$  inflow  $I_2$

water level $h = h_O$

research

FIG. 11  CARD INDEX
(information store)

new ($c_n$)

feedback

discharge

$D_1$   $D_2$   $D_3$

$h = h_o$ constant when
$I_1 + I_2 = D_1 + D_2 + D_3$

number of index cards
$c = c_O$

obso-
lete
($c_O$)

number of index cards

$c = c_O =$ constant,
when $c_n = c_o$
(at present : $c_n > c_o$,
i.e., $c =$ inconstant)

time

—— new cards added   — — old cards discarded

– – – resultant increase of cards in the index

FIG. 12

# STATISTICS AND THERMAL PROCESSES

The introduction of the entropy concept into thermodynamics, as a criterion for the degree of order in a system, provides a very good illustration of the transition from the concept of continuity to the concept of discontinuity, a transition which is required for a statistical treatment of phenomena.

In accordance with earlier ideas on the subject, let us start by considering heat as a continuum, that is, thermal energy conceived as a fluid medium that will flow through a body from the hotter to the colder area (Fig. 1). It should be borne in mind that this is the only kind of heat flow that is ever observed in nature. It would, of course, be perfectly compatible with the principle of the conservation of energy to find that, in a closed system (a system shut off from energy exchange with its surroundings), thermal energy can also flow from the colder to the hotter part of a body, since this flow would not alter the total energy of the system (Fig. 2). Yet we find that nature imposes a restriction upon the flow of energy; its one-way directional tendency must therefore be embodied in an additional law of nature.

In formulating a new natural law it is, as a rule, necessary also to define a new physical entity: in this case it is entropy (represented by the symbol $S$). Entropy is a measure for the directional nature of thermal processes. For an actual process taking place in a closed system, the entropy must, by definition, always increase. How the definition of entropy fits into the continuum theory of heat will now be explained in greater detail. Such an explanation comes under the heading of thermodynamics, which can be defined as that branch of physics which is concerned with the various phenomena of energy, and especially the laws governing the transformation of heat into other forms of energy, and vice versa.

It was R. Clausius who arrived at the definition of entropy on the basis of the following considerations (published in two papers in 1850 and 1854 respectively):

Let $dQ$ denote the thermal energy supplied to a system (for example, a volume of gas, $V$), $dU$ the increase in the internal energy of the system (for example, on heating that volume of gas), and $\delta A$ that proportion of the energy which leaves the system, for example, in the form of heat radiation, or by transformation into other forms of energy (for instance, into work done on expansion of the gas). Then the following equation (energy theorem) is valid:

(1)     $dQ = dU + \delta A$

Equation (1) is integrable only for the above-mentioned special case, in which work is done in expanding a gas against a constant pressure $p$, at constant temperature. Only then does it constitute a total differential (since then $\delta A = pdV$):

(2)     $dQ = dU + pdV$

In general, equation (1) is not integrable, inasmuch as $dQ$ — because of the behavior of $\delta A$ and $dU$ — is an incomplete differential. However, by introducing the so-called reduced thermal energies, or reduced heat quantities, $dQ/T$, $dU/T$ and $\delta A/T$ (Fig. 3, page 23), where $T$ denotes the absolute temperature, it is possible to transform equation (1) into an integrable form:

(3)     $dQ/T = (dU/T) + (\delta A/T)$

Mathematically speaking, $1/T$ is an integrating factor for the incomplete differential of equation (1). Since $dQ/T$ is now a total differential, we can introduce a new physical entity $S$, which is so defined that its differential is equal to (3), that is:

(4)     $dS = dQ/T$

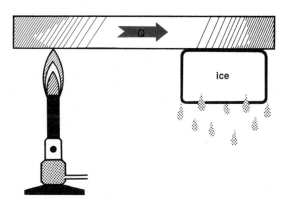

**FIG. 1 FLOW OF THERMAL ENERGY (Q) IN A METAL ROD FROM THE HOTTER TO THE COLDER END**

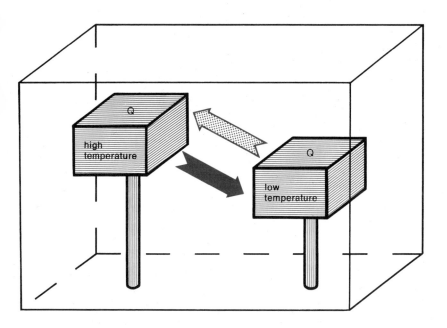

**FIG. 2 IN A CLOSED SYSTEM THE ENERGY THEOREM WOULD BE CONFORMED TO, EVEN IF THERMAL ENERGY Q TRANSFER OCCURRED FROM LOWER TO HIGHER TEMPERATURE ▨ INSTEAD OF FROM HIGHER TO LOWER AS ACTUALLY OCCURS ▬**

From (4) we obtain for $S$:

$$(5) \qquad S = S_2 - S_1 = \int_1^2 \frac{dQ}{T}$$

where the limits of integration, 1 and 2, characterize the transition from state 1 to state 2. Since thermal processes in closed systems normally proceed in such a manner that $T_2 < T_1$, that is, in the direction of diminishing temperatures (or more precisely: so as to bring about an equalization of temperature differences), it follows that $S$, as defined by equation (5), must increase (Fig. 4):

$$(6) \qquad S \geqq 0$$

With the aid of the entropy concept, the restrictions that have to be imposed upon the energy theorem — the first law of thermodynamics — are adequately specified. They constitute the content of the second law of thermodynamics: "For irreversible processes the entropy increases; in the isothermal limiting case (that is, for processes in which the temperature remains constant) it remains unchanged (such processes are reversible)." From this original definition of entropy, it is not easy to see how this criterion for the directional nature of thermal processes can be linked to a measure of the degree of order of a collective — what has, in the foregoing, been defined as information entropy.

To establish this link we must consider L. Boltzmann's statistical explanation of heat phenomena. According to his interpretation, these phenomena are conceived as being caused by a multitude of only statistically analyzable mechanical processes, involving the transfer of energy and momentum by collisions between molecules (Fig. 5). Thus he bases his approach on the molecule as the statistical element. These individual elements (the molecules) are in no way different from one another, in other words, they are totally de-individualized and may be interchanged without causing any external change in the overall state, which is characterized by a particular, statistical, distribution of energy over the aggregate of molecules. As illustrated in Fig. 6, in which the energy values of the individual molecules are the abscissae, and the numbers of molecules possessing these energy values are the ordinates, there are a number of molecules with very low energies (low velocities), a very large number of molecules having medium energies, and finally a small number of molecules with high and very high energy values (Boltzmann assumes the molecular energy to be kinetic energy — the energy of motion). Fig. 6 represents the so-called Maxwell-Boltzmann distribution.

The greater the total energy of the system, the farther is the maximum of the distribution curve shifted towards the molecules having the higher energy values, corresponding to a higher mean molecular energy (which is equivalent to stating that the molecules' mean velocity increases with the increasing total energy of the system). At the same time, the curve becomes wider, and the maximum becomes lower. In other words: more molecules have an energy that is equal (or approximately equal) to the mean energy per molecule. For a thermal process, higher total energy signifies a higher temperature, and lower total energy signifies a lower temperature. The definition of temperature can, indeed, be based on the mean value of molecular energy, as determined by the sum of the kinetic energies of all the molecules involved in the thermal process.

Undoubtedly the various possible statistical distributions of energy, over the aggregate of molecules simultaneously, represent states having different degrees of order. More particularly, the state with greater total energy (higher temperature) constitutes a state having a higher degree of order than does the

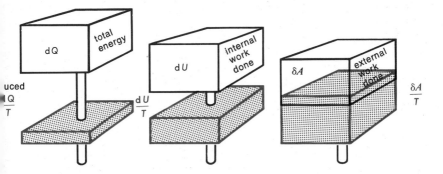

**FIG. 3   REDUCED HEAT QUANTITIES AS A MEASURE FOR THE ENTROPY S**
(only heat energies of equal temperature can be added together)

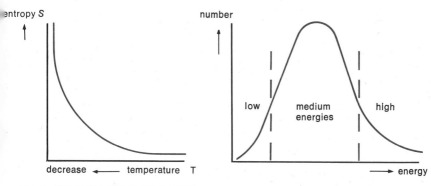

**FIG. 4   INCREASE OF THE ENTROPY S WHEN THE TEMPERATURE T OF CONSTANT ENERGY Q DECREASES:**

$$S = \frac{Q}{T} \; (ST = \text{constant})$$

**FIG. 6   THE ENERGY DISTRIBUTION IN THE MOLECULES OF A GAS (ACCORDING TO BOLTZMANN)**

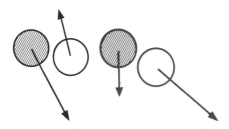

**FIG. 5   MOLECULES BEFORE (−) AND AFTER (+) COLLISION: THE ENERGY QUANTITIES ARE PROPORTIONAL TO THE SQUARE OF THE LENGTH OF THE ARROWS REPRESENTING THE VELOCITIES**

state with a lesser total energy and therefore a lower temperature (Fig. 7). A higher degree of order corresponds to a more uniform distribution of the total energy over the aggregate of molecules, and reveals itself in a widening of the distribution curve at higher temperatures.

The directional nature of heat flow that is manifested in natural closed-system thermal processes — in other words, the transition from higher-temperature to lower-temperature states, or the equalization of temperature differences within the system — accordingly corresponds to the transition of the energy distribution in the aggregate of molecules, from a more highly ordered to a less highly ordered (and therefore more probable) state. Thus the state with the higher degree of order corresponds to the higher, and that with the lower degree of order corresponds to the lower temperature.

These considerations provide us with the key to the statistical interpretation of entropy in Boltzmann's theory of heat. The second law of thermodynamics can thus be alternatively expressed as follows: a closed system, left to itself, will tend towards a state of greater disorder, in the sense envisaged above (Fig. 8), and will, in the limiting case, at best preserve the existing degree of order. With this interpretation of entropy, Boltzmann also liberated this concept from its purely thermodynamic context, and revealed it as a general concept relating to statistical distributions over aggregates. This opens up the possibility of appropriately generalizing it and so transferring its application to other phenomena and processes that are susceptible of interpretation as aggregates of statistical elements, and which are thus statistically analyzable (see page 12 et seq.).

In order to arrive at a mathematical characterization of entropy, starting from these statistical notions, we must look for an indicator, or criterion, for characterizing the "degree of order" of any particular state. Undoubtedly, the more highly ordered state is the less probable one, as compared with the disordered state. Thus if we define a thermodynamic probability to be (in the sense conceived here) associated with the degree of order of a state, the functional relationship between the entropy $S$ and this thermodynamic probability $W_{th}$ will have to be so conceived that the lower entropy corresponds to the lower probability. This requirement is fulfilled by the following relation:

(7) $\qquad S = k \ln W_{th}$

where the constant $k$ is known as Boltzmann's constant, and has the experimentally determined value:

(8) $\qquad k = 1.38 \times 10^{-16}$ erg/degree

while ln denotes the natural logarithm with base $e = 2.71828\ldots$. $W_{th}$ must be greater than, or at least equal to, unity ($W_{th} \geq 1$) (thermodynamic probability is based on a different definition from that of ordinary probability, which must be less than, or at most equal to, unity).

This relationship, and the connection between this statistical interpretation of entropy and its thermodynamic interpretation as given in the foregoing pages, will now be further elucidated for the benefit of those readers of this book who may be interested in the mathematical background.

As we have seen, the state of order of a system having thermal energy $Q$ is determined by a particular distribution of this total energy over the aggregate of molecules comprising the system. Let the number of these molecules (conceived as statistical elements) be $N$. It will be further assumed that, within a given energy distribution, $n_i$ molecules out of the total of $N$ molecules have each the energy $E_i$

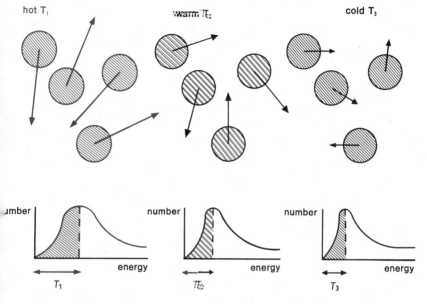

FIG. 7 DIFFERENT THERMAL STATES (—,--,—) HAVE DIFFERENT TEMPERATURES
($T_1$, $T_2$, $T_3$), VELOCITY, AND ENERGY DISTRIBUTIONS

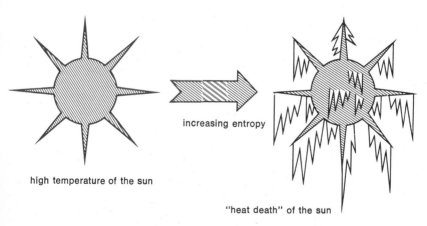

increasing entropy

high temperature of the sun

"heat death" of the sun

FIG. 8 CONSISTENT APPLICATION OF THE SECOND LAW OF THERMODYNAMICS
(RELATING TO THE INCREASE OF ENTROPY IN CLOSED SYSTEMS) LEADS TO
THE HYPOTHESIS OF THE "THERMAL DEATH OF THE UNIVERSE"

(Fig. 9). The probabilities $W_1$ and $W_2$ of two such states of order, are defined by Boltzmann as the number of cases favorable to the occurrence of the state in question, which is determined by how frequently the molecules (which are de-individualized, in the sense of being indistinguishable from one another) can be interchanged, within the energy values, without causing any change in the overall distribution of energy within the system. Then, according to the rules of probability calculus, we obtain:

(9) $\quad W_1 = N!/\pi_{i_1}(n_{i_1}!); \qquad W_2 = N!/\pi_{i_2}(n_{i_2}!)$

where $N!$ denotes "factorial $N$", that is, $N! = N \times (N-1) \times (N-2) \times \ldots 3 \times 2 \times 1$, while $\pi_{i_1}$ and $\pi_{i_2}$ denote the product operation, thus for example: $\pi_{i_1}(n_{i_1}!) = (n_{1_1}!) \times (n_{2_1}!) \times (n_{3_1}!) \times \ldots$ Defined in this way, these probabilities which always have a value greater than unity ($> 1$), are designated as "thermodynamic probabilities," because, in contrast with the usual definition of probability, as adopted in probability calculus, their definition does not entail a division by the total number of possible cases. For this reason, too, they are — in contrast with probability as it is usually defined — never proper fractions. Since the two states of order, represented by the subscripts 1 and 2, differ in their respective thermal energy values $Q_1$ and $Q_2$, the two thermodynamic probabilities $W_1$ and $W_2$ can be conceived as functions of these thermal energies:

(9a) $\quad W_1 = f(Q_1); \qquad W_2 = f(Q_2)$

In a process consisting of the transition of the system from the first state to the second state, it is evident that the system must consecutively manifest both states. Now, a well known law of probability theory states that, the probability $W_{12}$ of the simultaneous occurrence of two events having, respectively, probabilities $W_1$ and $W_2$, is equal to the product of their probabilities (Fig. 10):

(10) $\quad W_{12} = W_1 \cdot W_2$

As we have previously stated, for a system such as we have postulated here, every process that entails a transition from one state to another state proceeds in only one direction (certain processes that are called "reversible" will be dealt with separately); no exceptions have ever been observed. It is logical then to assign to such processes a maximal probability and to deal similarly with reversible processes, with the additional remark that for reversible processes, either direction is to be considered equally probable. Thus in the present analysis we assume that $W_{12}$ takes on a maximum value. Now if $W_{12}$ is to take on a maximum value, the differential of $W_{12}$, that is $dW_{12}$, must become zero. Therefore:

(11) $\quad dW_{12} = d(W_1 \cdot W_2) = W_1 dW_2 + W_2 dW_1 = 0$

Hence, on dividing by the product $W_1 W_2$, we obtain:

(12) $\quad dW_1/W_1 + dW_2/W_2 = d(\ln W_1) + d(\ln W_2) = 0$

which is equivalent to:

(13) $\quad d(\ln W_1) = -d(\ln W_2)$

Since the principle of the conservation of energy (first law of thermodynamics) is valid in the closed system under consideration, the increase in thermal energy in the one state must be equal to the decrease in thermal energy in the other state; therefore:

(14) $\quad dQ_1 = -dQ_2$

On dividing (13) by $dQ_1$, and having due regard to (14), we obtain:

(15) $\quad d(\ln W_1)/dQ_1 = d(\ln W_2)/dQ_2$

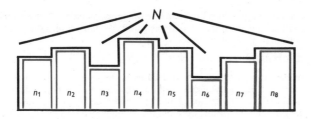

**FIG. 9 THE SUB-QUANTITIES $n_1 \rightarrow n_8$ WITH DIFFERENT RESPECTIVE PROBABILITIES FORM THE TOTAL QUANTITY $N$**

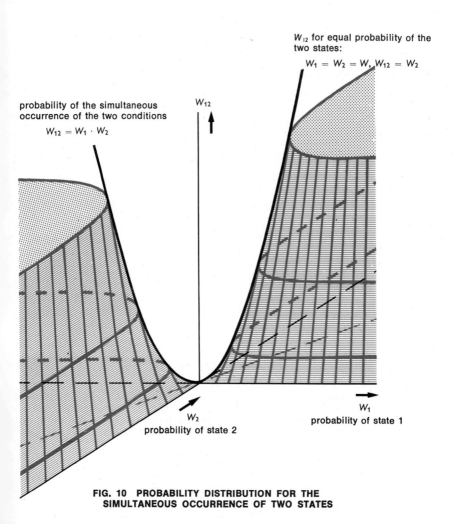

$W_{12}$ for equal probability of the two states:

$$W_1 = W_2 = W, \ W_{12} = W_2$$

probability of the simultaneous occurrence of the two conditions

$$W_{12} = W_1 \cdot W_2$$

$W_{12}$

$W_2$
probability of state 2

$W_1$
probability of state 1

**FIG. 10 PROBABILITY DISTRIBUTION FOR THE SIMULTANEOUS OCCURRENCE OF TWO STATES**

It follows that the expressions $\ln W_i$ can only be proportional to the thermal energies $Q_i$, and that therefore the derivatives $d(\ln W_i)/dQ_i$ must all be equal to the same proportionality factor $\beta$

$$d(\ln W_i)/dQ_i = \beta \quad \text{or} \quad \ln W_i = \beta Q_i$$

Because of the units of measurement used here, this factor $\beta$ must have the reciprocal dimension of energy; it can be shown that $\beta = 1/kT$, where $T$ denotes the absolute temperature. Hence we obtain the following differential equation expressing the general relationship between the thermodynamic probability $W_{th}$ of a state, and the thermal energy $Q$:

$$d(\ln W_{th})/dQ = 1/kT$$

In combination with equation (4), which states that $dQ = TdS$, we obtain:

(16) $\quad d(\ln W_{th})/dS = 1/k$

whence follows the equation $S = k\ln W_{th}$, already indicated, where $k$ is Boltzmann's constant. An integration constant, arising on integration of (16), has been omitted ($S_0 = 0$); using this constant, we may fix an origin (zero reference point) from which to reckon the entropy of a system. We assume an entropy of zero corresponding to a thermodynamic probability of one.

With the entropy equation (7), we have at our disposal a definition which can be generalized, and which shows us that the choice of the statistical procedure and the probability definition which we adopted – in other words, choosing the statistical element and stipulating the state – determine the content of the entropy concept.

Thus, for example, we get a reversal of the algebraic sign in (7) if, instead of the thermodynamic probability $W_{th}$, we introduce the conventional ("ordinary") probability $W$, or the frequency $h$, for characterizing a state of the collective:

(17) $\quad W \leqslant 1 \quad \text{and} \quad h \leqslant 1$

The entropy will, in such a case, always have negative values, since the logarithm of a proper fraction is always negative. This means that, in the thermodynamics of natural processes, the entropy will always tend to decrease in value. To reflect this characteristic, the term "ectropy" was proposed to denote this property (Fig. 11). However, this has not caught on, and at present the term "negentropy" (a contraction of "negative entropy"), proposed by A. Brillouin, has been widely adopted instead. The generalization of the concept of entropy, as a result of the statistical definition (7) has, not without reason, met with some criticism. With regard to the straightforward physical character of the entropy concept, it is felt by some that it should remain confined to thermodynamics. In its physical context, the term acquires a meaning which differs from its original thermodynamic significance. As we have already seen, conceived as "information entropy," it constitutes a measure for the information content of a source of information (see page 12 et seq.). In this sense, that is, expressed in terms of information entropy, the thermodynamic entropy is a measure of the lack of information as to the thermal state described. Viewed in this way, the second law of thermodynamics could be conceived as stating that every closed system will strive to attain a state of greater lack of information (Fig. 12).

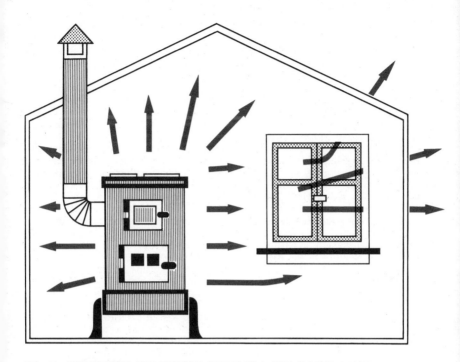

**FIG. 11   MAINTAINING THE THERMAL STATE IN A NON-CLOSED SYSTEM BY THE NEGENTROPY OF A HEATING SYSTEM WHICH COMPENSATES FOR THE INCREASE IN ENTROPY**

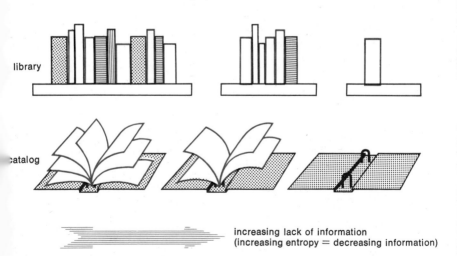

library

catalog

increasing lack of information
(increasing entropy = decreasing information)

**FIG. 12**

# CONTROL, SELF-CORRECTION AND AUTOMATION

The term "control" may be taken to designate the aimed and purposeful influencing of processes. The purposeful character of the operation neutralizes the occurrence of random variations. Control constitutes an outside intervention in the system under consideration. This can best be explained by reference to a simple example: a motorist at the wheel of his car. The car is a system subject to external influences; the driver influences its behavior by various interventions operating through the steering wheel, accelerator and gear shift. In this way he ensures that the car will not hit the curb, or collide with some obstacle in its path (Fig. 1). This example shows that we must distinguish between the external world and the system that is influenced by the external world. Control operations may, however, also occur within a closed system, a system that is not in communication with the external world. For example, consider a closed thermal system, such as a metal rod which, at the beginning of the experiment (time $t = 0$), is heated at one end and is then enclosed in some kind of enveloping sheath, or jacket, which prevents any heat exchange with the environment. A state of equilibrium (steady state) will then establish itself in the closed system. There will thus be a steady-state distribution of energy over the molecules of the rod.

The quantity, or variable, which is controlled in this example (technically known as the "controlled variable" or "controlled condition") is the steady-state energy distribution. The essential nature of control, as envisaged here, is embodied in the notion of "feedback," which signifies that part of the energy of the process is "fed back," that is, is diverted and utilized for controlling the process. More specifically, in cybernetics, it denotes the principle that part of the output of a process is fed back as input and thus acts as a control signal that enables the system to monitor its own actions and take self-correcting steps.

Possibly the oldest form of feedback control is exemplified by the oscillating chute for delivering cereal grains to millstones. The softer the grain, the faster the chute shakes, thus it delivers its grain at a faster rate. The harder the grain and more difficult it is to grind, the slower the chute shakes. This effect is achieved by utilizing the fact that, with harder grains, there is greater friction between the millstones, so that these rotate more slowly than when softer grain is being ground. The chute, driven by an eccentric cam from the mill shaft, will correspondingly oscillate with a lower or higher frequency (Fig. 2). In this case, the feedback action is extremely simple and direct. Another familiar example of a technical control system based on the feedback principle is James Watt's centrifugal governor, for regulating the speed of a steam engine. It comprises two balls attached to levers, which fly outwards when the shaft on which they are mounted is in rotation. The faster it rotates, the further apart the balls go. Through a linkage system this movement of the balls and levers actuates a control valve, which increases or decreases the supply of steam to the cylinders of the engine and thus regulates its speed, keeping it approximately constant at a value corresponding to the setting of the valves (Fig. 3).

The purpose of every control system is to maintain a certain "desired value" (also known as the "reference value" or "index value") of the controlled condition. This is very clearly exemplified by the thermostat, a device for the regulation of temperature (Fig. 4). Thermostats are extensively used in connection with present-day heating appliances, refrigerators, and so on. In most cases, the actual temperature-sensing element is a bimetallic strip, a composite strip which is formed when two metals, having different coefficients of thermal expansion, are bonded together. When the temperature changes, one of the metals expands, or contracts, more than the other, so that the strip becomes curved. When the temperature in a room, for example, exceeds the

FIG. 1 STEERING A CAR TO AVOID AN OBSTACLE

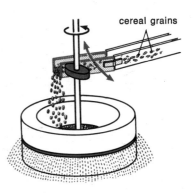

cereal grains

FIG. 2 HARDER GRAINS CAUSE THE MILLSTONES TO ROTATE MORE SLOWLY SO THAT THE RATE OF OSCILLATION OF THE CHUTE DECREASES

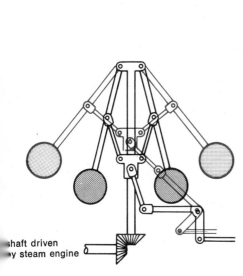

shaft driven by steam engine

FIG. 3 JAMES WATT'S CENTRIFUGAL GOVERNOR

● = valve open
● = valve closed

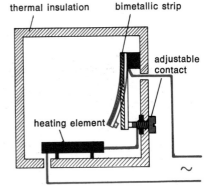

thermal insulation        bimetallic strip

adjustable contact

heating element

~

FIG. 4 THERMOSTAT

desired value, the bimetallic strip breaks an electric circuit and thus switches off the heating appliance. Then when the temperature in the room goes down and falls below the desired value, the strip straightens itself and thus remakes the circuit, so that the heating comes on again. In this way the room temperature is maintained in the vicinity of the desired value.

From the foregoing examples it will be evident that a control system based on the feedback principle cannot maintain the controlled condition at exactly the desired value. It is in fact the deviation from this value that initiates the controlling (self-correcting) action. Clearly, there must be some deviation before correction can take place.

Two more examples of self-correcting action are to be found in familiar toys: the water-drinking bird, and the motor car that cannot run off the edge of a table (Figs. 5 and 6). The bird is made up of two hollow glass spheres, interconnected by a tube and pivotally mounted at a point slightly above their overall center of gravity. The lower sphere is filled with liquid ether, and—since ether readily vaporizes at ordinary temperatures—ether vapor fills the entire space above the liquid. To "start" the bird, its beak is wetted. Evaporation of the water from the felt covering of the beak causes local cooling, so that ether vapor condenses in the beak and head (that is, in the upper sphere), while ether from the lower sphere evaporates. The result is that the upper sphere gradually becomes heavier and tips forward, plunging the beak into the glass of water. The felt is thus wetted again; at the same time the ether vapor pressure in the two spheres becomes equalized, and the liquid ether flows back again, into the lower sphere. This shift of weight causes the bird to swing back, lifting its beak out of the water, so that the initial state is restored. The process is now repeated. It is similar in principle to the operation of a heat engine in which, as a result of the evaporation of water, a temperature difference is maintained between the boiler (corresponding to the lower sphere of the drinking bird), and the cooler (the upper sphere).

The toy car that cannot run off the edge of a table has, in addition to its clockwork-driven road wheels, a fifth wheel mounted transversely. A "nose" at the front of the car normally keeps this transverse wheel slightly above the surface of the table; but when the nose slips off the edge, the body of the car drops slightly, so that the transverse wheel, which is also powered by the clockwork and is constantly rotating, now touches the surface and thus causes the car to swing away from the edge until the nose comes back on to the table and lifts the transverse wheel clear again.

These simple examples indicate that a multitude of possibilities are available for the design of automatic devices. In the foregoing examples only one parameter—one desired value—was specified. Far more complex automatic devices can be conceived, with a large number of specified parameters. These form, as it were, a set of instructions for the device and are assembled in programs. A modern washing machine provides an example of a device which is programmed to perform a specified sequence of operations (Fig. 7). The instructions issued to the device by the program may, in certain instances, be so numerous as to necessitate a statistical approach to enable their controlling and correcting actions to be predicted. This is particularly so in a case where not all the parameters are completely controlled, that is, when the instructions conform to a random distribution as, for example, the information contained in an information source can be considered to do.

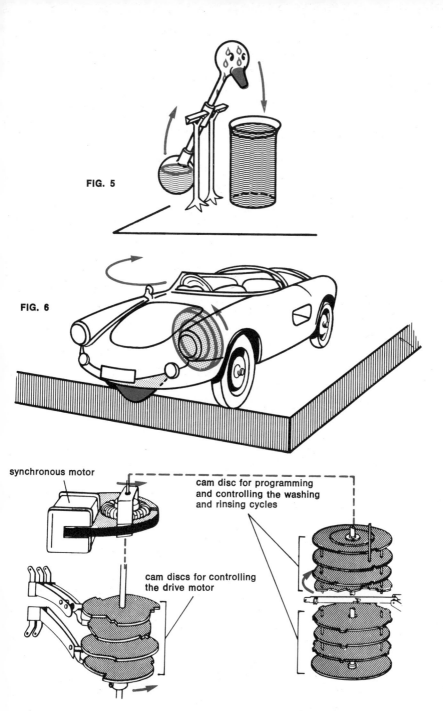

FIG. 5

FIG. 6

synchronous motor

cam disc for programming
and controlling the washing
and rinsing cycles

cam discs for controlling
the drive motor

FIG. 7  PROGRAMMING MECHANISM OF A WASHING MACHINE (SCHEMATIC)

# INFORMATION THEORY

In order to determine the mean information content of information obtained from a source which contains $N$ data (elements of information) of different statistical frequency, we shall first consider an information source containing a number of equally probable data, between which it is necessary to discriminate. Each element of information obtained from a source can be broken down into a series of bits (Fig. 1, see also page 12 et seq.); the information content will depend on the degree of order that characterizes these bit series, and can be expressed in terms of the information entropy. From Fig. 2 it appears that, in order to decide in favor of one of the four equally probable data envisaged there, we always require two bits. These may, for example, be represented electrically by making (L), or breaking (O), a circuit. The following functional relationship exists between the number of bits (binary digits), the information content $H$, and the number $Z$ of equally probable data:

(18) $\quad H = \mathrm{ld}\,Z$

where ld denotes the dual logarithm, that is, the logarithm of base 2. From Fig. 2 it is apparent that the number $Z$ (=4) of the equally probable data, and the number $H$ (=2) of the binary steps, are linked by the relationship $Z = 2^H$ (in this instance: $4 = 2^2$). The information content $H$ is identical with the information entropy.

If the information source contains data which are not all equally probable, but instead $N$ data composed of groups with $n_i$ equally probable data, then the mean (or average) information content, or entropy $\bar{H}$ of one of the data is expressed by:

(19) $\quad \bar{H} = -\sum_i h_i \mathrm{ld}\,h_i$

where $h_i = n_i / N$ is the statistical frequency (probability) of occurrence of the individual data (Fig. 3).

As appears from this formula, the mean information entropy $\bar{H}$ may (independently of the algebraic sign) have values which are not whole numbers, although only integral bit values have real significance in information theory. It means that bit series with different lengths must be associated with the various equally probable groups of data. This process is called coding (see page 46 et seq.).

By introducing the concept of (statistical) frequency $h_i$ we have based our considerations on the conventional probability concept with $W \leq 1$ and thus caused the negative sign to appear in equation (19). The mean information entropy defined by $\bar{H}$ is therefore a negentropy, in the sense conceived by Brillouin (see page 28).

Referred to the unit of time, the information entropy indicates the information yield, or information productiveness, of the source. The generalized concept of entropy, as adopted in information theory, is thus found to have acquired a visualizable meaning and is comparable with the concept of the yield of a source, or spring, in hydrodynamics. In the latter science, a distinction is made between zones where springs are present and those which contain drains. At the springs, additional liquid is introduced into the flow, whereas withdrawal of liquid from the flow occurs at the drains. For purposes of calculation, the region under consideration is enclosed within a spherical surface. The calculation determines how much more liquid flows out of this enclosed volume than into it. If the difference is positive, it means that the region contains

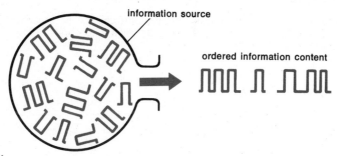

information source

ordered information content

FIG. 1

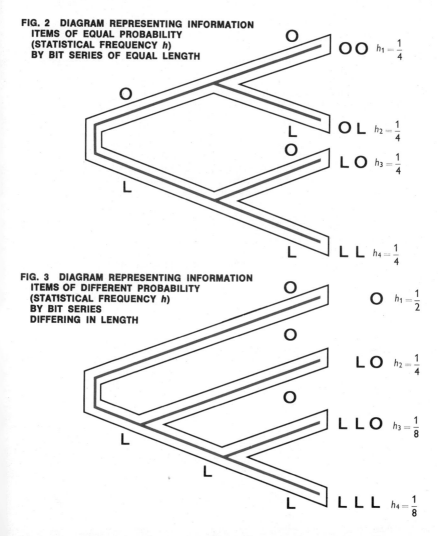

FIG. 2  DIAGRAM REPRESENTING INFORMATION
ITEMS OF EQUAL PROBABILITY
(STATISTICAL FREQUENCY $h$)
BY BIT SERIES OF EQUAL LENGTH

O  O  O O  $h_1 = \frac{1}{4}$

O  L  O L  $h_2 = \frac{1}{4}$

L  O  L O  $h_3 = \frac{1}{4}$

L  L  L L  $h_4 = \frac{1}{4}$

FIG. 3  DIAGRAM REPRESENTING INFORMATION
ITEMS OF DIFFERENT PROBABILITY
(STATISTICAL FREQUENCY $h$)
BY BIT SERIES
DIFFERING IN LENGTH

O  O  $h_1 = \frac{1}{2}$

O  L O  $h_2 = \frac{1}{4}$

O  L L O  $h_3 = \frac{1}{8}$

L  L  L L L  $h_4 = \frac{1}{8}$

springs; if it is negative, then drains are present; and if it is zero, then inflow and outflow are balanced. This difference between inflow and outflow is technically called the divergence (Fig. 4).

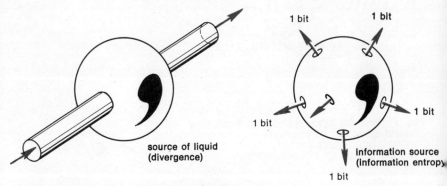

source of liquid
(divergence)

1 bit

1 bit

1 bit

1 bit

Information source
(Information entropy)

1 bit

**FIG. 4 COMPARISON BETWEEN INFORMATION ENTROPY (INFORMATION YIELD) AND DIVERGENCE**

In making a comparison with hydrodynamic phenomena, it was seen that a transmission channel is required to have a certain information capacity which is determined by, for example, its electrical properties if the flow of information — the bit stream — is represented by a pulse train, a succession of current surges and current interruptions. The higher the frequency of the pulses, the wider must be the frequency range that the transmission channel can carry; in other words, it must have a greater band width $B$. The band width is determined by the capacitance and the self-inductance of the channel (for electrical transmission). These two quantities are associated with a time constant which determines the build-up time $\tau$ of the transmission channel, and thus the band width (Fig. 5a). We see that the build-up curve is steeper and — because of the inverse proportionality — the band width $B$ is greater, according as the build-up time is less. A large band width means a wide frequency range; for $B$ tending to infinite magnitude ($B \to \infty$) this corresponds to a range of $f = 0$ to $f = \infty$; for $B$ tending to zero ($B \to 0$), only a single frequency $f$ is transmitted.

The transmission channel will be most economically utilized when its information capacity is equal to the information entropy (per unit time, thus expressed as information yield) of the information source. The following simple relation is obtained for the information capacity $C$ of a disturbance-free information channel:

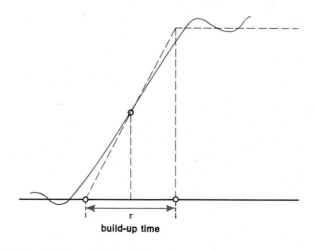

build-up time

**FIG. 5a RELATIONSHIP BETWEEN BUILD-UP TIME $\tau$ AND BAND WIDTH $B$ $(\tau = \dfrac{1}{2B})$**

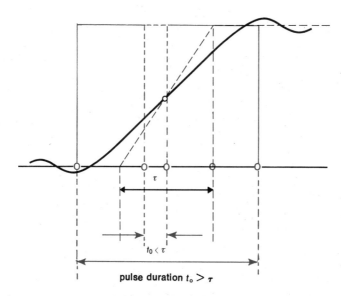

pulse duration $t_o > \tau$

**FIG. 5b RELATIONSHIP BETWEEN BUILD-UP TIME AND PULSE DURATION $t_o$; IF THE PULSE DURATION IS TOO SHORT ($t_o < \tau$), THE TRANSMISSION CHANNEL CANNOT BUILD UP TO THE PULSE FORM AND THE PULSE BECOMES MUTILATED**

(20) $\quad C = 2B$

The derivation of this relation is given below for the benefit of those readers who are more especially interested in this aspect.

Equation (20) states, in effect, that the information capacity of an undisturbed channel is equal to twice the band width.

Let us suppose that the number of equally probable data that can be transmitted with maximum accuracy through a channel is equal to $Z$ (of duration $T$), and comprises $2\xi$ information elements (L, O) of duration $t_0$. Then the information capacity of the channel, that is, the maximum information flow (rate of transmission) that the channel can accurately convey, is expressed by:

(21) $\quad C = \lim_{T \to \infty} \mathrm{ld}Z(T)/T$

To arrive at this expression, we determine the information entropy (18), express this as a function of the information duration $T$, divide by $T$ (in order to become independent of this duration), and proceed to the limit as $T \to \infty$. In view of what has already been explained, we may put:

(22) $\quad Z(T) = 2^{\xi} \quad \text{and} \quad \xi = T/t_0$

For accurate transmission of the pulses, the information element duration $t_0$ must always exceed (or, in the limiting case, be equal to) the build-up time, as determined by the electrical properties of the channel (Fig. 5b), that is:

(23) $\quad t_0 \geqq \tau$

A well known principle in conventional communication theory, first formulated by K. Küpfmüller, states that the build-up time $\tau$ and the band width $B$ of a channel are linked by the relation:

(24) $\quad \tau = 1/(2B)$

Putting $t_0 = \tau$, and substituting (22) and (24) into (23), we obtain for the information capacity of a disturbance-free channel:

(20) $\quad C = \lim_{T \to \infty} \mathrm{ld}2^{2BT}/T = \lim_{T \to \infty} 2BT/T = 2B$

which is the relation already presented above.


The completely disturbance-free channel is an ideal case, not realizable in actual practice. For even at best there is an irreducible minimum of disturbance, so-called thermal noise, due to the thermodynamic interchange of energy between a material and its environment, associated with random irregularities and fluctuations in the electron stream. With sufficient amplification these disturbances can be made audible in a loudspeaker. This sort of noise is, for example, heard in VHF reception when the receiver is adjusted to maximum sensitivity and not tuned to a transmission.

Let $E_R$ denote the thermal noise energy (disturbance energy), and let the information energy $E_N$ be taken as the effective energy. Then, out of $Z$ information element amplitudes at the input end of the channel, only the proportion $Z'$ will be recognizable at the output end, after transmission through the channel. This means a decrease in the information content, therefore also a lowering of the information entropy and, consequently, a decrease in information capacity to the value:

(25)     $C = B\mathrm{ld}(1 + (E_N/E_R))$

for the disturbed channel.

**FIG. 6**
**LOSS OF INFORMATION DUE TO THERMAL NOISE (DEFORMATION OF THE PULSES)**

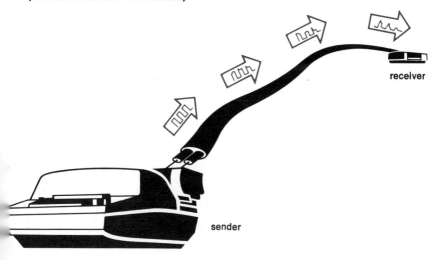

receiver

sender

For high values of the disturbance energy ($E_R \gg E_N$) the following approximation can be introduced into equation (25):

(26)    $1 + (E_N/E_R) \approx e^{E_N/E_R}$

and we thus obtain:

(27)    $C \approx B(E_N/E_R)\mathrm{lde} \approx 1.443 B(E_N/E_R)$

The expression for the information capacity of the disturbed channel (25) is obtained by means of a simple calculation based on considerations as to the proportion $Z'$ of information that is recognizable at the output end of the channel in relation to the information $Z$ fed into the input end (Fig. 7). We obtain the number $Z'$ of distinguishable amplitude ranges, or amplitude levels, on considering that the total energy $E_N + E_R$ flowing through the channel is proportional to the square of the amplitude. On dividing the total energy by the disturbance energy, we obtain the number of square-amplitude ranges which are distinguishable, in other words, the number of amplitude levels is determined by the square root of this quotient. Therefore:

(28)    $Z' = \sqrt{(E_N + E_N)/E_R}$

According to (18) we now obtain for the information yield for these $Z'$ information element amplitudes:

(29)    $H = \frac{1}{2}\mathrm{ld}(1 + E_N/E_R)$

Hence we find for the information capacity:

(25)    $C = B\mathrm{ld}(1 + (E_N/E_R))$

An interesting insight into the transmission conditions for an information channel is obtained by using the equation (25) (which relates to the information capacity of the disturbed channel) to find the expression for that information quantity $M$ which can at most be transmitted through the disturbed channel in the time $t$. Thus we obtain:

(30)    $M = Ct = Bt\mathrm{ld}(1 + (E_N/E_R)) = Bt\rho$

where the dual logarithm is represented by the abridged notation $\rho$, and is designated as the signal-to-noise ratio (high values of the disturbance energy are associated with low values of $\rho$).

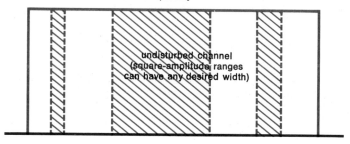

total quantity

undisturbed channel
(square-amplitude ranges
can have any desired width)

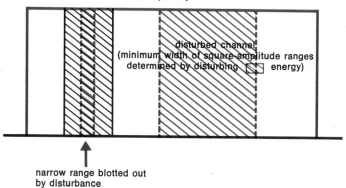

total quantity

disturbed channel
(minimum width of square-amplitude ranges
determined by disturbing  energy)

narrow range blotted out
by disturbance

**FIG. 7  DISTINGUISHABLE AMPLITUDE LEVELS
AT EXIT OF CHANNELS WITH AND WITHOUT DISTURBANCES**

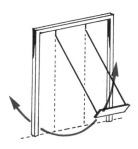

**FIG. 8  DYING-OUT OF OSCILLATIONS OF A SWING**

According to equation (25), the quantity of information is represented by the volume $M$ of a parallelepiped in a three-dimensional co-ordinate system (with axes $B$, $t$ and $\rho$). Any particular volume $M$ can be produced by any number of different combinations of the three co-ordinates $B$, $t$ and $\rho$, as shown in Fig. 9.

In terms of communication engineering this means that the transmission of an equal quantity of information (volume of the parallelepiped) with large band width and high signal-to-noise ratio (low disturbance energy) requires a shorter time than it does with small band width and low signal-to-noise ratio (high disturbance energy). Transmission channels of the first type are expensive, whereas those of the second type are relatively cheap to construct.

By suitable choice of information capacity, it is possible always to select the most economical transmission channel for dealing with any particular communications engineering problem. For extreme conditions—for example, for a 1000:1 ratio of disturbance energy to effective energy—it is, for a band width of 3400 cycles/sec., as employed in telephony, still possible to transmit at a rate of 4 bits/sec. This means that even with very severe disturbance the channel can still transmit 4 elements of information per second quite intelligibly (Fig. 10).

In practice we often encounter the case where it is necessary to decide be-

FIG. 9   THREE-DIMENSIONAL REPRESENTATION
OF AN INFORMATION QUANTITY OF 12 BITS

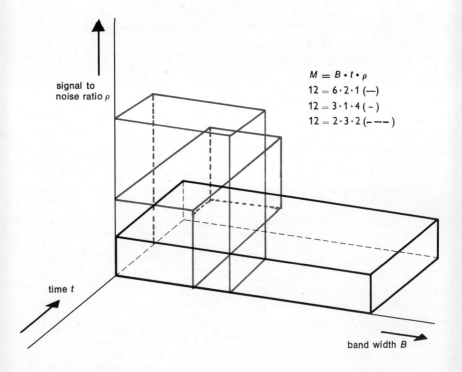

signal to
noise ratio $\rho$

$M = B \cdot t \cdot \rho$
$12 = 6 \cdot 2 \cdot 1 \,(\text{—})$
$12 = 3 \cdot 1 \cdot 4 \,(\text{–})$
$12 = 2 \cdot 3 \cdot 2 \,(\text{---})$

time $t$

band width $B$

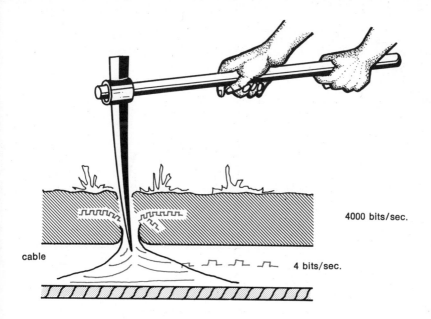

4000 bits/sec.

cable

4 bits/sec.

**FIG. 10   DISTURBED TELEPHONE LINE**

tween two alternatives, that is, where there are two equally probable sets of data. We first calculate the information entropy as a function of the (statistical) frequency. For this purpose, we take the frequency of one of the data sets as $h$, that of the other set will then be $(1 - h)$. The mean information entropy $\bar{H}$ as a function of the frequency $h$ is therefore:

$$(31) \qquad \bar{H}(h) = -[h\,\mathrm{ld}\,h + (1 - h)\mathrm{ld}(1 - h)]$$

We are more particularly interested to know for what values of the frequency $h$ the information entropy $\bar{H}$ acquires an optimum value. In the present case, the optimum value of $\bar{H}$ is identical with the maximum value, since $\bar{H}$ is dependent only on one parameter, namely, the frequency $h$. $\bar{H}$ attains this value for $h = \frac{1}{2}$. This value is obtained as a result of the following considerations. If the information entropy $\bar{H}$ as a function of the statistical frequency $h$ is to have a maximum value, the first derivative of $\bar{H}$, with respect to $h$, must become zero, thus, the following condition must be satisfied:

$$(32) \qquad \mathrm{d}\bar{H}/\mathrm{d}h = -[\ln 2 + \mathrm{ld}\,h - \ln 2 - \mathrm{ld}(1 - h)] = \mathrm{ld}\,h/(1 - h) = 0$$

Hence:

$$(33) \qquad h/(1 - h) = 1\cdot$$

or

$$(34) \qquad h = \tfrac{1}{2}$$

Thus we obtain equal probability for the two sets of data, as already indicated above.

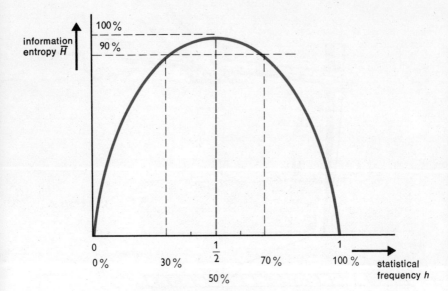

**FIG. 11 PARABOLIC DISTRIBUTION OF INFORMATION ENTROPY FOR TWO EQUALLY PROBABLE DATA SETS**

The curve representing the information entropy as a function of $h$ is given in Fig. 11 (cf. Fig. 10, p. 27). We see that it has a maximum for $h = \frac{1}{2}$. The two processes, characterized by the data sets, therefore have a 1:1 probability ratio. As appears from the curve, deviations of $\pm 20\%$ from the 1:1 ratio cause only a 10% decrease in the information entropy. This favorable behavior of the entropy is, for example, reflected also in weather forecasts, when they are reduced to a simple formula or phrase — as embodied in popular dicta such as the traditional German one suggested in Fig. 12: "When the cock crows on the dunghill, the weather will change or will remain just as it is."

**FIG. 12**

To conclude these considerations, it is of interest to reflect why these principles of information theory were not clearly understood until cybernetics provided fresh insight. After all, it might equally well have occurred that the experimental discovery of the thermodynamic entropy change associated with an information quantity of one bit led on to the concept of information entropy (Fig. 13). A simple calculation shows the thermodynamic entropy change to be equivalent to $10^{-16}$ erg per degree centigrade. This is an exceedingly small quantity. Even in television broadcasting, in which the entropy changes between the individual points of information are very small indeed, these are (converted to the thermodynamic scale) still on the order of $10^{-9}$ erg/degree.

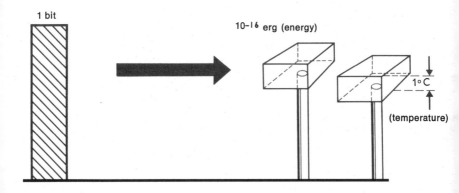

**FIG. 13  BINARY DIGIT AND THERMODYNAMIC ENTROPY**

According to Brillouin, the relationship between the units of measurement for thermodynamic entropy $S$ and information entropy $H$ can be calculated from the equations for $S$ and $H$, namely, equations (7) and (8). It is thus possible to determine the decrease (in erg/degree) of the thermodynamic entropy when the information entropy increases by one bit. Let $Z$ denote the number of equally probable states, or data, respectively. Then the equations for $S$ and $H$ are:

(35)  $S = k \ln Z$  and  $H = \operatorname{ld} Z = \ln Z / \ln 2$

For the ratio of the dimensional units, we obtain:

(36)  $\mu = S/H = k \ln 2 \approx 10^{-16}$

where we conceive the temperature expressed in energy units $k$, so that the ratio $\mu$ becomes a dimensionless quantity. We have thus obtained the value indicated above, and it is understandable that this entropy change, because it is so very small, at first escaped experimental detection.

The co-ordination between data (for example, numbers, letters, or syllables) and pulse trains is called coding. The value of the information entropy, and therefore of the utilization of the information yield of the source, that is, of the information flow, in bits, coming from it, depends on the coding (Fig. 14). The coding whereby each item of information can, on average, be transmitted with the least number of bits can be regarded as the optimum coding. In that case, the information flow conveys the maximum amount of information, and the information entropy attains its maximum value $H_{max}$. This is always so if the source only contains data (items or elements of information) that are all equally probable. It is different, however, if the data contained in the source differ in probability. This will be elucidated by the following example:

We have already established the relation $\bar{H} = -\Sigma h_i \mathrm{ld} h_i$ (see equation (9), page 34), which gives us a mean value for the information entropy $\bar{H}$ per item of information. This value $\bar{H}$ depends to a great extent on the coding. Undoubtedly the information entropy will increase if the more probable data (that is, the data occurring with higher statistical frequency) are assigned a smaller number of bits than the less probable ones. Thus a larger number of data can be expressed by the same "bit stream," which is determined by the yield of the source. An example will clarify this. Suppose that a source contains four items of information in the form of the letters $A$, $B$, $C$, $D$, having the statistical frequencies $h_A = \frac{1}{2}$, $h_B = \frac{1}{4}$, $h_C = \frac{1}{8}$, $h_D = \frac{1}{8}$. The information entropy $\bar{H}$, and therefore the yield of the source according to (19), is then expressed by:

$$(37) \qquad \bar{H} = -\tfrac{1}{2}\mathrm{ld}\tfrac{1}{2} - \tfrac{1}{4}\mathrm{ld}\tfrac{1}{4} - \tfrac{1}{8}\mathrm{ld}\tfrac{1}{8} - \tfrac{1}{8}\mathrm{ld}\tfrac{1}{8} = \tfrac{7}{4}$$

For equal frequency of the letters: $h_A = h_B = h_C = h_D = \frac{1}{4}$ the source would – both according to (18) (with $Z = 4$), and according to (19) – have the maximum value of its information entropy:

$$(38) \qquad \bar{H} = 2$$

This maximum entropy would correspond to a coding in which two bits are assigned to each of the equally probable data, that is, to each letter (Fig. 15).

If we choose the same coding for the first case (with letters of unequal frequency), we find this to be not the most favorable coding for that case. There must be some other coding that can manage with fewer bits per letter, and which corresponds to the entropy value expressed by (19). This is indeed so. For if we perform the coding in accordance with the scheme presented in Fig. 16, we find the average requirement to be $\frac{7}{4}$ bits per letter on determining the sum of the products of the frequencies and the number of bits assigned to each, in other words, the procedure for determining the entropy (31): $\frac{1}{2} \times 1 + \frac{1}{4} \times 2 + \frac{1}{8} \times 3 = \frac{7}{4}$. Thus the information yield of the source is fully utilized: $\bar{H} = \bar{H}_{max}$.

In the case where the coding chosen is not the optimum, the proportion $r$ of the information entropy of the source will remain unutilized, and there will be a certain amount of overdetermination of the data. This proportion is expressed by:

$$(39) \qquad r = (\bar{H}_{max} - \bar{H})/\bar{H}_{max} = 1 - \bar{H}/\bar{H}_{max}$$

Shannon applies the term "redundancy" to denote this proportion, or ratio, $r$. In the example considered here, we obtain for $\bar{H}_{max} = 2$ and $\bar{H} = \frac{7}{4}$, the following value for $r$:

$$(40) \qquad r = \tfrac{1}{8}$$

(corresponding to 12.5%).

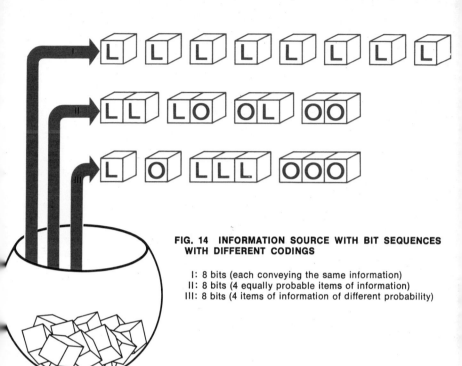

**FIG. 14 INFORMATION SOURCE WITH BIT SEQUENCES WITH DIFFERENT CODINGS**

I: 8 bits (each conveying the same information)
II: 8 bits (4 equally probable items of information)
III: 8 bits (4 items of information of different probability)

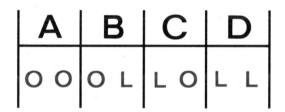

| A | | B | | C | | D | |
|---|---|---|---|---|---|---|---|
| O | O | O | L | L | O | L | L |

**FIG. 15 CODING FOR EQUALLY PROBABLE ITEMS OF INFORMATION**

| A | B | C | D |
|---|---|---|---|
| O | LO | LLO | LLL |

**FIG. 16 OPTIMUM CODING FOR ITEMS OF INFORMATION OF DIFFERENT PROBABILITY**

# REDUNDANCY

Data are always associated with redundancy if their coding is not the optimum, that is, so long as it is possible to establish a different coding for such data, which is able to manage with fewer bits. Since redundancy is a very important concept, it will be examined here in greater detail with reference to some examples. In everyday life, redundancy compensates to some extent for the shortcomings of the human data processing system: the brain. It compensates for the fact that people are forgetful, so that instructions that the brain ought to store without loss are nevertheless apt to be forgotten. This is one of the most significant functional differences between the human brain and, for example, the electronic data store. Certain familiar routine actions which we perform every day and which always proceed according to the same pattern, such as getting up in the morning, washing, dressing, shaving, having breakfast and going to school or work, in short, actions which we perform "mechanically," may nevertheless sometimes show gaps. Children, in particular, are prone to forget to do certain things: "Don't forget to brush your teeth" is the sort of redundant information that serves to bridge a frequently recurring gap in performance.

For the electrical transmission of a quantity of information, a certain amount of redundancy, such as occurs in speech and also in the written language, is also of great importance. For then any disturbances arising along the transmission channel will not entirely invalidate the information. Examples from the German and the English language will serve to illustrate this.

## FIG. 1 FREQUENCY WITH WHICH LETTERS OCCUR IN GERMAN

| letter | frequency | $-h_i \operatorname{ld} h_i$ |
|--------|-----------|------------|
| E | 0.1669 | 0.431 |
| N | 0.0992 | 0.331 |
| I | 0.0782 | 0.287 |
| S | 0.0678 | 0.283 |
| T | 0.0674 | 0.262 |
| R | 0.0654 | 0.257 |
| A | 0.0651 | 0.256 |
| D | 0.0541 | 0.228 |
| H | 0.0406 | 0.188 |
| U | 0.0370 | 0.176 |
| G | 0.0365 | 0.174 |
| M | 0.0301 | 0.152 |
| C | 0.0284 | 0.146 |
| L | 0.0283 | 0.146 |
| B | 0.0257 | 0.136 |
| O | 0.0229 | 0.125 |
| F | 0.0204 | 0.114 |
| K | 0.0188 | 0.108 |
| W | 0.0140 | 0.086 |
| V | 0.0107 | 0.070 |
| Z | 0.0100 | 0.067 |
| P | 0.0094 | 0.063 |
| J | 0.0019 | 0.017 |
| Q | 0.0007 | 0.007 |
| Y | 0.0003 | 0.004 |
| X | 0.0002 | 0.003 |
| total | 1.000 | $\bar{H}_{German} = 4.10$ bit/letter |

$$\bar{H}_{max, German} = \operatorname{ld} 26 = 4.70 \text{ bit/letter}$$

The German verb "ziehen" (meaning "to pull") contains six letters, three of which — the e h e in the middle of the word — are, in effect, redundant, in the information-theoretical sense envisaged here. The three letters z i n (with the i pronounced long) would suffice to transmit the meaning of the word. We see, however, that if the transmission is mutilated in consequence of disturbances, serious misunderstanding of the meaning of the word can very easily occur when it is thus transmitted in its non-redundant form. In ordinary written language, one of the letters can quite permissibly be mutilated: it will then still be perfectly possible to make out the word "ziehen."

The English written language offers some even more striking examples. The word "through" comprises seven letters, of which only three are essential, namely, a symbol for the English th, a symbol for r, and a symbol for u (ough). Here again, with non-redundant coding, any mutilation in transmission can quite easily make the message totally unintelligible, whereas with redundant coding it is still possible to make out the intended information even if one of the seven letters is mutilated.

Figs. 1 and 2 are tables giving the frequency with which the individual letters occur in the German and the English written language respectively. From these figures it is possible to make an assessment of the redundancy of these languages. We find that the mean information entropy $\bar{H}$ (calculated from the frequency) is 4.1 bits per letter for German and 3.87 bits per letter for English.

These figures relate to information entropy, taking account solely of the frequency of individual letters. It is a well known fact that both in German

## FIG. 2 FREQUENCY WITH WHICH LETTERS OCCUR IN ENGLISH

| letter | frequency | $- h_i \, \mathrm{ld} \, h_i$ |
|---|---|---|
| E | 0.105 | 0.323 |
| T | 0.072 | 0.272 |
| O | 0.065 | 0.254 |
| A | 0.063 | 0.250 |
| N | 0.059 | 0.238 |
| I | 0.055 | 0.228 |
| R | 0.054 | 0.226 |
| S | 0.052 | 0.218 |
| H | 0.047 | 0.206 |
| D | 0.035 | 0.178 |
| L | 0.029 | 0.147 |
| C | 0.023 | 0.124 |
| FU | 0.0225 | 0.122 |
| M | 0.021 | 0.117 |
| P | 0.0175 | 0.106 |
| YW | 0.012 | 0.076 |
| G | 0.011 | 0.071 |
| B | 0.0105 | 0.069 |
| V | 0.008 | 0.055 |
| K | 0.003 | 0.025 |
| X | 0.002 | 0.018 |
| JQZ | 0.001 | 0.010 |
| space between words | 0.233 | 0.535 |
| total | 1.000 | $\bar{H}_{\text{English}} = 3.87$ bit/letter |
| | | $\bar{H}_{\text{max, English}} = \mathrm{ld}\ 27 = 4.74$ bit/letter |

and in English there often occurs group formation. For example, in German such groups (letter combinations) are ei, au, eu, en, er, ie, ig, sch; while in English we have ou, gh, th, ed, ty, ing, sh. As a result of this grouping of letters, there is a further reduction of the mean information entropy. By carrying out counts of letter groups in German and English texts, Küpfmüller has shown that the mean information entropy in the German written language tends to the limit $\bar{H}_{g\ German} = 1.6$ bits/letter, while for English the corresponding limit is $\bar{H}_{g\ English} = 1$ bit/letter (Fig. 3). We can now calculate the redundancy from equation (39), using the maximum values for the information entropy (see Figs. 1 and 2, pages 48 and 49), thus we obtain, for the German and the English written language, respectively:

$$(41) \qquad r_{German} = 1 - \frac{\bar{H}_{g\ German}}{\bar{H}_{max\ German}} \approx 66\%$$

and

$$(42) \qquad r_{English} = 1 - \frac{\bar{H}_{g\ English}}{\bar{H}_{max\ English}} \approx 75\%$$

From these equations it appears that in written German two-thirds, and in written English three-quarters, of all the letters in a connected passage of text are redundant and make no real contribution to the transmission of the information content. To transmit an information content of 1.6 bits in German, $2^{1.6}$, or approx. 3 symbols, of equal frequency, in suitable coding, would suffice, while in English only $2^1$, or 2 symbols, of equal frequency (equal probability) would be required, assuming that, in both cases, the optimum coding is chosen and the redundancy is zero ($r = 0$). The optimum coding would admittedly result in economical utilization of the transmission channels (enabling the transmission rate of the information to be increased three- to four-fold), but the absence of any redundancy would make it much more difficult to determine correctly the information, in the event of mutilation, and would therefore increase the susceptibility to disturbance.

An example of coding with a very high degree of redundancy is afforded by the five-unit teleprinter code. This code was established before Wiener's cybernetics and the principles of information theory had been discovered. It operates with a relatively large information flow. All letters are treated as though of equal statistical frequency. From equation (18), on page 34, we thus obtain for the information entropy, in the case of the 26 letters of the German written language, the value $H = 4.7$, or approx. 5 bits per letter. Thus in the teleprinter code, each letter is transmitted by means of five bits, or information elements, corresponding to current impulses or current pauses of 1/50 second duration. At the beginning and end of each letter, one bit of 1/50 second duration is transmitted as a marker, thus the total duration of transmitting one letter is about 1/7 sec., and the teleprinter (or teletypewriter) can transmit up to 7 letters per second, or a maximum of 420 letters per minute. The teleprinter code is presented in Fig. 4; the bits are symbolized by L and O (see page 10). Because of the integral (whole-number) character of the bits, five information elements had to be adopted for this code. But since $2^5$ is equal to 32, it provides the possibility of transmitting six more elements than are necessary for reproducing the letters of the alphabet. These redundant five-unit groups are utilized for signaling purposes. The time interval of 1/50 sec. is designated as 1 band.

According to the principles of information theory it would, with maximum utilization of the information yield, be possible to establish a redundancy-free optimum coding—more particularly, a three-unit code—for the teleprinter. As appears from the special example, however, the use of a method of rep-

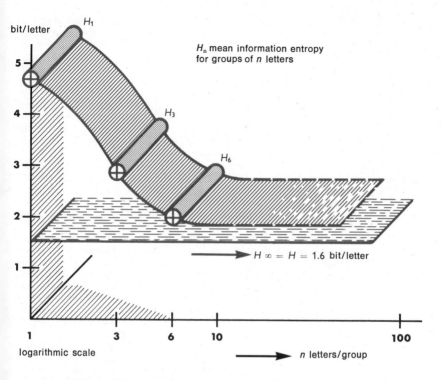

**FIG. 3 APPROXIMATE VALUES AND LIMIT VALUE OF THE MEAN INFORMATION ENTROPY FOR GROUPS OF $n$ LETTERS ($n \rightarrow \infty$) IN GERMAN (letter: $H_1$; syllable: $H_3$; word: $H_6$)**

| | | |
|---|---|---|
| A = LLOOO | J = LLOLO | S = LOLOO |
| B = LOOLL | K = LLLLO | T = OOOOL |
| C = OLLLO | L = OLOOL | U = LLLOO |
| D = LOOLO | M = OOLLL | V = OLLLL |
| E = LOOOO | N = OOLLO | W = LLOOL |
| F = LOLLO | O = OOOLL | X = LOLLL |
| G = OLOLL | P = OLLOL | Y = LOLOL |
| H = OOLOL | Q = LLLOL | Z = LOOOL |
| I = OLLOO | R = OLOLO | |

furthermore:     OOOLO     OLOOO     LLLLL
LLOLL     OOLOO     OOOOO

**FIG. 4 FIVE-UNIT CODE FOR TELEPRINTER ALPHABET**

resentation embodying a certain amount of redundancy is of great practical advantage, in that it provides a safeguard against the possibility of complete disruption of the information content of the message, in consequence of relatively minor disturbances in transmission. This is the reason why there has latterly been a change-over to a teleprinter code of even higher redundancy, namely, a seven-unit code (Fig. 5), which enables the machine to detect errors itself.

But the application of a redundant mode of representation is important, not only in the domains already referred to, in which it is sometimes possible to establish the redundancy in numerical terms, more particularly with the aid of equation (39), that is, the cybernetic method of calculation. Two further general examples will now be considered:

A lecturer, wishing to give a lecture that his audience can properly understand, cannot dispense with a certain amount of redundancy in his presentation of the subject. As a rule, this takes the form of repeating important points and recapitulating various sections of the subject, so as to give the audience an opportunity to digest and absorb the information given. It is indeed asking too much of any audience to expect them to remember every word of the lecture with the faultless accuracy of a tape recorder. The human listener grows tired, or his attention may briefly wander from the subject, so that he loses the thread of the argument. Hence it is essential that the lecturer should occasionally pause to recapitulate and lay special emphasis on important points. He must enable his audience to pick up the thread again and catch up with him. The more skilled the lecturer is in choosing the redundancy of his treatment of the subject (for example, by suitable use of the blackboard), the more readily intelligible will his lecture be. For the same reason, it is desirable always to end a lecture with a short retrospective survey of the whole subject treated, and thus bring the principal points once more into focus in the listeners' minds.

The same idea applies to communication in writing. It is, generally speaking, a good thing for the author of a book or article to use a redundant mode of presentation. In writing, however, it is not always necessary to revert in so much detail to earlier statements as in the case of a spoken discourse. Quite often, in writing, it will suffice to refer to a preceding page or statement by inserting some phrase such as "as already stated," or "as mentioned on page . . ." This sort of redundant writing will help more particularly those readers who use the book as a work of reference, that is, to look up information on particular subjects. Thus, depending on the state of their knowledge, they can "get into" the subject at any point in the book without having to wade through the whole of it (Fig. 6).

Particularly, a person who is already, to some extent, familiar with the subject can obtain the desired additional information quickly and conveniently from a book of this kind, if it is written with a suitable degree of redundancy. This book, too, aims at ensuring optimum utilization of its contents by means of an appropriate choice of redundancy. Thus redundancy is seen to have both a positive and a negative aspect. From the receiver's point of view it has the advantage of enabling him more easily to recognize and interpret the information transmitted to him, and to recall to mind certain facts that he may have wholly or partly forgotten. From the sender's point of view, on the other hand, redundancy appears to have more of a negative character; at all events, it reduces the economy with which he can operate, since it prevents optimum utilization of transmission channels. In considering the question as to how much redundancy should be provided in the transmission of information, we should remember what has been said about the information entropy of two equally probable sets of data (see pages 26 and 43). Clearly, the answer is that the "fifty-fifty probability" is the most advantageous choice.

```
A = LOLLOOO    J = OOLOLLO    S = OOLOOLL
B = OLLOOOL    K = OOOLLOL    T = LLOOLOO
C = LOOOLLO    L = OLLOOLO    U = LLOOOLO
D = LOOLLOO    M = LOLOLOO    V = OOLLOOL
E = OOOLLLO    N = OLLOLOO    W = LLOOOOL
F = LOOLOLO    O = LLOLOOO    X = OOOLOLL
G = OOOOLLL    P = OLOLOLO    Y = LOLOOLO
H = OLOOLLO    Q = OLOOOLL    Z = LOOOOLL
I = OLOLLOO    R = OOLOLOL
```

**FIG. 5  SEVEN-UNIT CODE FOR TELEPRINTER ALPHABET**
**(IN EACH CODE ARE THREE L AND FOUR O DIGITS,**
**i.e., THREE CURRENT PULSES AND FOUR PAUSES)**

**FIG. 6  REDUNDANCY IN A LECTURE (IMPORTANT FACTS ARE**
**WRITTEN ON THE BLACKBOARD, INFORMATION OF SECONDARY**
**IMPORTANCE IS RUBBED OUT) AND IN A BOOK**
**(HEADINGS AND REFERENCES)**

And here again we find that deviations of ±20% from this equal probability will reduce the information entropy by no more than 10%. We see that, as regards their own redundancies, the English and the German written languages likewise lie within the limits that we have indicated. The statement that the redundancy of the German language is 66% means that, from the sender's point of view, in building up an item of information from the letters of the alphabet, only 34% can be freely chosen; the other 66% will then be completely determined by the rules of the language. In English the free choice of letters is only 25%, the other 75% being determined by the rules. Of interest in this connection is the fact that the spoken language has a redundancy of 50%. Most sounds of speech take up a greater length of time than is necessary for their reception by the human ear and brain. The redundant parts of the information that are transmitted by the spoken language are either pauses or periods during which a tone is sustained at constant frequency. Neither of these elements contributes to the information content, but they do enable the hearer to compensate for any disturbances in his reception of the message or in his mental processes.

These redundancy analyses are carried out with the aid of acoustic spectrograms, in which the speech is "made visible" (they are, in fact, called "visible speech spectrograms"). In a spectrogram of this kind, the time duration of a spoken word or sentence is represented by the abscissae, and the acoustic frequencies of the spoken sounds are represented by the ordinates. An acoustic spectrogram of this type shows definite frequency bands for the vowels, but for the consonants it shows a noise spectrum spread over a wide frequency range. Fig. 7 represents the acoustic spectrum of the word "salmon." In the right-hand diagram, the acoustic spectrum has been redrawn schematically, in order to better reveal the time intervals that are redundant—which

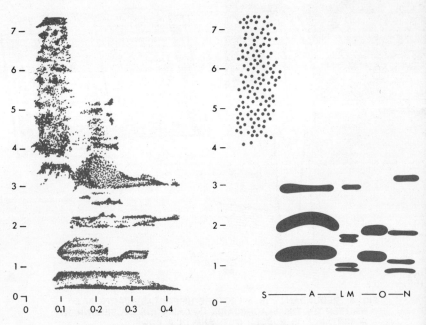

**FIG. 7 ACOUSTIC SPECTRUM OF THE WORD "SALMON"**

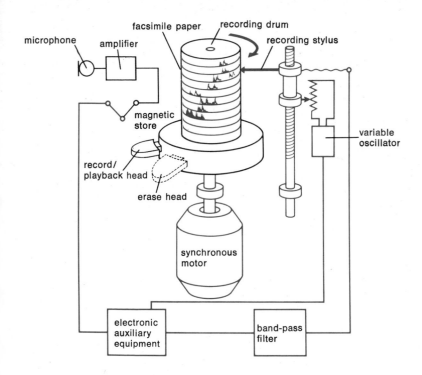

**FIG. 8 ACOUSTIC SPECTROGRAPH (SCHEMATIC)**

contribute nothing to the information content. These redundant portions constitute something like 50% of the speaking time. The apparatus for obtaining visible speech spectrograms is illustrated schematically in Fig. 8. The following is a description of its operation.

A strip of stress-sensitive facsimile paper is wrapped around a rotating drum, the speed of rotation of which determines the time scale (on the axis of abscissae) of the acoustic spectrum. A stylus, which is moved parallel to the axis of rotation of the drum (that is, in the direction of the ordinates) by an amount proportional to the acoustic frequency, records the frequencies. The latter are picked up by a microphone and amplifier, and filtered out by means of a band-pass filter. Recording is performed through the agency of a magnetic storage device which enables the recording operation to be speeded up by displacement to a different frequency position. From this example, it can be inferred that speech, too, is characterized by non-optimal utilization of information entropy, this being due to internal linkages and relationships peculiar to the spoken language.

In this sense, redundancy may be regarded as a measure for "internal linkages," associated with particular governing relationships and rules. This becomes very clear if we imagine the two theoretical extreme cases: first, the world constituted as something entirely without rules or laws of nature; second, the condition where we know all the rules that regulate a world controlled by its own inherent laws and governing relationships. In the first case it would mean that the receiver's behavior would be controlled in a completely determinate manner by the incoming data, whose redundancy in this case would be zero (Fig. 9a). In the second case everything that happens is predetermined and foreknowable; the receiver requires no information at all, so that the redundancy of all incoming data is 100% (Fig. 9b). The reality is somewhere intermediate between these two extremes. Every living creature, man included, constantly requires information to control its behavior. But information already received, and recorded in the creature's memory, is also utilized for guiding and shaping the pattern of behavior. We call such processes "learning." The more the creature has learned, the higher is the degree of redundancy of all subsequently received information. Considerations of this kind have led to a cybernetic definition of "learning." As MacKay puts it: "Learning is a discovering and utilizing of redundancies."

H. Frank gives a very useful example to illustrate this: the periodic system of the chemical elements. Before this system had been established, the discovery of a new element was an entirely new piece of information, with no redundancy. This situation was changed dramatically when the regular patterns and rules governing atomic structure, as embodied in the periodic system, had been discovered. It then even became possible to predict the existence and properties of elements which had not yet been found in nature, but whose presence was suspected on the evidence of blank spaces in the system. Such prediction was based on the redundancy properties of those elements. It is these redundancies, determined by the rules and governing relationships of atomic structure, that made it possible to fill in many of the blanks in the periodic system in a relatively short time, in other words, to track down the "missing" chemical elements. It also became possible to apply certain corrections to earlier observations, and to predict the properties of, and actually discover, the so-called transuranic elements (Fig. 10).

Another example to illustrate the significance of redundancy can be based on Ohm's law, which states that the voltage drop (that is, the potential difference) between two points of a conductor carrying an electric current is equal to the product of the current strength and the resistance of the portion of conductor between the two points. A source of information can be assigned an "information potential," which is here taken to mean the ability of the source to give a certain yield when it is connected to any particular information channel. The transmission of information through a channel can thus be conceived as analogous to the transmission of an electric current between two points differing in their electric potential (Fig. 11). In that case, the redundancy would correspond to the ohmic resistance of the current path. Zero redundancy would correspond to zero ohmic resistance, and 100% redundancy would correspond to an infinitely high resistance. The redundancy itself would be represented by the unutilized portion of the information that the sources are able to yield because of the difference of their information potentials, that is, it is equivalent — in this analogy — to the ohmic voltage drop. The electrical energy loss in the form of heat, which can admittedly be utilized for heating, would correspond to the redundant information, which, as we have seen, also has its useful aspects, namely, in enabling the receiver better to detect any errors or disturbances in the information transmitted to him.

In order further to elucidate the concept of information potential, it should be pointed out that we know of many information sources, such as the planets, whose information we cannot as yet utilize exhaustively, as it has hitherto only been possible to obtain very incomplete data from those sources through optical transmission channels (telescopes). In order to get more information from them, and thus avail ourselves more fully of their information potential, we now carry out landings on the moon and send out space probes to take close looks at the planets, more particularly Venus and Mars,

**FIG. 9a INFANT:**
**EVERY ITEM OF INFORMATION IS NEW**
**(0% REDUNDANCY)**

**FIG. 9b SUPER-EXPERT:**
**EVERY ITEM OF**
**INFORMATION IS KNOWN**
**(100% REDUNDANCY)**

**|. 10 PERIODIC SYSTEM OF CHEMICAL ELEMENTS AS AN**
**EXAMPLE OF A HIGH-REDUNDANCY SYSTEM**

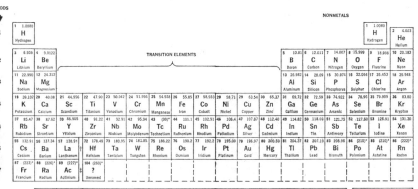

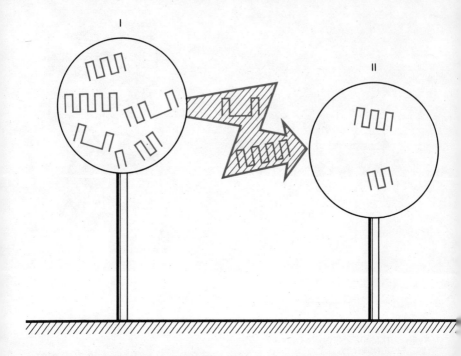

**FIG. 11    INFORMATION GRADIENT:** $U_\mathrm{I} - U_\mathrm{II} = R \cdot I$ **(REDUNDANCY • INFORMATION)**

and help to tap some of the information potential available there. In other words, the object of these space vehicles is to achieve better utilization of the distant information sources and supply us with a more ample flow of information about the planets (Fig. 12). Man himself, the most universal data processing system of all, effected a landing on the moon on July 21, 1969. The existence of redundancy therefore guarantees the existence of an information potential gradient, which in the case of 100% redundancy is unutilized and in the case of 0% redundancy would break down. It is thus comparable to an electric potential that is prevented from taking effect by the interposition of an insulator or that breaks down as a result of a short circuit. As we have seen in various examples, the most favorable value of redundancy is around 50%. This is also the reason why — as will be further explained (see page 59) — we do not fully utilize the possibilities of data processing equipment to reduce redundancy to something very near zero, but that, instead, we sometimes even artificially introduce redundancies. Why this is done will be explained with the aid of some comparative figures. A good typist — a human data processor — makes, on the average, about one mistake in every thousand keys she strikes on her typewriter. This performance therefore corresponds to an absolute error frequency of 1/1000. The requirements applicable to electrical transmission channels are substantially higher: an error frequency not exceeding 1/100,000 is usually specified for these. For data processing equipment, the frequency is even lower — less than 1/1,000,000; this would

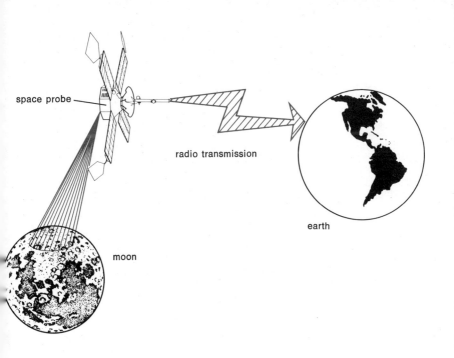

space probe

radio transmission

earth

moon

**FIG. 12  INFORMATION POTENTIAL OF THE MOON BEING TAPPED BY SPACE EXPLORATION**

be equivalent to one typing error in a text equivalent to about 250 normal pages of a book, assuming about 4000 typing strokes per page (Fig. 13). The difference between a human being and a data processing machine is that the former can detect logical relationships, whereas the machine cannot. For instance, when the context indicates that the circumference, $2\pi r$, of a circle has been referred to, and the letter $\pi$ has already occurred several times in combination with $2r$, a misprint—for example, $2\varphi r$—will at once strike the human data processor as being inconsistent and therefore incorrect. Data processing machines can indeed achieve optimum performance with regard to information entropy; but if we wish to make them resemble the human intelligence more closely in the detection of errors, the only way to achieve this is by dispensing with optimum utilization of the information entropy and introducing more redundancy into the information fed to the machine.

In teleprinting engineering, for example, this is in fact done in the case of overseas radio links. Instead of the usual five-unit code comprising five bits per letter, permitting 32 combinations (see page 51), a seven-unit code is employed, which has seven bits per letter and provides 128 possible combinations (see Fig. 5, page 53). With this large number of possibilities, letters and figures can each be represented by three pulses of current and four pauses, constituting a sequence of seven bits. So when the data processing machine receives a sequence containing more, or less, than three current pulses, it rejects it as erroneous, or affected by disturbances in transmission.

With increased redundancy, a larger number of bits will have to be transmitted per second if the rate of information transmission is not to be reduced. This in turn requires a greater band width, which, in practice, is not always possible with existing equipment (these aspects have already been considered on page 42 with reference to the three-dimensional diagram on that page).

The storage devices (memories) of data processing systems are, from time to time, relieved of information that has become superfluous or obsolete. In the human memory, too, this kind of thing happens in varying degrees, usually outside the control of our volition: we call it "forgetting." This process of forgetting is not without its positive aspects: it ensures that we never stop learning and that we continue to be receptive to new information from the environment. Finally, it should be noted that the quantity $(1 - r)$ is designated as the "information content" (Fig. 14). From equation (39) we obtain the following expression for the information content:

(43)     $1 - r = \bar{H}/\bar{H}_{max}$

FIG. 13  FREQUENCY OF ERRORS IN DIFFERENT DATA
PROCESSING SYSTEMS (PER MILLION STROKES)

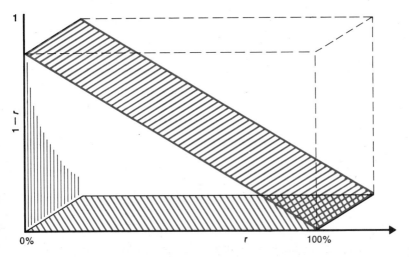

FIG. 14  DECREASE IN INFORMATION CONTENT $= 1 - r$
WITH INCREASING REDUNDANCY (R)

# CYBERNETICS AND LINGUISTICS

In the section dealing with redundancy (beginning on page 48), it has been shown that the cybernetic approach can be of great value to linguistic science. In those examples it was the information-theoretical, or the statistical, evaluation of the frequencies of letters occurring in the spoken or written language that enabled us to form numerical estimates of the redundancy inherent in English and German. However, letters are not the only fundamental elements that are statistically analyzable in a language. Other statistical information elements, in their hierarchic order, are the sounds (phonemes), syllables (composed of sounds), words (composed of syllables) and sentences (composed of words). The number of sounds in human speech is nearly twice as large as the number of letters.

For a mathematical analysis of the structure of a language the syllables are undoubtedly more advantageous and logically more appropriate than the letters as statistical information elements. The relative frequency distribution of the number of syllables per word for various languages will here be considered both empirically and theoretically. The empirical procedure consists in actually counting the numbers of syllables in given texts and then calculating their relative frequency. As examples for the German language we shall consider Goethe's "Wilhelm Meister," and Rilke's "Comet," and for Latin, Caesar's "De bello Gallico," and Sallust's "Bellum Jugurthinum." The results of these tests are presented in Fig. 1. It emerges that the curves have a characteristic shape for each language. The numbers of syllables occurring in the writings of other authors can also be counted and plotted in further curves of the same generally similar shape for any particular language. From such curves, we can determine a mean curve and then find the relative frequency distribution of the numbers of syllables per word that is characteristic of the language in question. Such characteristic curves for German and Latin are given in Fig. 2, while Fig. 3 shows characteristic frequency distri-

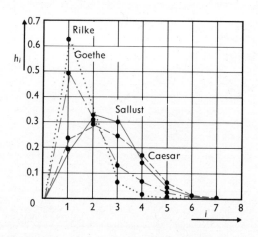

FIG. 1 RELATIVE FREQUENCIES *h* OF THE NUMBER OF SYLLABLES *i* PER WORD. WORDS OF ONE, TWO AND MORE SYLLABLES ($h_1$ O, 1; O, 2, etc.) ARE PLOTTED AGAINST NUMBER OF SYLLABLES PER WORD (*i* 1, 2, etc.)

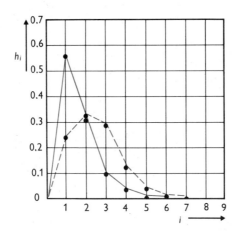

**FIG. 2 DISTRIBUTION OF THE RELATIVE FREQUENCIES OF THE NUMBERS OF SYLLABLES PER WORD FOR ONE GERMAN (———) AND ONE LATIN (– – –) AUTHOR**

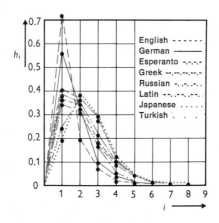

**FIG. 3 MEAN FREQUENCY DISTRIBUTION OF NUMBERS OF SYLLABLES PER WORD IN VARIOUS LANGUAGES**

bution curves for the numbers of syllables per word for eleven different languages, including one "artificial" language (Esperanto). Also stated in Fig. 3 are the average numbers of syllables $i$ per word; as will be explained later on, these figures play an important part in the theoretical consideration of the subject. A feature common to all the distribution curves in Fig. 3 is that they have a maximum, which is situated between 1 and 2 syllables per word. The actual magnitude of this maximum varies. These curves show that, for languages with a high maximum (high peak in the diagram), there is a rapid decrease in the frequency of words containing more syllables than correspond to that maximum. For languages with a lower maximum, this decrease is less rapid, that is, the curve plunges away less steeply to the right of the maximum.

For the experimental reproduction of such a distribution curve, it is necessary to consider what fundamental requirements must be fulfilled by all the individual languages. One condition is that a word must have at least one syllable. Another important requirement is to know the average number of syllables that is characteristic of the language in question.

For carrying out an experiment of this sort, we use a device known as Galton's board. At its upper edge this board has a number of "starting compartments," while an equal number of "target compartments" is disposed along its lower edge (Fig. 4). The intervening space is studded with rows of nails. Balls released from the starting compartments roll down towards the target compartments; during their descent, they encounter the nails and are tossed about in an entirely random manner. If an equal number of balls are placed in each starting compartment, the distribution of the numbers of balls that arrive in the target compartments will correspond to the so-called Gaussian frequency distribution, or normal distribution, which is expressed by the function $f(x) = ae^{-kx^2}$ (Fig. 5).

However, basing ourselves on the two above-mentioned initial conditions satisfied by every language, we obtain frequency distribution curves that do not conform to the normal distribution, but which, instead, have shapes such as those in Fig. 6. To use Galton's board we must therefore first place one ball in each starting compartment, thereby complying with the requirement that each word must comprise at least one syllable. Then we must distribute additional balls irregularly over the starting compartments, in such numbers as to conform to the relative frequency ratio. For example, if we wished to obtain the frequency distribution curve for German as a function of the number of syllables, we should thus have to add 63 balls. If, instead, we wished to reproduce, say, the Turkish language, we should additionally have to put 146 balls into the starting compartments. When the balls are allowed to roll down from these compartments through the rows of nails, the number of balls that arrive in the target compartments will represent a distribution curve which does, indeed, conform in character to the curves shown in Fig. 3. W. Fucks has derived the following mathematical relationship for the mean frequency distribution $h_i$ of $i$-syllabic words when the mean (average) number of syllables is $\bar{i}$:

$$(44) \qquad h_i = \frac{(\bar{i}-1)^{i-1}}{(i-1)!}\, e^{-(\bar{i}-1)}$$

Experimental data hitherto obtained would indicate that this relationship is valid for all languages. The only criterion that varies from one language to another is the empirically determined value $\bar{i}$ for the average number of syllables. The theoretical curves calculated with the aid of the distribution function (44), for values of $\bar{i}$ ranging from $\bar{i} = 1.2$ to $\bar{i} = 2.6$, have been plotted in Fig. 6. They are in very good agreement with the empirically determined

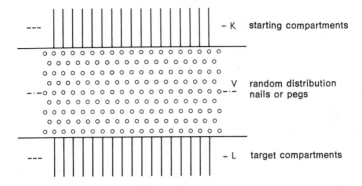

**FIG. 4   GALTON'S BOARD**

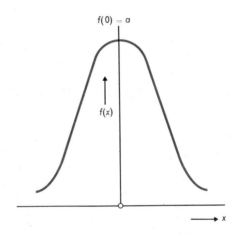

**FIG. 5   GAUSSIAN FREQUENCY DISTRIBUTION**
(x = error; f(x) = number of measured values with the error x)

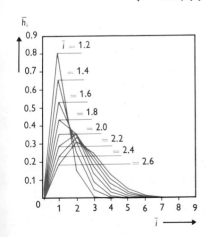

**FIG. 6   THEORETICAL FREQUENCY DISTRIBUTION**

curves. With the aid of (44) we can also calculate the mean information entropy, which, as we have seen, constitutes a measure for the information content (according to (19), page 34). We thus obtain the curve drawn in Fig. 7, which represents the relation between the mean information entropy $\bar{H}$ and the mean (or average) number of syllables $\bar{i}$ per word. The entropy values, calculated with the aid of the empirically determined values of the frequency, have been plotted as points in the same diagram. They are in fair agreement with the theoretically determined curve.

The precise numerical values for the mean frequencies of the syllables $h_i$ in the words of various languages, as well as the mean number of syllables $\bar{i}$ and the mean information entropy $\bar{H}$, are given in the table in Fig. 8. The satisfactory agreement between empirical observation and theory, as appears from Figs. 3, 6 and 7, shows that with his basic assumptions, which have led to the distribution formula (44), W. Fucks has indeed formulated the general statistical law governing the construction of human speech. The simplest words, which form the basis of every language, are in many cases mono-syllabic. Depending on the mental capabilities of the person concerned, further syllables are appended, in a completely random manner, to these monosyllabic words, so that polysyllabic words are formed. For any par-ticular language this is ascertained empirically, by carrying out syllable counts in characteristic and typical texts. As appears from Fig. 7, the English language contains the highest proportion of monosyllabic words, which means that it requires the least number of syllables to convey a given amount of information. This may be one reason why English has to so great an extent become adopted as an international language.

Besides the statistical approach associated with cybernetics, other sta-tistical conceptions, already known in physics, have also been applied to linguistic studies. For example, R. B. Lees describes the historical evolution of word stems, so-called morphemes, with the aid of an exponential equation which is exactly similar to the equation for radioactive disintegration. He compares the number of morphemes present in a language at a particular time with the corresponding number at another time, and finds that, as a re-sult of "morpheme disintegration" (Fig. 2), the number $N_0$ of morphemes initially present will, after the passage of a length of time $t$, have diminished to a number $N$ expressed by:

$$(45) \qquad N = N_0 e^{-\lambda t}$$

In this formula, the symbol $\lambda$ represents the so-called disintegration constant, which is a measure of the rate of disintegration of a morpheme, while $e^{-\lambda t}$ is an exponential function in which $e = 2.718. \ldots$ (the base of the natural logarithms). A similar function can be used for expressing the growth of capital or the increase of a debt by compound interest. From the statistical data at his disposal, Lees has calculated that for the transition from Egyptian to Coptic, a morpheme required about 760 years for its disintegration, and that the duration of a morpheme in the transitions from Old High German to New High German, or from Old Norse to Swedish, was about 850 years. He has also successfully applied his method to the life period of languages de-rived from a common origin and found, for example, a life period of 1236 years for the German/English language pair, while the corresponding figure for Osmanic/Azerbaijanic is 526 years. These values are in fair agreement with the historically ascertainable facts.

So far, objective aspects of linguistic phenomena have been considered. However, as was already apparent from Fig. 1, the subjective characteristics of the individual personality – the personality of the author – give rise to differences between the frequency distribution curves, though of course they bear an overall, distinctive resemblance to one another for authors writing in

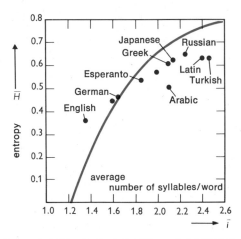

**FIG. 7 INFORMATION ENTROPY AS A FUNCTION OF THE AVERAGE NUMBER OF SYLLABLES**

| English | German | Esperanto | Arabic | Greek | Japanese | Russian | Latin | Turkish |
|---|---|---|---|---|---|---|---|---|
| 0.7152 | 0.5560 | 0.4040 | 0.2270 | 0.3760 | 0.3620 | 0.3390 | 0.2420 | 0.1880 |
| 0.1940 | 0.3080 | 0.3610 | 0.4970 | 0.3210 | 0.3440 | 0.3030 | 0.3210 | 0.3784 |
| 0.0680 | 0.0939 | 0.1770 | 0.2239 | 0.1680 | 0.1780 | 0.2140 | 0.2870 | 0.2704 |
| 0.0160 | 0.0335 | 0.0476 | 0.0506 | 0.0889 | 0.0868 | 0.0975 | 0.1168 | 0.1208 |
| 0.0056 | 0.0071 | 0.0082 | 0.0017 | 0.0346 | 0.0232 | 0.0358 | 0.0282 | 0.0360 |
| 0.0012 | 0.0014 | 0.0011 | — | 0.0083 | 0.0124 | 0.0101 | 0.0055 | 0.0056 |
| — | 0.0002 | — | — | 0.0007 | 0.0040 | 0.0015 | 0.0007 | 0.0004 |
| — | 0.0001 | — | — | — | 0.0004 | 0.0003 | 0.0002 | 0.0004 |
| — | — | — | — | — | 0.0004 | — | — | — |
| 1.4064 | 1.6340 | 1.8950 | 2.1036 | 2.1053 | 2.1564 | 2.2295 | 2.3920 | 2.4588 |
| 0.3670 | 0.4560 | 0.5350 | 0.5130 | 0.6110 | 0.6220 | 0.6470 | 0.6310 | 0.6290 |

**FIG. 8 MEAN FREQUENCY DISTRIBUTIONS OF SYLLABLES PER WORD FOR NINE LANGUAGES**

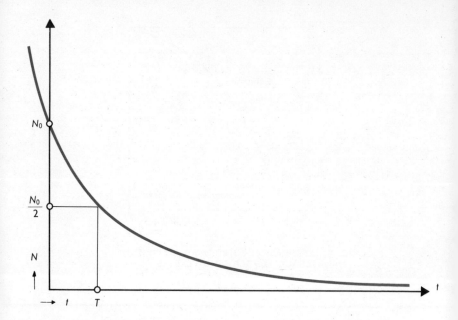

FIG. 9 $T = \dfrac{\ln 2}{i}$ HALF-LIFE PERIOD—THE TIME IT TAKES FOR THE INITIALLY EXISTING NUMBER OF MORPHEMES $N_0$ TO BE HALVED

the same language. The mean (average) number of syllables per word, and the information entropy, of a number of works by well known English, German and Latin authors are presented in the accompanying table (Fig. 10). It appears that the mean number of syllables varies by 7% in the English authors and by 29% in the German authors considered in this table. This is more clearly manifested in Fig. 11, which gives the relationship between the mean information entropy $\bar{H}$ and the mean number of syllables $\bar{i}$ for various authors.

An interesting question that arises in this connection is whether such $\bar{H}$-$\bar{i}$ diagrams can provide a criterion for deciding whether or not a controversial text is the genuine work of a certain author. It is not yet possible to give a definite answer to this question. It is, however, safe to say that the problem of authenticity is not a matter of linguistic structure alone and that considerations of meaningful content must also enter into it. But, in this respect, no clear-cut criterion has yet been found.

Similar difficulties are encountered in connection with the spoken language because, in addition to its text and objective structure, its information content comprises subjective components that are associated with the speaker's personality. Speech has a melodic quality, a certain "tone color" (timbre), which enables us to distinguish one speaker from another, as well as possessing a dynamic character (sound volume range)—all of which are features not found in the written language. K. Küpfmüller has attempted to estimate, empirically, the proportions of melody, tone color and sound volume range in the communication of the information content of spoken words. The table (Fig. 12) lists these speech components for different speaking

| author | title | i | H |
|---|---|---|---|
| Shakespeare | Othello | 1.294 | 0.2940 |
| Galsworthy | Swan Song I | 1.326 | 0.3215 |
| | Swan Song II | 1.338 | 0.3233 |
| | Forsyte Saga | 1.342 | 0.3344 |
| Huxley | Brave New World | 1.397 | 0.3675 |
| | Antic Hay | 1.409 | 0.3777 |
| Rilke | Cornet | 1.451 | 0.3836 |
| Carossa | Geheimnisse des reifen Lebens | 1.749 | 0.4783 |
| Hesse | Steppenwolf | 1.725 | 0.4710 |
| Mann | Buddenbrooks | 1.738 | 0.5054 |
| | Zauberberg | 1.757 | 0.5159 |
| Jaspers | Der philosophische Glaube | 1.887 | 0.4968 |
| Sallust | Epistula II | 2.482 | 0.6411 |

FIG. 10   (according to W. Fucks)

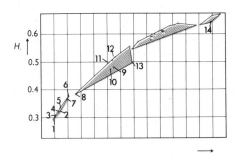

1 Shakespeare
2 Galsworthy
3 Swan Song I
4 Swan Song II
5 Forsythe Saga
6 Antic Hay
7 Brave New World
8 Rilke
9 Carossa
10 Hesse
11 Buddenbrooks
12 Zauberberg
13 Jaspers
14 Sallust

FIG. 11   (according to W. Fucks)

| speaking speed | contributions in bits from | | | | total flow of information | total entropy |
|---|---|---|---|---|---|---|
| | text | speech melody | tone color | sound volume range | | |
| 6   letter/sec. | 9.6 | 3.3 | 10 | 1 | 23.9 | 4.0   bit/letter |
| 12          '' | 19.2 | 6.3 | 9 | 1 | 35.5 | 3.0      '' |
| 18          '' | 28.8 | 8.5 | 7 | 1 | 45.3 | 2.5      '' |
| 24          '' | 38.4 | 9.3 | 5 | 1 | 53.7 | 2.2      '' |

FIG. 12

speeds. Fig. 13 shows the information flow rate as a function of speaking speed, split up into components corresponding to melody, personal characteristics, sound volume range and total flow. An information flow of 40 bits per second, at a mean speaking speed of 14 letters per second, conveys 42.5% more information than the written text alone. Language is not just a physico-acoustic process but also a linguistic one. This was already apparent when we were considering questions of speech analysis in dealing with the subject of redundancy (see page 54). This duality is still more clearly manifested below, where we consider the problems of speech synthesis.

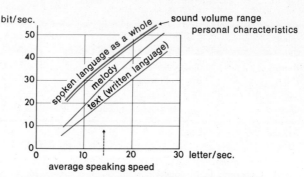

**FIG. 13   INCREASE OF INFORMATION CONVEYED BY THE SPOKEN LANGUAGE AS COMPARED WITH THE WRITTEN**

Strictly, "synthetic language," refers only to a set of acoustic effects which, although it is perceived as "speech" by human beings because it bears an acoustic resemblance to human speech sounds, is produced without the intervention of the human voice. A synthesis of this kind can be achieved by electrical simulation of the speech organs or by imitative reproduction of speech spectra, as has already been described (see page 54, Fig. 7). A third possibility, whereby quasi-synthetic speech is produced, is the utilization of "speech elements," that is, the process of building up words from individual sounds, which are "dissected" from spoken language recorded on magnetic tape, for example.

In simulating the human organs of speech, it must be remembered that only three cavities in the head participate in producing the sounds of speech, namely, the throat, the mouth and the nasal cavity. This system is illustrated schematically in Fig. 14. It can be simulated by an electrical equivalent circuit, as in Fig. 15. The "throat" and the "nasal cavity" are composed of 35 oscillating circuits, connected in series. The various tone colors, which are produced by changes in the size and shape of the cavities in the human speech system, must be reproduced in the simulating system by variations in the self-inductance $(L)$ and capacitance $(C)$ of the individual oscillating circuits.

With regard to the construction of a synthetic language with the aid of acoustic spectra we must remember the description already given of how an acoustic spectrograph functions (see page 55, Fig. 8). It was shown there how the significant properties of an acoustic spectrogram can be schematized. This means that it is possible to construct artificial spectrograms that can be converted into sounds with the aid of a playback apparatus. Acoustic spectrograms produced in this way, drawn by hand, are shown in Fig. 15.

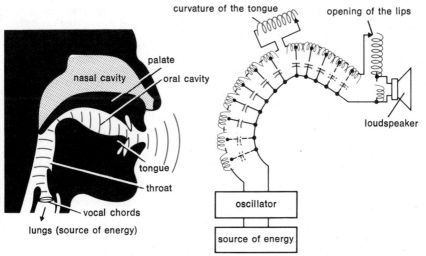

FIG. 14  THE HUMAN ORGANS OF SPEECH

FIG. 15  ELECTRICAL SIMULATION OF THE VOICE-PRODUCING SYSTEM

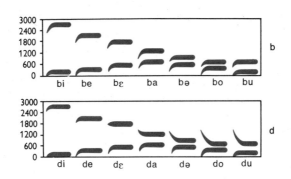

FIG. 16  SPECTROGRAMS OF SOUND COMBINATIONS DRAWN BY HAND

A suitable apparatus for converting such spectrograms into sounds has been designed by F. S. Cooper (Fig. 17). Its principle is that the spectrogram is depicted on a transparent film, which is moved past a photo-electric cell. In this way, the variations in light and shade produced in the scanning field of the photo-electric cell are converted into corresponding variations of electric current which, after undergoing amplification, are made audible by a loudspeaker. The schematic diagram of the playback apparatus shows how a wide flat beam of light, focused by a cylindrical lens, is modulated by a disc rotating at a certain speed and comprising 50 circular "sound tracks." In this way 50 bands of light are formed, side by side, whose frequencies are whole multiples of 120 cycles/sec. (the fundamental tone), and which cover the range from 120 to 6000 cycles/sec. These light images are projected, by a system of lenses, on to a scale that corresponds to the frequency axis of the spectrogram and is disposed at right angles to the direction of movement of the film. Now when an artificially produced spectrogram is interposed in the path of the light beam, the reflection of the rays will conform to the shape and position (corresponding to the duration and acoustic frequency) of the spectrogram patterns. The light reflected in this way is focused on to a photo-electric cell and converted into sounds.

As already stated, synthesis based on the utilization of "speech elements" will produce quasi-synthetic speech. The basic idea of building up speech from individual spoken sounds, which are stored up and used as required, was soon found to be impracticable. Words produced in this way remained largely unintelligible. The main reason for this failure was that the smooth transitions between the individual sounds (phonemes), which are characteristic of real speech, were absent because they had not been included in the synthesis.

Realizing this shortcoming, K. Küpfmüller and O. Warns have devised a method in which, instead of single sounds, double sounds are used for speech synthesis, that is, the "elements" they employ consist of combinations of two sounds with their transition. By joining such double sounds together with a certain amount of overlapping, it proved possible to synthesize something resembling natural speech (Fig. 18). The German language requires about 40 individual phonemes (sounds, including diphthongs) for its phonetic description. This means that, for this kind of speech synthesis, it is necessary to store 1560 double phoneme combinations. If it is desired to provide, over and above the purely textual information, additional information as characterized by melody, tone color and sound volume range, the required number of individual phonemes, and therefore the number of double phoneme combinations, will have to be increased to nearly 4000. To achieve this degree of elaboration with technically workable equipment, however, becomes prohibitively expensive.

Attempts have accordingly been made to reduce the requisite number of speech elements by appropriate methods. That this is indeed a possibility has been proved by B. Cramer, who succeeded in achieving speech synthesis by the combining of single phonemes, at the same time interposing a connecting sound between the successive speech elements. The duration of this connecting sound must, however, be so short as not to disturb the flow of speech. The vowel |ə|, known as the "shwa" sound in Hebrew, has been found to provide the most favorable connecting sound. For technical feasibility, this system requires only 40 speech elements, which consist of the phonemes of the phonetic alphabet. A "shwa" sound is interposed before and after each sound, so that the word "salmon," for example, is reproduced by the following assembly of elements:

(46)    |əsə|, |əaə|, |ələ|, |əmə|, |əoə|, |ənə|

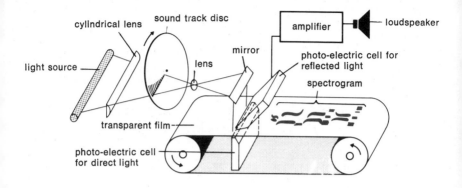

**FIG. 17  PLAYBACK DEVICE DESIGNED BY F. S. COOPER (SCHEMATIC)**

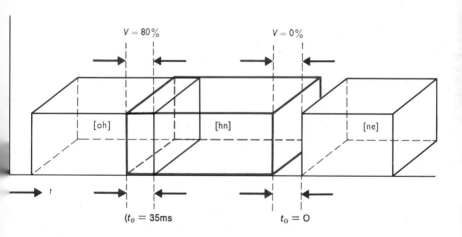

**FIG. 18  OVERLAPPING SPEECH ELEMENTS AS REQUISITE FOR INTELLIGIBILITY (V) OF A SYNTHETIC LANGUAGE ($t_o$ = overlapping time)**

With Cramer's method, it becomes possible to achieve speech synthesis at acceptable cost, so long as the aim is to obtain exact reproduction of the content, and additional information—as communicated by tone color, melody, sound volume range and personal characteristics—is dispensed with. All this shows that the statistical approach to information in cybernetics also opens up fresh prospects in the study of linguistics. Especially the field of structural linguistics readily fits into the general cybernetic pattern of thinking. This is because the rational aspects of speech are bound up with its structural character. Typically, when it comes to evaluating the creative character, which manifests itself in the meaningful content of the language used, the cybernetic method reaches the limits of what it can do. This becomes apparent more particularly in attempts to establish the authenticity of controversial texts by style analysis based on structural criteria. This is not really very surprising when we consider that every rational procedure is perforce restricted to the rational characteristics of the processes that it sets out to analyze. Processes such as intuitive and creative achievement, which do not belong to the domain of the rational (in the sense envisaged here), are fundamentally inaccessible to the cybernetic technique. We thus find ourselves up against the limits of this approach. It helps us to get closer to the transcendental core by enabling us to remove, as it were, a rationally manipulable enveloping layer, but we cannot thus get to the core itself. Fucks's equation (44), for example, states the general scheme of the speech formation process, but it tells us nothing about the "why" and "how" of the mean value of the number of syllables, which is characteristic of any particular language. In this formula, it appears merely as an empirical value that has to be determined from the language itself.

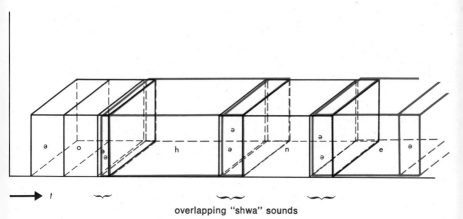

overlapping "shwa" sounds

FIG. 19 SYNTHETIC LANGUAGE FORMED WITH THE AID
OF A CONNECTING SOUND

# CYBERNETICS IN PHYSIOLOGY

The interactions between the external world and the actions of a human being who receives information about that world through the senses can be understood with the aid of the concepts and principles of cybernetics. This is illustrated by a simple experiment that we can perform for ourselves. (See Figs. 1a and 1b). I place an object — a pencil, for example — on the table and then pick it up. I perceive the position of the pencil through my sense of sight. This visual information is transmitted through nerves to the appropriate center in my brain, where it is "processed," and whence the necessary instructions to grasp the pencil are issued, through other nerves, to the muscles of my arm and hand. In performing this action, the movements of the arm are monitored by the eyes and optimally guided. When I close my eyes, this monitored guidance of my movements is absent. My hand now no longer goes unerringly to the pencil, but has to grope about until the pencil reveals itself to another of my senses, namely, the sense of touch. This experiment shows that the control exerted over these movements through visual feedback is much more effective than the control provided by tactile feedback. The latter is in fact so poor that my hand does not perform a direct movement at all, but oscillates about while seeking the pencil. This illustrates the typical behavior of a control loop with a very low degree of feedback: it oscillates. Thus we here have a process eminently suited for study by the methods of information theory, or cybernetics. But the transmission of sensory stimuli by the nervous system is not merely a process formally describable in terms of information theory; it is also, in reality, a form of electrical transmission (Fig. 2). The sensory nerve cells, for example, in the eye or ear, receive a stimulus from the external world. This stimulus is converted into an electrical potential and is transmitted, in the form of impulses, to the next nerve cell. The whole nervous system is composed of nerve cells (neurons) which are its structural and functional units.

Each neuron consists of the cell-body, a single long nerve fiber (axon), which carries impulses away from the cell-body, and a number of short dendrites, which receive impulses from the axons of other neurons. The axon, which is the actual information channel, may be several feet in length and has a diameter of about 0.0001 cm (0.00004 inch). The cell-body itself may be compared to an amplifier with two states of equilibrium. It can be either in the state of rest or in the working state, operating in the manner of a relay with an "off" and an "on" position (see also the flip-flop described on page 148 et seq.). The state of the cell at any given instant, therefore, corresponds to a binary digit or bit (see page 10). The extremity of the axon terminates at a dendrite, or at the cell-body of the next neuron. At the actual junction, the current path is interrupted by a discontinuity called the synapse, which is comparable to a toroidal transformer that serves as a galvanic separation between transmission channels and forms an inductive connection between them. Inside the synapse, a form of electrolytic transmission takes place, the actual "gap" being approximately a hundred-thousandth of a millimeter wide. At the synapse, the impulse is passed on by acetylcholine, a substance that is secreted there and which stimulates the adjacent neuron. Like every flip-flop circuit, the neuron, too, has a relaxation time, that is, it requires a certain length of time before it is ready to respond to another impulse. In physiology this is known as the refractory period, and it is of the order of 0.5 to 1 millisecond.

The velocity of propagation of an impulse in a nerve cell is approximately 120 m/sec. (400 ft./sec.), corresponding to about one-third of the velocity of

FIG. 1a PHYSIOLOGICAL FEEDBACK THROUGH SENSE OF SIGHT

FIG. 1b PHYSIOLOGICAL FEEDBACK THROUGH SENSE OF TOUCH

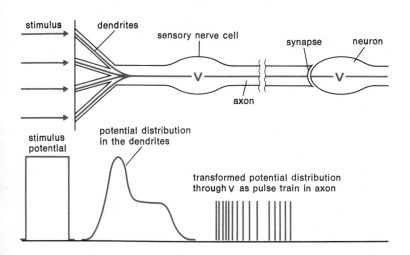

FIG. 2 TRANSMISSION OF A SENSORY STIMULUS

sound. A number of neurons serving as successive amplifier cells are connected between the receptor (sense-organ, such as eye, ear, and so on) and the brain. Fig. 3 illustrates a neuron with its dendrites and axon. The resting potential has a negative value: approximately −60 to −80 millivolts; the action potential is positive: +90 to +100 millivolts. The axons, often as many as two or three thousand, are grouped together in bundles (the nerves), which resemble cables and form complex intermeshed and interlinked networks. The intermeshing ensures that the sensory stimuli are transmitted not just by one nerve, but by a number of nerves, so that the error rate is reduced, and transmission to the brain and central nervous system is duly achieved. These analogies with electrical transmission systems constitute a highly schematized interpretation of the actual physiological process. Nevertheless, such considerations have yielded valuable insight into the precise location of nervous diseases—something that had not previously been ascertainable by other means. It has thus been possible to distinguish whether a disease is in the peripheral nervous system, that is, the nerves that carry the information to the central nervous system (brain and spinal cord), or in the central nervous system itself.

We have already referred to the act of picking up an object with our eyes open, that is, with a high degree of feedback, and with our eyes closed, so that visual control is lacking and oscillatory groping movements are performed in order to locate the object (see page 76). Such lack of control also manifests itself as a disease condition known as intention tremor. The patient, wishing to extend his hand and grasp an object, finds that his hand trembles and sways to and fro, so that he cannot correctly bring it into position to grasp the object. There is, however, another form of pathological tremor, called Parkinson's disease in which the behavior pattern is roughly the opposite to that associated with intention tremor. This disease, which generally occurs late in life, is characterized by tremors, particularly when the patient is at rest. In the earlier stages of the disease, the tremors cease when voluntary movements are performed; later they occur at all times except during sleep. In the case of intention tremor, there is evidently a disturbance in the feedback and thus in the brain's response to the sensory messages it receives. The disease is therefore located in the brain, whereas in Parkinson's disease the defect is in the nerves that transmit the feedback impulses.

On the basis of these cybernetic considerations, it is possible to devise an apparatus that demonstrates the typical behavior patterns associated with the two diseases just referred to. It consists of a small, three-wheeled carriage whose rear axle is driven by an electric motor. The front wheel is steerable. The carriage is provided with a pair of photo-electric cells directed obliquely forward and arranged in a bridge circuit. The bridge voltage is proportional to the difference in the intensity of the light entering the two photo-electric cells, and it can have its polarity reversed before being fed to an amplifier. Through this amplifier, the bridge voltage is used to drive a small motor that controls the sliding contact of a potentiometer. A second sliding contact of the same potentiometer is connected to the steerable front wheel by means of a lever the movements of which are controlled by a second small motor. This motor is driven, through an amplifier, by the voltage difference between the two sliding contacts. Depending on the polarity of the bridge voltage, the carriage will either seek the light (positive phototropism) or shun it, (negative phototropism). According to which of the two behavior patterns is displayed, the device can be said to behave like a "moth" (attracted to light) or like a "roach" (repelled by light). The circuit in which the photo-electric cells, the bridge, the first amplifier, and the first control motor are located corresponds to the transmission

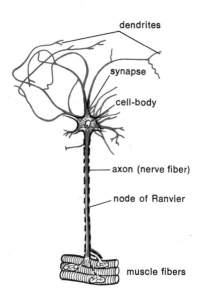

**FIG. 3   DIAGRAM OF A NEURON**

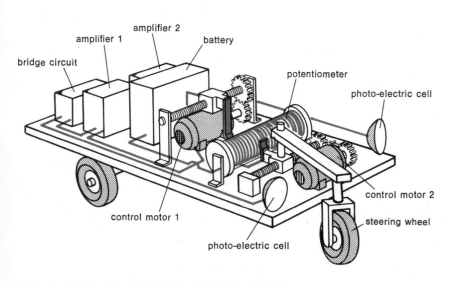

**FIG. 4   MODEL FOR SIMULATING INTENTION TREMOR AND PARKINSON'S DISEASE**

path of the stimulus through the nerves and the associated part of the brain. The second circuit, which is actuated by the voltage difference of the potentiometer and which ultimately manipulates the steering lever through the agency of the second control motor, corresponds to the feedback path. Disturbances in the two circuits may produce oscillations, in which case the steering lever will swing to and fro. When there are disturbances in the first circuit, the behavior will correspond to intention tremor, while disturbances in the second circuit cause a behavior pattern corresponding to Parkinson's disease in human beings. We must not, however, make the mistake of supposing that this model accurately simulates actual physiological behavior. The latter is a much more complex process. Yet the schematization, adopted for the purpose of the cybernetic interpretation, does reflect the significant features of the symptoms of these diseases.

The occurrence of such feedback phenomena are to be observed in a great many biological processes. The physiological control loops are eminently suited to a cybernetic interpretation. They serve primarily to control the vital conditions of the organism, in order to eliminate the influence of disturbances. These include, for example, blood pressure, body temperature, and the contraction or dilation of the pupil of the eye (see page 100 et seq.).

The way in which the pupil functions is illustrated in Fig. 5. In this case, the visual feedback causes contraction of the iris, so that the pupil (the opening in the iris) is reduced in size proportionally to the increase in light intensity, and vice versa. This cybernetic process can be observed very strikingly by means of an experiment that anyone can perform for himself. Stand in front of a mirror in a semi-darkened room. Look into the reflected image of your eyes and observe that the pupils are wide open when the eyes have had time to grow accustomed to the semi-darkness. Then shine the beam of a flashlight into one eye and note that both eyes immediately react by a contraction of the iris, so that the pupil becomes smaller (Fig. 6).

The examples that have been presented show that, from the cybernetic standpoint, the human brain plays the part of a control center. For a power consumption of about 25 watts, and a memory storage capacity of about $10^{14}$ bits, it has a volume of about 1500 cm³ and weighs about 1.5 kg (3.3 lb.). Via the senses the data are collected periodically, day by day, and thus add to the stored information content of the brain. Against this there is a simultaneous process of steady loss, or wastage, of stored information in consequence of forgetting, so that the average contents remain approximately in the vicinity of the above value. Of course, the precise brain capacity and amount of stored information vary from one person to another. Besides, it must once again be emphasized that the cybernetic approach to physiological problems can only provide schematic, average interpretations. At the same time, however, the advantage of this approach lies in the uniformity of its pattern of interpretation, which can be applied to a wide variety of processes.

Comparing the brain to a control center leads us to seek analogies with communications engineering—for example, similarity between the brain and some vast telephone exchange. There is, indeed, an apparent analogy between the telephone system and the complex network of nerve fibers that constitute the connecting paths between the many nerve centers, and which, by intermeshing and by providing alternative paths, serve to obviate errors and disturbances as far as possible. The functions of the brain are not equally divided between the two halves of that organ. In people who are right-handed, the left half of the brain is the dominant one. In left-handed people, the right half of the brain dominates. In either case, the dominant side of the brain performs the higher functions.

The predominance of one side of the brain may, for example, manifest it-

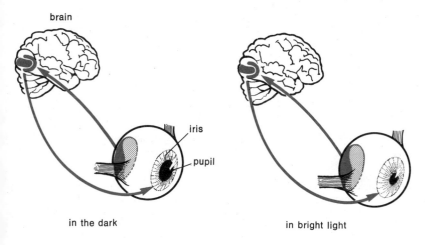

FIG. 5   PUPIL REACTION

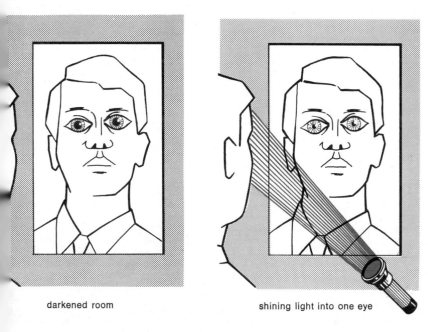

darkened room

shining light into one eye

FIG. 6   EXPERIMENT TO DEMONSTRATE PUPIL REACTION

self as the result of a brain injury. If the nondominant side of the brain is damaged in an adult, the consequences are much less serious than if the damage occurs on the dominant side. Early in his career the great bacteriologist Louis Pasteur suffered a cerebral hemorrhage that left one side of his body slightly paralyzed. After his death, an autopsy revealed that the right side of his brain had suffered such severe damage as to have been rendered virtually useless. Nevertheless, on recovering from his illness, he went on to make his most important scientific discoveries. If the dominant left side of his brain had been damaged to the same extent, it might well have been fatal or at least have reduced him to almost total mental incapacity.

In this context it is of interest to note that the "re-education" of left-handed children to right-handed behavior can sometimes cause serious disturbances of their vital functions. This may include various defects in speech, reading and writing. For such re-education does nothing to change the physiological basis of the dominance of one side of the brain (in this case the right side) over the other. However, in the normal person the non-dominant side of the brain is by no means devoid of purpose. Apart from the fact that such functions as seeing are two-sided, the practice and skill acquired by the "secondary hand" (usually the left hand) is associated with a corresponding degree of "training" of the non-dominant side of the brain. For such processes there must be connections between the two sides of the brain. Actually there are bundles of nerves linking them together, but in relation to the vast network of nerve cells within each part of the brain, these linking fibers are very few. "Detour connections," via the brain stem, are possible, however, though their precise paths are not fully known. Doubtless they are more liable to disturbance than the relatively few direct connections between the two sides of the brain. It would appear that the human brain has already reached a stage of development where it can no longer achieve optimum utilization of the anatomically available possibilities. The brain has become so large, and so complex, that it is unable to use all the organs simultaneously (Fig. 7).

This state of affairs suggests an analogy with an overloaded telephone exchange (Fig. 8) whose internal lines of communication — corresponding to the bundles of nerve fibers in the brain — cannot cope with all the messages they have to carry. In automatic telephony, this condition is manifested by the "busy" signal, which is already heard after the first few digits have been dialled.

The process of remembering items of information, such as a name or a number, may take some time to accomplish while the mind "searches" for the required data. There is a direct analogy with the process of information retrieval from a data store — for example, the process of obtaining information from the "directory assistance" service of the telephone system. Only one communication channel leads to the store, and when I try to remember a particular fact or figure, I use this channel to retrieve the information from the store, that is, from my memory. However, while I am thus using the channel in this interrogatory capacity, I temporarily block the channel whereby the remembered item of information is brought into my conscious mind. At some time or other we have all had the experience that, if we cannot remember a fact at once, we need merely wait a few minutes until the communication channel has been "cleared," that is, until the nerve path in question has been relieved of its interrogatory function; the desired fact then suddenly comes to mind.

Relatively little is yet known in detail about the functioning of the human brain. In particular, we do not know how the stimuli communicated by the sense organs are converted into conscious perceptions. For this reason the general cybernetic interpretation is all the more welcome in that it gives us at least some approximate clues as to the functional characteristics and how they are interlinked. Behavioral research has also made a major contribution. Sci-

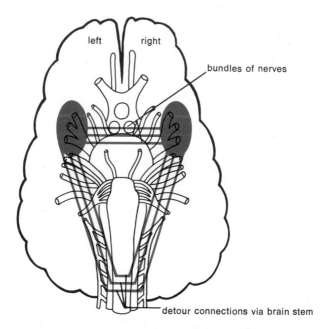

**FIG. 7 NERVE PATHS CONNECTING THE TWO SIDES OF THE BRAIN**

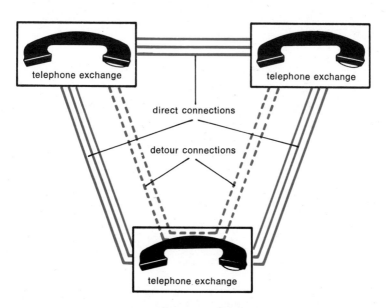

**FIG. 8 DIRECT AND DETOUR CONNECTIONS BETWEEN TELEPHONE EXCHANGES (NUMBER OF AVAILABLE LINES APPROXIMATELY 10% OF THE NUMBER OF SUBSCRIBERS)**

entists have studied the way in which the brains of lower animals work and have made important discoveries. For example, research by J. Z. Young has shown that the common octopus can be taught to take hold of geometric patterns made of plastic and to distinguish particular shapes, so that the creature's sense of sight and touch can be deduced from its reactions. The octopus can

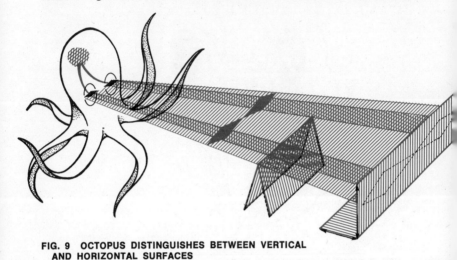

**FIG. 9  OCTOPUS DISTINGUISHES BETWEEN VERTICAL AND HORIZONTAL SURFACES**

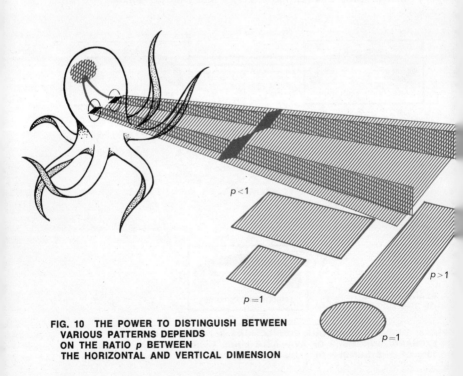

**FIG. 10  THE POWER TO DISTINGUISH BETWEEN VARIOUS PATTERNS DEPENDS ON THE RATIO $p$ BETWEEN THE HORIZONTAL AND VERTICAL DIMENSION**

distinguish between rectangles standing upright and lying horizontal, but it can detect no distinction between two obliquely placed rectangles, even if their respective planes are perpendicular to each other (Fig. 9). These experiments confirm the validity of the supposition that the octopus's ability to recognize and respond to shapes depends on the ratio of the vertical to the horizontal dimension of the object perceived. The creature is unable to distinguish between various geometric shapes (circles, squares) which do not differ from one another in their dimensions in the vertical and the horizontal direction. It appears that the horizontal dimension is of primary importance in this respect. A rectangle that is placed with its long side "horizontal," i.e., transversely to the creature's sight direction, is distinguished from a square with a side length equal to the shorter side of the rectangle; but if the rectangle is placed with its long side "vertical," i.e., parallel to the sight direction, then the octopus fails to distinguish it from the square (Fig. 10). Evidently the ratio $p$ of the horizontal dimension to the area of the geometric pattern plays a decisively important part. If we take this ratio as being 1 for the square, then $p > 1$ will correspond to the rectangle placed transversely, and $p < 1$ to the rectangle placed parallel with respect to the sight direction. The larger the value of $p$, the better is the octopus able to distinguish the shape, whereas shapes for which $p \leq 1$ are indistinguishable from one another. The importance of the vertical and horizontal dimensions of the visually observed image indicates a particular structure of the organs of sight. Confirmation of this is provided by the fact that the retina of the octopus's eye shows a rectangular arrangement of light-sensitive elements (Fig. 11a). The preference for the horizontal direction in the creature's visual function is in fact apparent from an external inspection of its eyes: the pupil is shaped like a horizontal slit. Also, the nerve fibers in the part of the brain concerned with visual perception extend in two preferred, mutually perpendicular, directions (Fig. 11b). These observations give indications as to how the processes in the much more complex brains of higher animals can be explained. More particularly, they show how greatly the "world-picture" that a creature forms in its mind is dependent on the structure of its sensory organs. To the octopus, the "world" presents itself as something composed essentially of horizontal features.

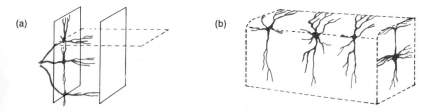

(a)          (b)

**FIG. 11  LOCATION OF DENDRITES IN MUTUALLY PERPENDICULAR PLANES IN THE RETINA (a) AND THE BRAIN (b) OF THE OCTOPUS**

# CYBERNETICS IN PSYCHOLOGY

The psychological school that works with cybernetic methods of investigation is sometimes referred to as "information psychology." It differs from other schools of thought in psychology in that it attempts to approach reality from a different direction, by making use of a cybernetic model conception of reality. In any case, the cybernetic outlook on the manner in which information is taken into the mind and made conscious yields some interesting new results. Thus it emerges that the number of information items that are mentally perceived (brought into consciousness) is fewer than the total number taken in. This can be verified by means of the following experiment. For a short period, for example, half a minute, a series of symbols (letters or figures) having a high information content, and others having a low information content (that is, with a high degree of redundancy), are projected on a screen. The person acting as the subject of the experiment is asked to watch the screen and then write down what he has seen. It is found that "messages" with a high information content are observed, and taken in, to a lesser extent than "messages" with a low information content. In Fig. 1, the observed symbols of four different series differing in redundancy have been plotted. With increasing redundancy, a higher percentage of the symbols is observed. If the ordinates are taken to represent the mentally perceived information (expressed in bits) instead of percentages, the curves are found to coincide into one curve (Fig. 2). This signifies that in each case the same amount of information has been brought into consciousness in the subject of the experiment. Actually, the curve in Fig. 2 would have to be a straight line passing through the origin of the co-ordinate system. Since this is not so, we can infer from the course of the curve that we take in more information than comes into our consciousness. The "intake time" is therefore shorter than the "apperception time" (the time needed for mentally perceiving the information, that is, for bringing it into consciousness). The length of time it takes to mentally perceive one bit of information is designated as the subjective time quantum and is equal to approximately 0.1 second. This represents the minimum interval required between two successive sensory stimuli to enable them to "register" individually in the subject's consciousness. If periodically emitted sounds, for example, follow one another in more rapid succession, so that they are separated by intervals of less than about 0.1 second, they are perceived as a single continuous sound. Fig. 2 shows that, in half a second, about 8 bits of information can be made conscious, that is, the information flow that the subject of the experiment can mentally perceive is approximately 16 bits per second. A mentally perceived item of information remains conscious for about 10 seconds and then disappears from the (conscious) memory or is stored in the (preconscious) memory. This length of time — about 10 seconds — is the awareness time. As the flow of incoming information is 16 bits per second, only 160 bits of mentally perceived information is accumulated in the conscious memory in a period of 10 seconds. Putting the amount of information transmitted by each individual letter at, say, 5 bits, it means that not more than about 32 letters can be present in the consciousness at one and the same time. If the information is taken in at a faster rate, not all of it can be made conscious: a proportion of it goes to waste because of this limit to the capacity of the consciousness at any particular time (Fig. 3).

We know that the conscious memory can cope with an information flow of 16 bits per second. Part of its contents are stored in the so-called preconscious memory, which has an information intake rate of 0.7 bits per second. This preconscious memory must in turn be subdivided into a short-term memory, which stores the information for periods of up to a few hours, and a long-term memory, which has an even lower intake rate of only about 0.05 bits per sec-

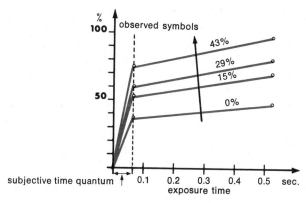

**FIG. 1 OBSERVED SERIES OF SYMBOLS WITH DIFFERING DEGREES OF REDUNDANCY (ACCORDING TO H. FRANK)**

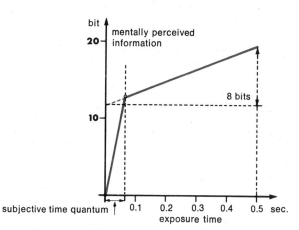

**FIG. 2 SERIES OF SYMBOLS BROUGHT INTO CONSCIOUSNESS (ACCORDING TO H. FRANK)**

**FIG. 3 THE CONSCIOUS MIND CAN COPE ONLY WITH A CERTAIN LIMIT OF INFORMATION AT ANY GIVEN TIME, SO THE MOTORIST CANNOT TAKE IN ALL THE TRAFFIC SIGNS HE PASSES IN QUICK SUCCESSION**

ond. This means that the stored information is present in the quantitative ratios of 320:23:1 — that is, only 1/320 part of the information that is brought into consciousness is stored in the long-term memory. In other words, everything that seems to be of lesser importance (and this comprises by far the greater part of the information intake) is fairly quickly forgotten (Fig. 4).

In the chapter dealing with linguistics, reference has been made to a phenomenon called the disintegration of morphemes (page 66). The process of forgetting conforms to an exponential function similar to that presented by radioactive disintegration. Since it can, in analogy with comparable communications engineering equipment, reasonably be assumed that the human brain has a finite memory storage capacity, it is evident that such a store must get rid of stored information — by forgetting — at the same rate as fresh information comes flowing into it. Since the information intake into the long-term memory within the preconscious memory is very small, the need for making room there to accommodate fresh incoming information is less. Thus, the information stored in the long-term memory is forgotten at a correspondingly slower rate. This cybernetic conclusion, which H. Frank has formulated in the statement that "forgetting" is merely the process whereby stored information is replaced by fresh information, is also in agreement with the theoretical concepts of certain schools of psychological thought. This theory is confirmed by the observed fact that, during sleep, we forget substantially less than during an equal period of time when we are awake. In a period of 8 hours about 20,000 bits flow into the short-term store of the preconscious memory, whence 1000 to 2000 bits are passed into the long-term memory, requiring an equivalent amount of stored information to be "run to waste" by forgetting. The loss of information (forgetting) conforms to a mathematical relationship similar to that which governs "morpheme disintegration," namely:

(47) $$G = G_0 e^{-mt}$$

where $G_0$ denotes the contents of the memory at time $t = 0$ and $m$ is a measure of the rate of disintegration. With the aid of the so-called half-life period, it is possible to calculate the capacity of the preconscious memory (Figs. 5 and 6). It is found to be somewhere between $10^6$ and $10^8$ bits and consists almost entirely of the long-term memory, whose capacity exceeds that of the short-term memory by several powers of ten.

The preconscious memory is of importance for bringing into consciousness items of information that are of particular significance. When such information arrives in the conscious memory, the preconscious memory supplies the appropriate concepts stored in it to associate themselves with the newly arrived information and thus transform it into meaningful awareness. As already stated, the conscious memory can cope with an information flow of no more than about 16 bits per second, so that this represents the limiting rate at which it can absorb information from the outer world and bring it into consciousness. On the basis of considerations such as these, H. Frank and P. R. Hofstetter have come to the conclusion that the information flow of language for average speeds of speaking is in the region of 8 to 10 bits per second. The remaining 6 to 8 bits per second, which go to utilize the full intake capacity (16 bits per second) of the conscious memory, are evidently those additionally supplied by the preconscious memory.

These facts and considerations suggest the following possible explanation of how the human memory functions. The discovery of closed neuron paths within the nervous tissue of the brain suggests a dynamic interpretation of memory, whose mode of functioning can be represented by the model illus-

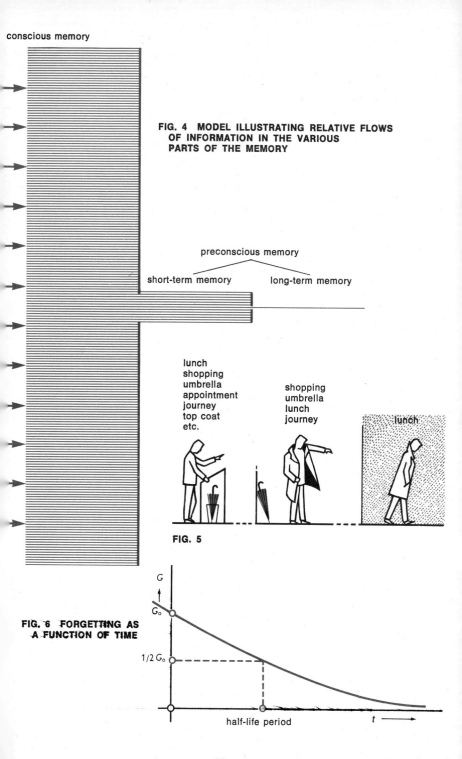

conscious memory

FIG. 4   MODEL ILLUSTRATING RELATIVE FLOWS
OF INFORMATION IN THE VARIOUS
PARTS OF THE MEMORY

preconscious memory

short-term memory          long-term memory

lunch
shopping
umbrella
appointment
journey
top coat
etc.

shopping
umbrella
lunch
journey

lunch

FIG. 5

FIG. 6  FORGETTING AS
A FUNCTION OF TIME

$G$

$G_0$

$1/2\,G_0$

half-life period

$t$

trated in Figs. 7a and 7b. In the "dynamic memory," the stored items of information (shown as white and red balls, each of which represents a bit) circulate in increasing succession in the closed neuron paths. From time to time, bits of information are retrieved from the memory, or are forgotten (Fig. 7c). In this way storage space becomes available, and fresh bits can enter and be stored.

This model could, however, provide an acceptable interpretation only of how the conscious memory or the short-term part of the preconscious memory perhaps functions. The circulatory motion within the closed neuron system will immediately be modified if, for example, the flow of blood through the brain is in any way disturbed. Yet investigations have shown that the long-term memory possesses a notably high degree of stability with regard to disturbance of the brain's blood circulation. This fact shows that the dynamic model conception can provide only an inadequate explanation of the long-term part of the preconscious memory. To obtain an idea of how the long-term memory functions, it is necessary to develop a static interpretation. This is not difficult to conceive, since the synapses, which are present at the end of each axon (nerve fiber) and which form a discontinuous transition to the next nerve cell, are regions where electric potentials can be stored (see page 76). Thus the "static memory" can conveniently be represented by an electrostatic model of a potential distribution within the nervous tissue.

The cybernetic approach to the representation of psychological relationships is best illustrated by the behavior of living creatures with regard to entirely new items of information. For example, when an adult human being finds himself or herself in totally unknown surroundings, for example, in some remote foreign land or, indeed, on some other planet, or when a new-born infant starts using his sensory organs to sound out the information potential of his environment, the movements that the individual performs will at first be of a purely random, tentative character. The results of these experiments are stored, and the sequences of actions which produce successful results, are retained in the memory as a kind of program. In this way the individual familiarizes himself with the form and manifestations of his surroundings. From the items of information received from the environment in response to the individual initially random movements, those items are screened out which are meaningful and useful to the individual and are stored in the memory. Items of information that are not particularly useful are retained for a time in the short-term memory, while those which are found to be important and which have to be kept available at all times are stored in the long-term memory.

Basing his work on information psychology, A. A. Moles has evolved a theory of "information aesthetics," whose fundamental law states that the information flow from a work of art which has a time dimension, such as a musical composition, a play or the recitation of a poem, is of the order of magnitude of the conscious intake capacity of the human mind (16 bits per second, see page 88, in order not to overload the mind with too much information and yet not to cause boredom as a result of too low a rate of information input (Fig. 8).

H. Frank has extended this "law" by applying it also to non-temporal works of art. In this case the criterion is not the rate of flow of the information but, instead, the information storage capacity of the conscious memory, which amounts to about 160 bits. The fundamental law can, for this situation, be now suitably stated as follows: for the purpose of aesthetic information, it is important that the "information configuration" of the work of art should possess redundancy; on the one hand, it should remain within the capacity of the ob-

FIG. 7a DYNAMIC MEMORY
BEING FILLED

FIG. 7b FILLED
DYNAMIC MEMORY

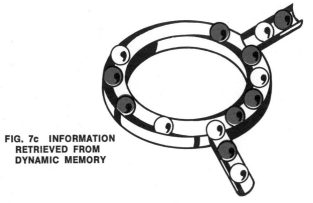

FIG. 7c INFORMATION
RETRIEVED FROM
DYNAMIC MEMORY

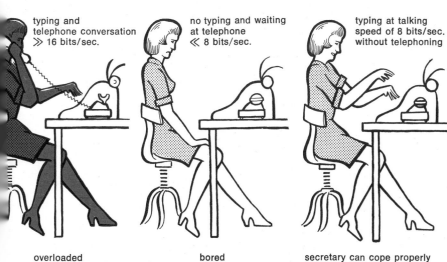

typing and
telephone conversation
$\gg$ 16 bits/sec.

no typing and waiting
at telephone
$\ll$ 8 bits/sec.

typing at talking
speed of 8 bits/sec.
without telephoning

overloaded

bored

secretary can cope properly
with information flow

FIG. 8

FIG. 9 THE RANDOM DISTRIBUTION OF THE RED AND WHITE
SQUARES PROVIDES A MAXIMUM OF INFORMATION AND
CORRESPONDS TO A HIGHLY PROBABLE STATE

FIG. 10 THE SAME NUMBER OF RED SQUARES ARRANGED IN A
PARTICULAR PATTERN GREATLY REDUCES THE INFORMATION AND
CORRESPONDS TO A HIGHLY IMPROBABLE STATE

server's mind to form an overall concept of it, and on the other, it should be pleasingly stimulating. This principle is illustrated by Figs. 9 and 10. The upper diagram (Fig. 9) represents a random checkerboard distribution which imparts a maximum of information. In Fig. 10 the same number of red squares have been arranged in a definite pattern, in such a way that they form crude pictures of a tree and a house. The amount of information (in the cybernetic sense) supplied by this arrangement of the squares is much smaller. The difference between the degrees of redundancy of the information flows supplied by the two diagrams (Fig. 9 and Fig. 10, respectively) is referred to as statistical redundancy. This is essential to aesthetic appreciation. The purely random distribution in Fig. 9 is the most probable distribution, whereas any other distribution is a less probable or indeed a highly improbable one. The most improbable, and also the most highly aesthetic, is the representation of mathematical irregularity in an ornamental feature.

According to M. Benze, the aesthetic effect increases with the improbability of the distribution. From this it can be inferred that the production of aesthetic information opposes the tendency towards attaining a uniform distribution or random distribution (which is the most probable condition in the statistical sense). Therefore we have here a process which acts in opposition to the general entropy and which can be termed "ectroscopic" (see page 28). As a creative process, it does admittedly yield less statistical information, but, on the other hand, it produces a more highly ordered state. This redundancy theory of aesthetics, evolved on the basis of information theory, could point the way to an objective formulation of aesthetic judgments. The assertions based on this redundancy theory are of course applicable to works of art generally, including musical compositions.

The information-theoretical approach may, however, also be applied to music in quite a different way. In the chapter on linguistics (see page 62 et seq.) it was shown how, by means of frequency analyses, the characteristics of individual authors become amenable to objective formulation. A similar procedure can be applied to music. In Fig. 11, the relative statistical frequencies of the tone pitches for four instrumental musical compositions are indicated. Even the psycho-acoustic parameter of pitch (which has nothing to do with the other parameters so important to musical appreciation — such as melody, harmony, rhythm and sound volume range) in itself already yields a pattern that is characteristic both of the composition and of the composer. In each of the four diagrams, the pitch pattern for "equal probability" of the tones (uniform or rectangular distribution) is indicated by the dotted lines. It is notable that the distributions obtained for the two modern composers writing in the twelve-tone scale approximate much more closely to this uniform statistical distribution, whereas the music of Bach and Strauss deviate very considerably from it.

It is of interest to note that in the evolution of music in the last four hundred years, the variation in the statistical frequency distributions for tone pitch has manifested a definite shift from low values of around 3.5 to a maximum of 13. The compositions belonging to different periods in the history of musical art can thus be arranged into several groups. It emerges that small amounts of variation now hardly occur in present-day music and that further development is tending towards increasingly large variations in the statistical frequency distributions for tone pitch. It seems likely that this evolution will continue to manifest the exponential character that appears in Fig. 12.

In discussing the human being confronted with an unknown "information configuration" of his environment (see page 90), we touched upon a process which really belongs to the domain of educational theory. In the conventional

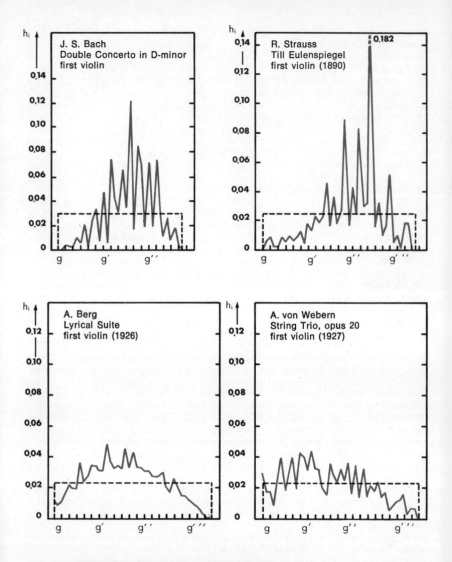

**FIG. 11 STATISTICAL FREQUENCY DISTRIBUTIONS
FOR TONE PITCH FOR FOUR INSTRUMENTAL COMPOSITIONS;
$h_i$ = RELATIVE FREQUENCY (ACCORDING TO W. FUCKS)**

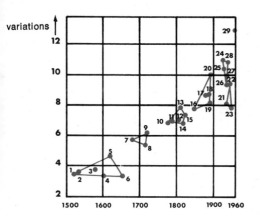

variations

| | 1. Willaert, Fantasies |
| 2. de Modena, Fantasies |
| 3. Palestrina, Ricercari |
| 4. Hassler, Preludes |
| 5. Schein, Sulten |
| 6. Rosenmüller, Studies |
| 7. Corelli, Concerto Grosso 8 |
| 8. Vivaldi, Concerto Grosso 3, 2 |
| 9. Bach, Concerto for Two Violins |
| 10. Mozart, Violin Concerto K 219 |
| 11. Mozart, Symphony in G-minor |
| 12. Beethoven, Fifth Symphony |
| 13. Beethoven, String Quartet 74 |
| 14. Spohr, Violin Concerto |
| 15. Schubert, Eighth Symphony |
| 16. Schumann, Second Symphony |
| 17. Brahms, Violin Concerto |
| 18. Tchaikovsky, Fifth Symphony |
| 19. Strauss, Till Eulenspiegel |
| 20. Tchaikovsky, Sixth Symphony |
| 21. Hindemith, Mathis the Painter |
| 22. Bartók, Suite II |
| 23. Egk, Orchestral Suite |
| 24. Berg, String Quartet 3 |
| 25. Webern, String Trio 26 |
| 26. Berg, Violin Concerto |
| 27. Webern, String Quartet 26 |
| 28. Schoenberg, Violin Concerto |
| 29. Nono Varianti |

**FIG. 12 DIAGRAM SHOWING TREND OF STATISTICAL FREQUENCY DISTRIBUTIONS FOR TONE PITCH IN MUSICAL COMPOSITIONS FROM THE 16TH CENTURY TO MODERN TIMES**

theories of learning it is customary to refer to "learning by trial and error." The object of the educationalist is to induce his pupils to store ordered information in their memories and help them with their intake of information from the — to them as yet unknown — information configurations presented to them. The pupil's adaptable learning system interacts with the teacher's adaptable teaching system. Appropriate application of the cybernetic approach to such processes ultimately always brings us back to the statistics of information theory, that is, the statistics of "binary decisions," as embodied in binary digits (bits). So it is hardly surprising that didactics (the science of teaching) also makes use of this method and has attempted to apply it in various systems of programmed teaching, both with and without the aid of teaching machines (see page 104).

Of course, in this field too, the cybernetic techniques, being purely rational methods, have their limitations. All technical systems operate without consciousness, whereas the human individual absorbs meaningful information and does not make his decisions merely on the basis of rationally stored programs but, instead, allows his actions to be determined, in part, also by the judgments of his conscience and by the creative urges that come flowing into his mind. These idiosyncrasies of personality are very clearly manifested in the statistical frequency distribution curves that emerge from the analysis of individual style in literary works and musical compositions (see Fig. 11 and page 66). In those curves, it is precisely these elements — not ascertainable on rational criteria — that give the statistical frequency distributions of the individual artists their specific character. Indeed, such characterization is so pronounced that it would appear by no means unreasonable to regard these differences in the frequency distribution as a significant part of the proof of authenticity. We thus see that the cybernetic approach provides a suitable pattern of thought for incorporating the rationally analyzable part of the complex of processes of psychological science into our overall world conception.

# CYBERNETICS IN BIOLOGY

The cybernetic method of interpretation has also found fruitful application in biology. More particularly, it has helped to explain how the proliferation and replication — the production of exact copies — of complex organic molecules, of which all living creatures are composed, are accomplished in such processes as protein synthesis, genetic inheritance, and virus infections, with the aid of a pattern encoded in the nucleus of the living cell. Proteins are composed of twenty different amino acids. An amino acid contains an amino group (consisting of hydrogen and nitrogen) and an acid group (consisting of oxygen, hydrogen and carbon). A compound formed of two amino acids is called a peptide; when more than two amino acids are combined in this way, the compound is called a polypeptide. Very large numbers of amino acids (more than 1000) may be joined together to form giant molecules. A very wide variety of different proteins can be built up by different combinations and arrangements of the twenty kinds of amino acids. If a protein is assumed to comprise only 100 amino acids, there are theoretically $20^{100}$ or approximately $10^{130}$ possibilities — a number expressed by the figure one followed by 130 zeros!

Living creatures receive the amino acids they need for their specific protein synthesis from the food they consume. Since the animal, or vegetable, proteins contained in the food derive from other species of living creatures (animals or plants), they cannot be directly assimilated into the consumer creature's system. In the digestive process they first undergo decomposition into the individual amino acids, which are then rearranged and recombined — by a process to be discussed in due course — into proteins specific to the creature concerned (Fig. 1). This protein synthesis is performed in the nucleus of the cell under the influence of nucleic acids, which serve as patterns and in which the amino acid sequences are encoded with the aid of four basic groups. Referring back to equation (18) (page 34), we must consider that 20 is a number situated between $4^2 = 16$ and $4^3 = 64$. It follows that a binary code is not sufficient for the representation of 20 different amino acid components, while on the other hand the number 64 is far too large (Fig. 2). Nature accordingly utilizes several ternary groups for one and the same amino acid. The amino code is therefore said to be degenerated, and several ternary groups may signify the same acid (Fig. 3).

In contrast with the amino acids, all 20 of which possess the same basic group (the amino group), the nucleic acids contain four basic groups:

(48)     adenine (A), cytosine (C), guanine (G), and thymine (T).

Thymine may be replaced by uracil (U). Besides, the nucleic acids contain an acid group, namely, phosphoric acid, and also a sugar. The latter is either ribose or deoxyribose (which contains one oxygen atom less than ribose). According to the nature of the sugar they contain, the nucleic acids are named ribonucleic acid (RNA) and deoxyribonucleic acid (DNA) respectively. The simplest combination of a basic group with a sugar and the phosphoric acid group is called a nucleotide, which is the building block (the elementary constituent unit) from which the nucleic acids are composed. Choosing adenine (A) as the basic group, ribose (Rb) as the sugar, and phosphoric acid (P) as the acid group, we can designate this nucleotide by the following "formula":

(49)     A/Rb/P

The individual nucleotides can combine to form long chain molecules, which are the nucleic acids and in which the successive links consist of phosphoric acid. Three such combined nucleotides (a triplet), with their

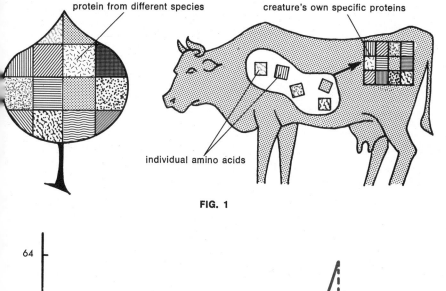

individual amino acids

protein from different species

creature's own specific proteins

**FIG. 1**

64

number of amino acids

20
16

4
1

1          2          3    code (with basis 4)

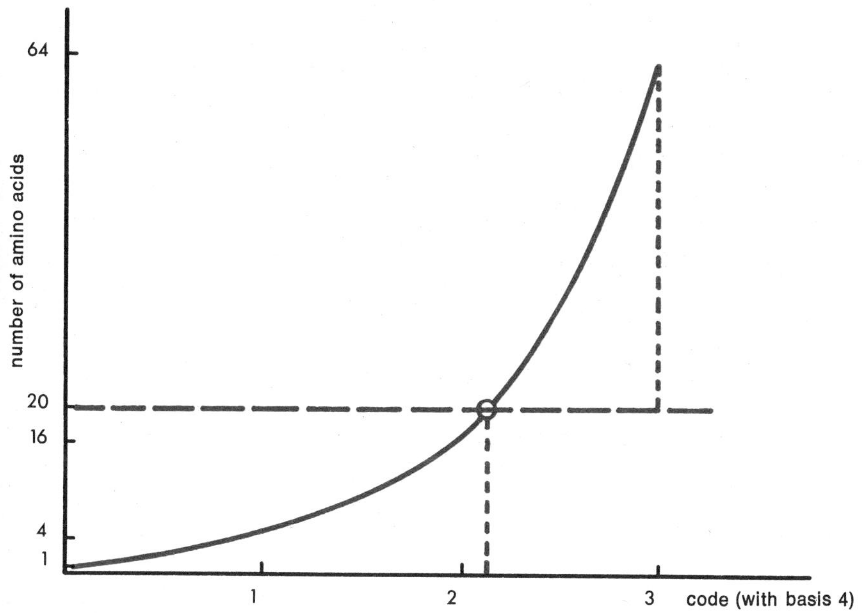

**FIG. 2  DIAGRAM SHOWING BREAKDOWN ( --- ) OF AMINO ACID CODE
IN THE SYNTHESIS OF AN ORGANISM'S OWN SPECIFIC PROTEINS**

ACG TAC GUA CGT ACG
ACG GTA ACG GUA ACG

**FIG. 3  TRIPLET FORMATION WITH NON-OVERLAPPING CODE (RED);
FOR COMPARISON: OVERLAPPING CODE (BLACK)**

three basic groups, contain the code for a special amino acid. For example, the formula:

(50)    $\underset{\text{Rb}-\text{P}-\text{Rb}-\text{P}-\text{Rb}}{\overset{\text{G}\quad\quad\text{A}\quad\quad\text{U}}{\big| \qquad \big| \qquad \big|}}$

contains the code GAU for the amino acid sequence which is characterized by it and constitutes the special protein to be formed.

The nucleic acid strands, composed of nucleotides, always occur in pairs in which the two strands are linked together parallel to each other and coiled into a helix. This linkage is due to base pairing, that is, the two strands are held together by bonds between specific pairs of the bases contained in their nucleotides. The schematic model of these combined giant molecules thus resembles a spiral staircase (Fig. 4). Only certain bases form these lateral bonds, namely:

(51)    adenine – thymine
adenine – uracil
cytosine – guanine

Thus the sequence of the bases in one helical strand determines the sequence of the bases in the other. The structures of the two nucleic acid strands are therefore complementary to each other, i.e., they are interdependent and interdetermined. They belong together like a photographic positive and its negative, a printing block and its impression (Fig. 5), or, indeed, as a lock and its key. Besides, the structure pattern in Fig. 4 explains why the nucleic acid strands are always found embedded in an envelope of protein, which is built up – in accordance with the basic code – from the various amino acids linked together to form chains. Stored in these nucleic acid double helixes is the code, and therefore the pattern, that determines the primary structure of the proteins. In the process of cell division in the living organism this pattern must be transferred to the two daughter cells produced in each normal cell division (mitosis). This transfer is of decisive importance in connection with protein synthesis, genetic inheritance, and virus infection. The doubling of the giant molecules – which is called replication, i.e., the production of exact copies – can be satisfactorily explained with the aid of the double helical model of the structure of the molecular chains.

The hereditary factors (genes) which are responsible for the inheritance of specific characteristics from cell to cell and ultimately from parent to offspring are located in the chromosomes, which are present in the nucleus of the cell. The genes consist of deoxyribonucleic acid (DNA). The process of replication may be conceived as follows. The double helix splits longitudinally – more or less in the manner of a zipper – into two separate helixes which are, as already stated, complementary to each other in the manner of a lock and its key. Each of the two helixes now builds itself a complementary partner and thus becomes a double helix once again. Free amino acids, phosphoric acid and sugar molecules are present in the cell. From this reservoir each nucleic acid helix obtains the materials for building its partner (Fig. 6). As a result of this process, each DNA molecule in the original cell has produced two identical DNA molecules, one in each of the two new cells into which the original cell has divided. Each new DNA molecule thus automatically has the genetic code transferred to it.

Research into viruses has been particularly valuable in this connection. Viruses are sub-microscopic agents that may cause disease in animals or plants. The mature virus consists of nucleic acid within a protein coat. The nucleic acids in such simple organisms contain less information stored in their

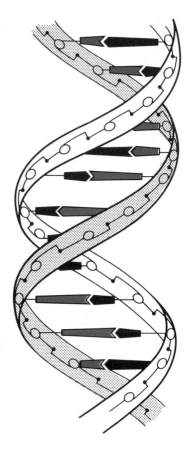

FIG. 4  DOUBLE HELICAL STRUCTURE
OF NUCLEIC ACID STRANDS

**BI**

FIG. 5  PRINTING BLOCK AND IMPRESSION
AS AN EXAMPLE OF
COMPLEMENTARY INTER-ASSOCIATION

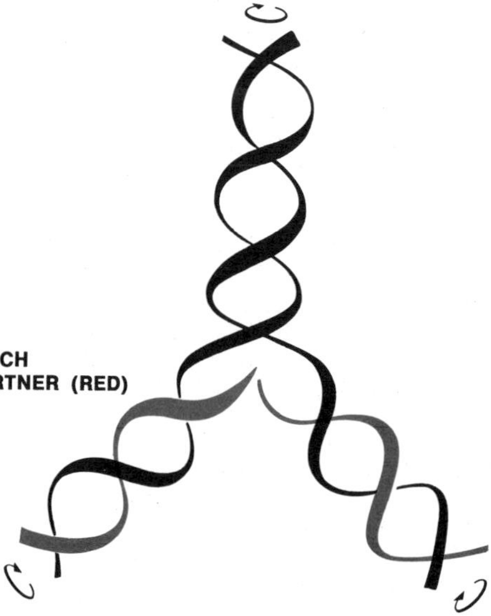

FIG. 6  REPLICATION OF A NUCLEIC
ACID BY DIVISION INTO TWO
INDIVIDUAL HELIXES, EACH OF WHICH
PRODUCES A COMPLEMENTARY PARTNER (RED)
FROM MOLECULES OBTAINED
FROM THE PROTOPLASM

code than those in higher organisms. Their nucleic acid chains are correspondingly shorter and easier to study.

It has proved possible, more particularly in the case of tobacco mosaic virus, to alter the genetic code by chemical means. Sudden changes in the hereditary factors are called mutations. The genetically changed organism (in this case, the virus) is called a mutant; it transmits the altered code to its descendants. As a result of such alteration of the code, which in turn brings about the formation of different amino acids, the composition of the protein formed from the amino acids is correspondingly changed.

Having explained the functional aspects of inheritance and protein synthesis, we can make use of the cybernetic model concept also to explain the manner in which viruses cause infections. The virus retains its protein coat and injects the double helix of nucleic acid directly into the cell that it invades (Fig. 7). In the cytoplasm (the liquid contents of the cell), this injected nucleic acid captures – in accordance with its own inbuilt genetic code – amino acids from the host cell to form nucleotides and thus reproduces the virus protein. As a result, the host cell's normal protein synthesis and its vital functions are disturbed, so that the cell becomes "sick."

These and similar results of research enable us to unravel, step by step, the structure of this so important genetic code and thus eventually decipher it. In this way, the cybernetic approach has helped the science of biology to make significant progress towards elucidating the mystery of life. Now that the formation and replication of the giant nucleic acid molecules has been discovered, there remains the still unanswered question as to how the nucleic acids are able to collect biologically meaningful information. To what extent science will succeed in finding rational explanations for these remaining problems and mysteries is something that the future must reveal.

But in another respect, too, the cybernetic approach has provided biologists with valuable new insights, namely, with regard to biological control processes.

The pupil reaction, in which the size of the pupil of the eye is controlled by the iris according to the intensity of the light entering it, is an instance of automatic control. Indeed, automatic control processes are very numerous in living organisms, for example, the control of the breathing function (Fig. 8). In this function, oxygen from the air drawn into the lungs is transferred to the blood stream, which distributes it through the arteries to those parts of the body where the oxygen is consumed, more particularly the muscles. In the latter the requisite energy is produced by oxidation processes in chemical reactions with the products of metabolism. In these reactions carbon dioxide is formed, which is absorbed into the blood, transported by the veins to the lungs, and exhaled. At periods of peak energy demand, for example, when a sportsman makes a major effort of physical exertion, the demand for oxygen by the muscles increases, and the rate of breathing is speeded up to match this demand. First, the carbon dioxide concentration in the blood rises; this rise is detected by sensing organs in the walls of the arteries and communicated to the control center in the brain. This in turn issues the command, through the nervous system, to increase the rate of breathing and the heartbeat. As a result, more oxygen enters the blood, and the faster blood circulation causes the rate of carbon dioxide exhalation to be speeded up. In consequence of this breathing control, the normal carbon dioxide content is restored. The biological control of the breathing function is therefore based on keeping the carbon dioxide content of the blood constant.

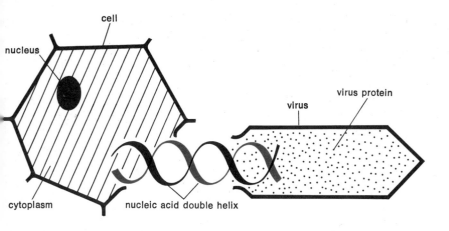

**FIG. 7  DIAGRAM ILLUSTRATING VIRUS INFECTION**

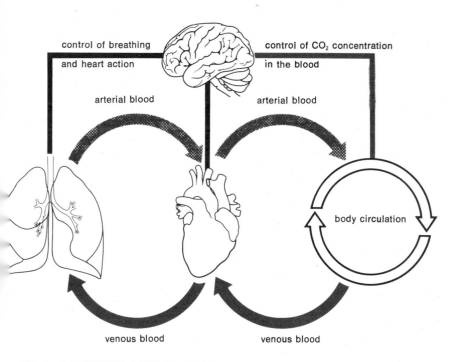

**FIG. 8  RESPIRATORY CONTROL SYSTEM**

A similar control process operates in maintaining the human blood-sugar (glucose) concentration at 1 mg per cm³. When the concentration of sugar in the blood rises, an increased quantity of insulin is secreted into the bloodstream by the islets of Langerhans, which are groups of special cells in the pancreas. Insulin converts the sugar into insoluble glycogen, a substance which is stored in the liver. When the sugar concentration falls, the adrenal (or suprarenal) glands are stimulated to secrete more adrenalin, which converts glycogen back into soluble sugar (glucose). The sugar is reintroduced into the bloodstream by the liver. In addition, this biological control loop actuates other stabilizing mechanisms. The kidneys excrete excess sugar from the body, and the central nervous system (brain and spinal cord) causes feelings of desire for, or aversion to, sugar in food if the blood-sugar level is upset and becomes too low or too high. The regulation of constant body temperature is another very important biological control process (Fig. 9). To meet a high energy requirement, the oxidation processes take place at a higher rate, so that more heat is evolved. If this causes the normal temperature (about 36.8° C, or 98.6° F) to be exceeded, the heat regulating system immediately intervenes. The body is cooled by the excretion of moisture (sweat), which evaporates from the skin.

One feature that characterizes all control processes that have to keep a certain quantity at a constant value (as in the biological control circuits already described) is that they can never be perfect, in the sense of maintaining absolute constancy. The controlling intervention always has to be initiated by a disturbance, or deviation, of the controlled variable from its reference value (or desired value). This causes the system to restore the controlled variable to the reference value. But there is, inevitably, always a certain amount of over-compensation, so that the actual value always oscillates about the reference value.

The amplitude attained by the disturbing deviation that initiates the intervention by the control system will depend on the response speed of that system. For instance, although the iris controls the amount of light admitted into the eye, a very bright flash of light may nevertheless constitute a hazard to eyesight, because the iris cannot respond quickly enough. External stimuli get through to the living organism by means of the available information transmission channels and thus initiate various control processes. This is very clearly demonstrated by the following example relating to the instinctive actions of the organism in a case where a biological and a technical control loop operate in combination with each other, as when a man steers a motor vehicle (Fig. 10). The "desired value"—determined by the motorist's will—in this case consists in driving in an exactly straight line on a road. A beginner at the wheel will be able to achieve this only with considerable difficulty. He will react slowly, and the vehicle will follow a wavy path. The more the motorist's responses become subconscious instinctive actions, the less will he deviate from the straight path. The vehicle then travels with only minor oscillations about the desired value, while the motorist makes the necessary steering corrections swiftly and almost automatically. Similar conditions apply to the other functions associated with driving a car. Thus, the sound of the engine tells the motorist just how much throttle to give, while the traffic conditions dictate his use of the brakes. All these fairly complex control interactions between technical equipment and biological organism take place almost as unconsciously as do the purely biological control operations within the organism (the human body) itself.

normal condition

the rise in body temperature due to
physical effort is compensated by
evaporative cooling (sweating)

**FIG. 9   REGULATION OF BODY TEMPERATURE WHEN PHYSICAL EFFORT
CAUSES OVERHEATING**

center line of road as guide line

path of wheels

**FIG. 10   COMBINED CONTROL OPERATIONS IN STEERING A MOTOR VEHICLE**

# CYBERNETICS IN TEACHING

The main function of teaching is to impart knowledge—items of information—to persons who receive the instruction given (Fig. 1). Teaching and learning are therefore concepts that have to be properly defined. Whereas it is a fairly simple matter to define teaching as the transmission of knowledge by establishing and maintaining an optimum flow of information, the concept of learning is more complex. Accordingly, quite a number of definitions of learning have been suggested at one time or another, depending on which educational, or psychological, school of thought devised them. A definition that in its conciseness is very well suited to the elegant formulations of cybernetics has been given by H. Frank: "Learning is the discovery and utilization of redundancies." Another definition that is likewise appropriate to cybernetic requirements is K. Steinbuch's, which specifically characterizes the relationship of teacher and pupil. It states: "Learning is a change in behavior or function in response to information about the external world; this change must be conducive to improvement in a sense to be defined." This definition is still incomplete in that it leaves undecided the precise nature of what constitutes "improvement." At this point irrational views may enter and considerably affect the definition. Nearly all experts are, however, agreed in asserting that it consists in "better adaptation to the environment," that is, more purposeful and useful behavior which helps to achieve better life prospects. Cybernetic considerations, such as those relating to the human memory (see page 86 et seq.), suggest the possibility of letting automatic machines perform the actual task of teaching and thus relieve the teacher from much tedious routine work, such as teaching his pupils the multiplication tables or simple rules of arithmetic or correct spelling. According to K. Steinbuch, between 20 and 30% of the teaching at primary school level could be undertaken by automatic machines (Fig. 2). For this, the teaching program has to be pre-recorded on magnetic tape. The subject matter is subdivided

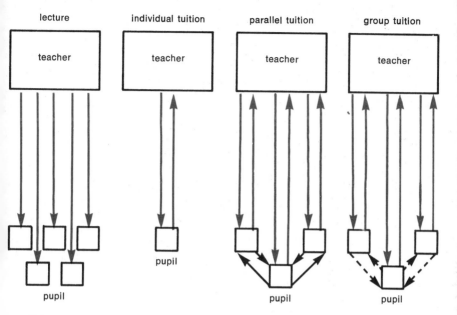

FIG. 1  POSSIBILITIES OF INFORMATION TRANSMISSION BETWEEN
TEACHER AND PUPILS AND FROM PUPIL TO PUPIL
(━━▶ DISTURBANCE; ┈▶ INFORMATION)(ACCORDING TO H. FRANK)

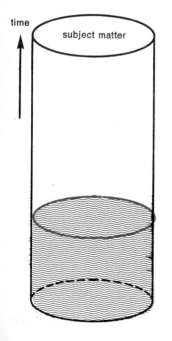

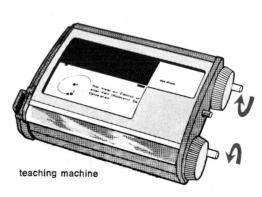

FIG. 2  PROPORTION OF THE TEACHING
THAT CAN BE DONE BY TEACHING MACHINES
IN PRIMARY SCHOOLS

into a succession of small steps. After each step, questions are automatically put to the pupil, who can then, from indications given by the machine, judge for himself whether he has suitably absorbed and memorized the information he has received in that program step. If so, he can go on to the next step; otherwise he can let the machine repeat the step just completed. As a rule, these machines operate on the "multiple choice" principle, whereby the pupil's knowledge is tested by letting him choose between several correct and incorrect answers.

Teaching machines of this type provide a very suitable means of imparting instruction, as they are readily adaptable to the pupil's mental ability and power of retention (Fig. 3). These methods have particularly gained wide acceptance in the teaching of foreign languages. The student can continually check his own pronunciation and may, if he wishes, record his own voice on tape and listen to it being played back. Alternatively, he can communicate directly with a teacher if he wants to ask questions that the machine cannot answer. Also, teaching machines have been developed which provide visual as well as acoustic instruction, the picture being presented by a small slide projector controlled by the machine or formed on the fluorescent screen of a television picture tube (Fig. 4). While cybernetic aids thus provide progressive teaching methods, they also lead to a model simulation of the biological data storage system—the memory—by a technical system which can perform similar functions, that is, which is capable of learning. A device of this kind developed by K. Steinbuch and his co-workers is the so-called "learning matrix," which is able to form associations, so that it can be said to "learn" how to establish these interconnections.

The problem was to construct an electrical network which, under the influence of electric currents that can be equated to the environmental influences, establishes lasting electrical connections as analogies to the associations. This electrical network comprises two mutually perpendicular systems of wires—the column wires and the row wires (see Fig. 5). The points of intersection are bridged by an electrolytic element which normally has a high ohmic resistance, that is, functions as an insulator. If there is a voltage difference at an intersection of two wires, movements of ions occur in the electrolyte; in consequence, a deposition of metal occurs at the negative wire (cathode). These metal deposits grow, like dendrites, through the electrolyte and reach the positive wire (anode), thus establishing a permanent, electrically conducting connection. In Fig. 6 the grid is assumed to consist of silver wires. The wires of one system of this grid (for example, the vertical column wires) have a coating of silver bromide (AgBr) which is in contact with the wires of the other system (the row wires) at the intersections. At those intersections where a voltage difference is applied, the filaments of deposited silver grow from the cathodic to the anodic wire. The "learning matrix," constructed on this principle is able to give specific responses to certain coded signals and is, conversely, able to emit certain code signs when a current is fed into it. The duration of the learning phase of the matrix depends on the growth time of the metallic filaments (dendrites) within the electrolytic substance (silver bromide, in this example) and is essentially a function of the voltage applied. The learning matrix is an excellent model for the study of theoretical problems in information psychology and, more particularly, the functioning of the human memory.

FIG. 3  TEACHING MACHINE FOR LANGUAGES

FIG. 4  TEACHING MACHINE WITH
VISUAL INFORMATION

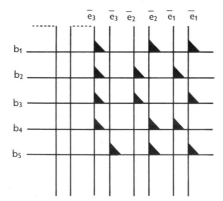

FIG. 5  LEARNING MATRIX
(SCHEMATIC)

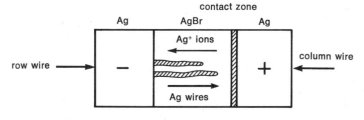

FIG. 6  ELECTROLYTICALLY ACTIVE ELEMENT
FOR FORMING THE NODES
OF THE "LEARNING MATRIX"

# CYBERNETICS IN SOCIOLOGY

A fundamental question relating to the organization of large administrative bodies, such as public authorities and major companies, is: Which of the two forms of organization is preferable — vertical or horizontal (Fig. 1)? Administrative bodies generally tend to develop a system of strictly vertical organization in which the chains of communication and command (down and up) have to conform to a specified pattern. Horizontal organization, that is, the co-ordination or lateral linking-up of departments and individuals belonging to different vertical sectors is, in such systems, ignored, or actually prevented, and sometimes even viewed with suspicion. In the light of what has been said about information entropy (see page 16 et seq.), it is evident that this tendency is conducive to the commission of administrative errors (bureaucracy, red tape). Thus, for example, the co-ordinated treatment of a set of problems by two different departments is unlikely in such an organization. This is not necessarily due to any inherent fault of the organization. Other factors are often involved, such as doubts about a colleague's authority in a certain matter, a deficient sense of responsibility, or the reluctance to make decisions — all arising from weaknesses of human nature, and all conspiring to increase the risk of errors by reducing the amount of available information. It is of course essential to issue only such instructions as do not further aggravate this natural tendency but, instead, counteract it. On the other hand, however, too much horizontal organization can be just as detrimental as excessive vertical organization. Whereas in the latter case the individual employee seeks refuge behind, or within, the cocoon of his special task or duty, without adequate contact with his colleagues, with too much horizontal contact he goes from conference to conference and tends to neglect his desk work. These opposing forms of organization each represent an equally probable set of information items whose maximum efficiency, in terms of information theory, is attained with equal statistical frequency (each 50%) (see page 44). From this can be deduced a practical guiding rule for the managerial staff of large administrative bodies: The most effective arrangement is achieved when the working capacity of the employees is equally divided between vertical and horizontal organization.

Besides reducing mistakes, the consistent application of cybernetic principles will also lead to proper treatment of the individual and not hold him responsible for such mistakes as arise within the collective of the large administrative body and happen, merely by chance, to be associated with him. The blame for such mistakes must be laid on the shortcomings of the organization itself.

Very informative possibilities for future development emerge from investigations conducted by W. Fucks, which have attracted much notice in professional circles. Starting from the trends displayed by the figures for the excess of births over deaths, steel production and electric power consumption, he draws inferences as to the future development of the economic power of various nations. On the basis of statistical evidence relating to the last two hundred years, it can be shown that for all the nations for which information is available, the transition from the agricultural to the industrial pattern of economy is attended by an initial increase in birth rate, which subsequently decreases again. This typical behavior for a number of European countries (Great Britain, France, Belgium, Germany) is represented by the average "European" curve in Fig. 2.

The present and probable future course of the excess of births over deaths in China is indicated in Fig. 3. Since statistical data relating to the increase of the Chinese population are available from as far back as the 5th century B.C., the future increase can be predicted with fair accuracy with the aid of

purely vertical organization

half vertical, half horizontal organization

purely horizontal organization

**FIG. 1 POSSIBLE FORMS OF ORGANIZATION FOR LARGE ADMINISTRATIVE BODIES ( ▒▒▒ = EFFICIENCY IN TERMS OF INFORMATION THEORY)**

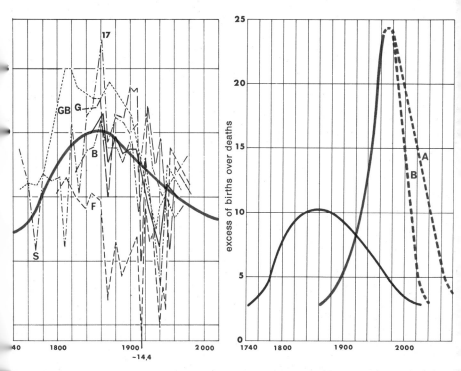

**FIG. 2 EXCESS OF BIRTHS OVER DEATHS FOR EUROPEAN COUNTRIES.**
**—— = AVERAGE CURVE FOR EUROPE (ACCORDING TO W. FUCKS)**

**FIG. 3 COMPARISON BETWEEN EXCESS OF BIRTHS OVER DEATHS FOR EUROPE AND CHINA (ACCORDING TO W. FUCKS)**

the pattern that will probably be manifested by the excess of births over deaths. On this basis, the population of China can be expected to approach the 2000 million mark by the year 2000.

As the significant criteria for economic power W. Fucks chooses steel production and power consumption. Economic power is determined by people and things, so that if we take the figure for steel and power (electrical energy) consumption per head of population and multiply it by the population figure (number of inhabitants), we obtain a measure for the estimation of a nation's economic potential. W. Fucks has chosen steel production because, at the present time, it best characterizes the level of industrial development. Perhaps at some future time the production of plastics will become more significant as a criterion than steel production.

For the various countries it is fairly accurately known up to what point of time in their history they still had no steelmaking industry, so that on the basis of statistical data, the evolution of steel production per head of population up to the present time is known with fair precision and can, therefore, also be confidently extrapolated into the future. Fig. 4 shows the evolution over the past 80 years in a number of countries (U.S.A., U.S.S.R., Belgium, Germany, France, Great Britain). From these data the dotted red curve can be determined, which will be further utilized for the purpose of the present discussion of the subject. If we adopt this functional relationship as representing also the growth of the Chinese steel industry, we can obtain, for the probable future evolution of that country's steel production, the curve presented in Fig. 5. It indicates that by the year 2000 China will be producing more steel than any other country.

Fig. 6 shows curves for the power consumption per head of population up to the present time (in megawatt-hours per year). The extrapolation of these trends to the year 2040 is presented in Fig. 7. Here again we see the extremely rapid growth of electrical energy production in China in the second half of the 20th and the first half of the 21st century. On the basis of the known data—steel production, energy production, population—it can now be ascertained whether production and population must be accorded equal importance in the calculation of economic power.

Basing his work on the statistical data, W. Fucks shows that the simplest relation, namely, economic power = production × population, is not in accordance with the facts. The functional relationship revealed by the statistics is best represented by the production multiplied by the cube root of the population:

(52)    $M = P\sqrt[3]{Z}$

where $M$ denotes the (economic) power, $P$ the production and $Z$ the population (number of inhabitants). This expression is valid both for the power calculated on the basis of steel production ($M_{ST}$) and calculated on the basis of energy production ($M_E$). It would thus appear appropriate to take the effective economic power $\bar{M}$ as the average value of $M_{ST}$ and $M_E$:

(53)    $\bar{M} = \frac{1}{2}((M_{ST})_n + (M_E)_n)$

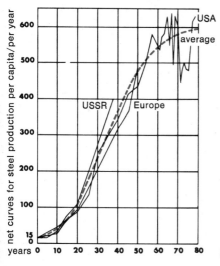

**FIG. 4  STEEL PRODUCTION PER CAPITA**

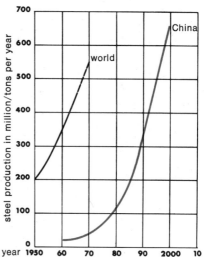

**FIG. 5  DEVELOPMENT OF STEEL PRODUCTION IN CHINA AND THE WORLD UP TO THE YEAR 2000**

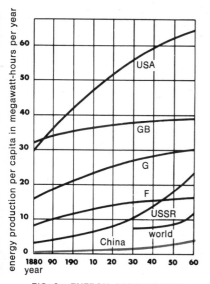

**FIG. 6  ENERGY CONSUMPTION PER CAPITA**

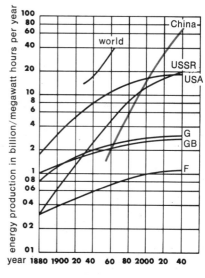

**FIG. 7  EXTRAPOLATION OF ENERGY PRODUCTION FOR VARIOUS COUNTRIES UP TO THE YEAR 2040**

(all according to W. Fucks)

In this expression the subscript $n$ relates to the various countries considered. Curves calculated in this way are given in Fig. 8. The economic power of the U.S.A. in 1960 has been taken as 100, and the calculation of all the values has been referred to this. It should be noted that the ordinates are plotted to a logarithmic scale, so that when the ordinate is doubled it means that the value of the power is quadrupled. According to these results, the economic power of China will, by about 1990, be equivalent to the combined power of the U.S.A., the Soviet Union and the whole of Western Europe. We see also that, from then onwards, there will be practically no further change in the relative economic power pattern of the U.S.A., the Soviet Union, Japan, Germany, Great Britain and France. Only the economic power of China will continue to grow, so that by the year 2010 it will be equal to double the combined power of the U.S.A., the Soviet Union and Western Europe. To what extent the pattern of growth of economic power will also determine political power will largely depend on the development of military weapon technology. It appears reasonable to suppose, as W. Fucks does, that in about twenty years' time the military technology of the major countries can be taken as proportional to their economic power. In particular, it should be noted that the overall development of the economic power pattern is primarily bound up with the future evolution of the population figures (Fig. 9). From this analysis it emerges that China, which today already has about $3\frac{1}{2}$ times as many people as the U.S.A. or the Soviet Union, will have something like $8\frac{1}{2}$ times as many people as those countries by the year 2040. From the formula:

$$(54) \qquad M = p(Z)^{4/3}$$

where $p$ denotes production (steel or energy) per head of population it appears that when the population is doubled, the economic power is increased by a factor 2.26.

However interesting and startling Fucks's results are, they also show how difficult the application of statistical methods of information analysis is to social sciences. This is due, more particularly, to the large number of parameters involved and the far greater difficulty, as compared with the natural sciences, of rationally establishing and defining them. Another factor that affects the issue is that, for the social scientist, it is much more difficult to approach his subject with complete objectivity. The appropriateness and correctness of the choice of parameters are affected by much possible variation and uncertainty, and the observer's subjectivity inevitably has considerable scope to assert its influence.

This manifests itself in the assessment of patterns of social behavior when an attempt is made to describe them in terms of cybernetic concepts, for example, the reaction of a single individual who attracts attention by behavior deviating from the accepted social norm. A very simple example will serve to illustrate this: A man arrives late for a lecture because he was not aware that its starting time had been brought forward. He feels embarrassed by his late arrival. He strives to compensate for this uncomfortable feeling by means of an internal regulating process. Quite automatically, all sorts of excuses occur to him: "It could have happened to any one"; "They ought to have let me know"; "Actually, I was doing the right thing, because I came at the time I was originally told." The control system that thus spontaneously comes into operation strives to compensate for this momentary loss of self-esteem by a process of rationalization, followed by feelings of aggression and, finally, of substitute self-satisfaction. In this way the latecomer rehabilitates himself, in his own esteem, as a member of the community. The foregoing example, which is H. Frank's, describes an individual reaction manifested by a member of a collective.

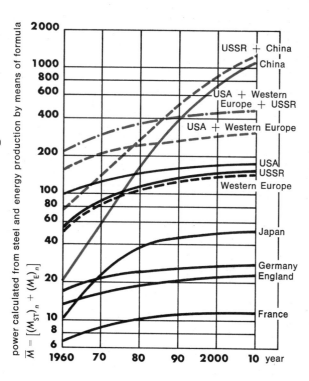

8 HYPOTHETICAL CURVES SHOWING HOW CHINA'S ECONOMIC POWER WILL OUTSTRIP ALL OTHER COUNTRIES BY THE YEAR 2000

power calculated from steel and energy production by means of formula

$$\overline{M} = [(M_{ST})_n + (M_{E^2})_n]$$

USSR + China
China
USA + Western Europe + USSR
USA + Western Europe
USA
USSR
Western Europe
Japan
Germany
England
France

1960   70   80   90   2000   10   year

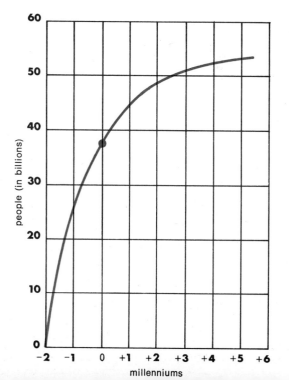

9 CURVE SHOWING WORLD POPULATION INCREASE AS A TOTAL OF THE NUMBER OF PEOPLE WHO HAVE LIVED FROM 2000 B.C. TO THE PRESENT TIME (0 = birth of Christ)

people (in billions)

−2   −1   0   +1   +2   +3   +4   +5   +6

millenniums

Of greater interest from the cybernetic viewpoint, however, are the social behavior patterns in which the individual merges into, and becomes part of, the collective, thereby acquiring and showing different properties within the collective. Thus we all know from our own experience that as members of a community of human beings, we react differently than as individuals (Fig. 10). For the sake of the community, and the standards it imposes, we put up with disagreeable circumstances, or go along with activities to which we, as individuals, would not lend our approval. This sort of reaction is referred to as "group effect."

Such group effects can be studied particularly well in communities of insects. Bees, ants and termites are social insects that live in large communities. Of course, each individual bee is a biological entity with its own respiratory system; but the hive as a whole also "breathes": To ventilate the interior of the hive, worker bees at the entrance set up a current of air by the motion of their wings (Fig. 11). In general, there is advanced function division of labor among the worker bees: honey gatherers, wax makers, nurses for the larvae, guard bees, cleaners, and so on. One may justifiably speak of the hive as having a collective intelligence. This is entirely in analogy with the fact that in information statistics the aggregate can be considered to have additional, and different, properties over and above those of the individual item of information.

individual

member of a collective

**FIG. 10   GROUP EFFECT IN MAN**

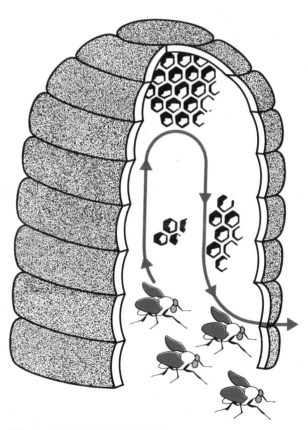

**FIG. 11   GROUP EFFECT IN BEES:
VENTILATION OF THE HIVE THROUGH COLLECTIVE ACTION**

# CYBERNETICS IN ECONOMICS

Closed systems — whether in thermodynamics or whatever — will, when left to themselves, always strive towards the state of maximum disorder, or in other words, towards the most probable statistical distribution. Only a non-closed system can oppose this trend, namely, if the disorder can be transformed into a more ordered state as a result of the entry of information from outside. This fundamental principle corresponds to the second law of thermodynamics, which may alternatively be formulated as follows in terms of information statistics: A closed system, left to itself, will tend towards the state in which the lack of information becomes a maximum (corresponding to the state of maximum thermodynamic entropy or minimum information entropy). These cybernetic considerations can also be applied to economic systems. In general, it can be stated that an industrial undertaking that closes itself to information from the outer world is doomed to decay from lack of information. An undertaking lives by the interaction of its internal information and the information that comes flooding in from outside, and no decisions involving the future can be made without taking due account of the external world and the information it contributes.

We see that here, too, we have an optimization problem, namely, to attain the optimum efficiency of two equally probable sets of information — the internal and the external information (Fig. 1). Optimum efficiency, in terms of information theory, is obtained if the two sets participate equally in the information process. With regard to the problem of handling the information available to industrial undertakings, it is possible to give a practical rule similar to the one already stated with reference to senior executives in an undertaking who are faced with the decision whether a vertical or a horizontal form of organization of their administrative machinery is preferable (see page 108). Applied to economics, the rule becomes: Make your decisions in such a manner that you utilize external and internal information equally in arriving at them. Of course, this rule will be all the more accurately valid according as the number of information items concerned is greater, that is, the larger the undertaking is that has to be optimally managed. This is because the validity of statistically-based rules is borne out with greater probability according as the statistical collective to which they apply comprises a larger number of individual elements. In the present case, this is the aggregate of the internal and the external information, that is, the total amount of information.

The interaction of an industrial undertaking with the industrial environment in which it operates shows other features that are typical of a cybernetic behavior pattern: the characteristics of controlled processes. To illustrate this, let us consider one such process with which we are all familiar: the interaction of supply and demand (Fig. 2). If we conceive the equilibrium between these two quantities as the reference value (or desired value) of the control system comprising production and sale of the product, we find that deviations from this reference value mean either an excess of goods for sale or a shortage of goods. In a free (capitalist) economy, a criterion — a measurable quantity — for this exists in the price of the goods in question. Just as in any other controlled process, the actual value will oscillate around the ref-

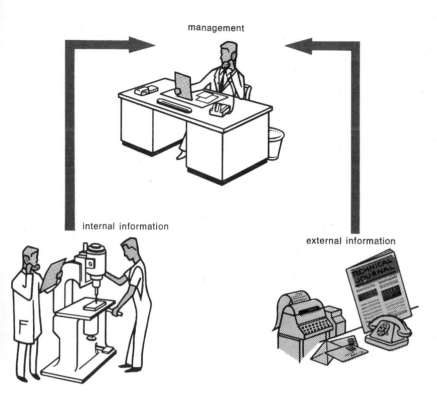

management

internal information

external information

TECHNICAL JOURNAL

**FIG. 1  INTERNAL AND EXTERNAL INFORMATION IN AN INDUSTRIAL
ENTERPRISE OR OTHER LARGE ORGANIZATION**

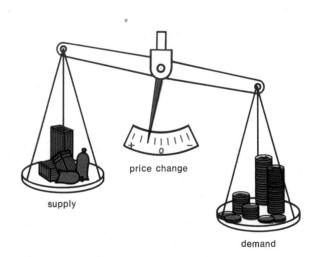

price change

supply

demand

**FIG. 2  INTERACTION BETWEEN SUPPLY AND DEMAND**

erence value, thus the available quantity of goods will swing to and fro a little between surplus and shortage (Fig. 3). The actual control is effected through the attendant phenomenon of a rise in price when goods become scarcer; the higher price encourages producers to turn out more goods until a surplus brings about a drop in price. The price thus acts as a regulator. Incidentally, this control process, which is characteristic of a free market economy, can be modified and manipulated by external intervention, for example, by government measures to restrict production or artificially control prices. However, this example does show that, in principle, economic phenomena manifest all the features suggesting that the cybernetic approach can validly and advantageously be adopted.

The multiplicity of internal and external information influences and the resultant obscuring of the individual parameters have, in the past, led to conventional economics being discredited in that it appeared impotent to give reliable predictions of the consequences of decisions by policy-makers in industrial and commercial undertakings. But here the cybernetic approach offers fresh potentialities and enables economic activities to be viewed from a new angle giving better predictability.

Because of the increasingly rapid developments that are taking place in every field and are causing rapid changes in economic patterns, which used to be constant for generations, the economic decisions in major industrial undertakings must not only meet the requirements of present production and marketing control, but must also prepare and plan ahead for problems and situations that lie in the relatively distant future. The structure of the economy is now no longer static; it has become dynamic. In a static economic structure, the producers of commodities found an existing and continuing demand for their products. In terms of forward planning, they were not much concerned about the future. Nowadays, on the other hand, producers often have to take a hand in promoting and creating a future demand for their products. Whereas in former days the industrialist could rely on intuition and inspired guesswork, his modern counterpart must avail himself of planning and research, conducted on cybernetic principles, to provide the rational basis for the future successful management of his undertaking.

If an undertaking is viewed as a cybernetic system, it must be presupposed that the information with which it operates presents a random statistical distribution. This signifies that the hierarchic forms of administrative organization, which have evolved traditionally, do not satisfy the basic conditions for a cybernetic approach or, conversely, that they are disturbing factors within the statistical information system. More particularly, it exercises a negative influence on the information control loops, in that the incoming information is supplied almost exclusively to the management (Fig. 4a). The lack of information in the lower echelons of the staff gives rise to mistakes, which cause economic harm to the undertaking; also, it tends to stifle the employees' interest in their work and lowers their efficiency and productivity.

But a dynamic economic structure, which is the only one that fits in with cybernetic principles, requires a dynamic organization and therefore a suitable statistical distribution of responsibility, characterized by the situation that each of the undertaking's employees, in his position within the organization, can be interested in optimizing his activities. With this kind of organization, a great deal of unproductive work is eliminated, especially much merely supervisory work. In such a dynamic organization, the individual employee receives fairer treatment because he is not held responsible for mistakes that are due to faulty overall organization.

The cybernetically necessary information for a dynamic organization is provided by an input-output analysis. An optimally dynamic organization also produces favorable results from the social and work-psychological stand-

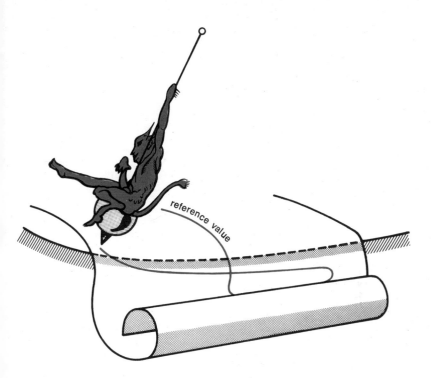

**FIG. 3  PRICE OSCILLATIONS VERSUS REFERENCE VALUE**

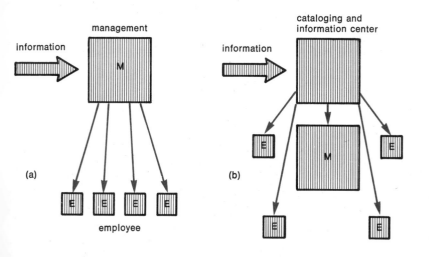

**FIG. 4  HIERARCHIC AND COLLECTIVE INFORMATION**

points. Since the individual employee receives an adequate supply of information, he has a sense of certainty about his decisions and thus about his place in the organization. Besides, he derives satisfaction from his work, since he has a share of responsibility, which boosts his self-confidence (Fig. 4b).

These cybernetic considerations on the optimum organization of industrial and commercial undertakings can be further generalized by applying this approach to sets of problems with the aim of arriving at optimum utilization of available resources. The term "operations research" is widely used to denote this. Operations research usually involves very long numerical computations. These became a practical proposition only when electronic computers became generally available to perform them quickly and economically.

Norbert Wiener describes how the British Admiralty, faced with the hazards of submarine warfare in the Second World War, had the problem of deciding the optimum size of convoys so that losses due to sinkings would be minimized. On the basis of statistical analysis and calculations — which nowadays would be called "cybernetic" — they arrived at the result that convoys should be as large as possible (Fig. 5). The Admiralty put this principle into practice and found it very successful.

Many wild animals live in herds. Within the collective of the herd, the individual animal is more secure than if it led a solitary existence. Wolves, lions, or other beasts of prey that attack a herd, always try to isolate a straggler from the herd. Conversely, in order not to abandon a handicapped member — a wounded animal, or a damaged ship — the collective (the herd, or the convoy) adjusts its speed to that of the slowest individual (Fig. 6).

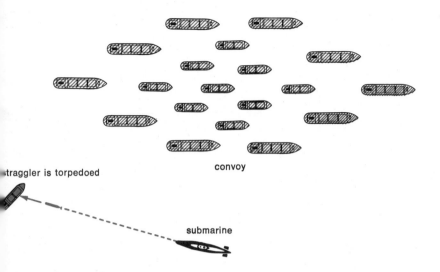

straggler is torpedoed

convoy

submarine

**FIG. 5  PROTECTIVE EFFECT OF A LARGE CONVOY OF SHIPS**

**FIG. 6  THE ESCAPE SPEED OF A ZEBRA HERD IS GOVERNED
BY THE SPEED OF THE FOAL**

# DOCUMENTATION

On page 18 the hydromechanical analogies were considered that helped to explain the mode of functioning of documentation stores. With the cybernetic approach it is possible also to draw inferences as to the optimum arrangement to be adopted for documentation projects. This will now be considered in greater detail for the benefit of readers more particularly interested in these problems.

Let $N$ denote the number of documents to be dealt with ("processed"), and let $b_1N_{c1} + b_2N_{c2}$ be the constant proportion added per unit time (where $b_1N_{c1}$ represents the incoming new documents, for example, journals, and $b_2N_{c2}$ represents documents obtained from a store, for example, for research purposes). Then the rate of change per unit time in the number of documents is expressed by the following first-order differential equation:

(55) $\quad dN/dt = -aN + b_1N_{c1} + b_2N_{c2}$

The solution of this differential equation gives the following expression:

(56) $\quad N = N_{c1}\ [e^{-at}\ (1 - b_1/a) + b_1/a] + N_{c2}\ [e^{-at}\ (1 - b_2/a) + b_2/a]$

Equation (56) becomes more convenient to work with by the introduction of some reasonable simplifications, which in no way restrict the generality of the present considerations. We shall assume that at $t = 0$ the number of new documents $N_{c1}$ is equal to the number of research documents $N_{c2}$, so that:

(57) $\quad N_{c1} = N_{c2} = N_0/2$

and furthermore, that the proportions $b_1$ and $b_2$ per unit time are likewise equal:

(58) $\quad b_1 = b_2 = b$

Equation (56) then becomes:

(58a) $\quad N = N_0\ [e^{-at}\ (1 - b/a) + b/a]$

In Fig. 1 the total documentation work has been plotted according to this relation for $b = 0.1$ and various values of $a$; here $b = 0.1$ represents the proportion of the literature intake per unit time, while $a = 0.001$ to $0.5$ represents the "processing rate."

For determining the economic effectiveness of a documentation project, it is necessary to subdivide the processing rate $a$, namely, into the proportion $a_D$ corresponding to the literature research done by professional documenters, and the proportion $a_F$ done by ordinary scientists or technologists:

(59) $\quad a = a_D + a_F$

The documenter's work is more effective on account of his special training. This difference will be taken into consideration by means of a factor $\eta$. The documenter carries out literature research as his main occupation, whereas the scientist or technologist can devote only a relatively small proportion of his time to such research; this is reflected in the reciprocal $\omega$ of that proportion. A further factor in the documenter's favor is that he operates from a central position in satisfying the documentation requirements of the organization to which he is attached and thus eliminates duplication of work by individual scientists or technologists in different departments of the organization acting in an uncoordinated manner. This is taken into account by a third factor $\epsilon$ (Fig. 2). We thus have:

(60) $\quad a_D = \epsilon\eta\omega a_F \quad$ and so $\quad a_D/a_F = \epsilon\eta\omega$

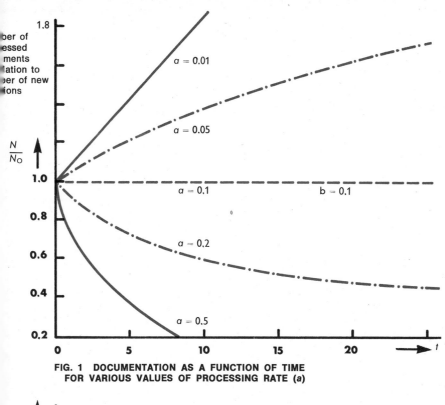

ber of
essed
ments
lation to
ber of new
ions

$\frac{N}{N_O}$ ↑

FIG. 1 DOCUMENTATION AS A FUNCTION OF TIME
FOR VARIOUS VALUES OF PROCESSING RATE (a)

$\frac{a_D}{a_F}$ ↑

f
ssing
of
sional
enter vs.
t
list

number of subject specialists $\varepsilon$

FIG. 2 EFFECTIVENESS OF DOCUMENTING BY PROFESSIONALLY-
TRAINED STAFF ($\eta$ w = EFFECTIVENESS FACTOR)

and (59) then becomes:

(61)     $a = a_F(1 + \epsilon\eta\omega)$

The following values may be adopted for the three factors: $\epsilon = 3$; $\eta = 5$; $\omega = 10$. These are empirical values, and they state that the professional documenter can devote ten times more time to documentation work than the ordinary scientist or technologist ($\omega$), that his special training enables him to work five times as fast as the latter ($\eta$), and that the documenter can be assumed to span the fields of work of at least three scientists or technologists ($\epsilon$). It then follows from (60) that a well-trained professional documenter can perform the literature research work of 150 ordinary scientists or technologists who only incidentally engage in such research (Fig. 3). This result is all the more surprising in that the assumptions made for $\epsilon$, $\eta$, and $\omega$ represent quite plausible values.

To sum up, it can be said that the processing of the analytical problems — evaluating, collating, translating — is still the exclusive preserve of human activity; machines that can simulate the analytical capacity of the human mind are still only in the infancy of their development.

In the sphere of documentation, the use of machines therefore continues to be confined to routine operations. However, it does result in a considerable saving in time, and it greatly speeds up the work. The preparation of references and abstracts of documents, which are analytical processes that cannot as yet be done by machines, is indeed the weak link in the chain of documentation. In this domain, in which the subjectivity of the human individual (the documenter) has the greatest amount of latitude, the greatest variations occur, as emerges when different documenters prepare abstracts and references for the same document. It is true that scientific papers are usually accompanied by a short preliminary synopsis and/or final summary prepared by the author. But the author is not the most objective interpreter of his own work. Quite conceivably, his paper or report may contain valuable incidental information — a sort of by-product of the main theme — which the author himself may regard as being of minor significance and which he therefore fails to mention in his summary. For example, a communications engineering paper, concerned with the production of microwaves in high-vacuum tubes, may also give valuable information on methods of measuring the vacuum, or of producing high vacuums, which are indeed important in themselves, but secondary to the main subject. The documenter, who by virtue of his training is not specialized in a relatively narrow field of science, will in such a case give a short reference to these methods. Thus this reference, when transferred to the references store, will be designated not only as being concerned with communications engineering, but also with vacuum engineering.

On the other hand, the documenter, having only a limited knowledge of any particular field of science or technology, is often faced with the difficult question as to which of the often synonymously employed concepts of the specialized technical language he should adopt in his characterization of the documentary information. To help him, so-called thesauruses — lists of systematically arranged scientific and technical concepts — have been compiled in a wide range of subjects by the collaboration of many expert contributors (Fig. 4). These compilations are used for guidance in the establishing of references. In this way uniformity is introduced into the references, with the certainty that the concepts (descriptions) employed will in turn be unambiguously understood by the users of the documentation.

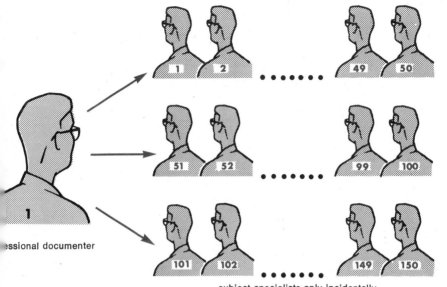

essional documenter

subject specialists only incidentally
engaged in document processing

**FIG. 3 RATIO OF OUTPUT BETWEEN PROFESSIONAL DOCUMENTER
AND SUBJECT SPECIALISTS (1:150)**

ELECTROCHEMICAL DRILLING

ELECTROCHEMICAL DRILLING
USE DRILLING
ELECTROCHEMISTRY

ELECTROCHEMISTRY
UF ELECTROCHEMICAL DRILLING
ELECTROLYTIC PROCESSES
BT CHEMISTRY
RT CHEMICAL ENGINEERING
ELECTRODEPOSITION
ELECTRODES &
ELECTROLYSIS
ELECTROLYTES
ELECTROLYTIC CELLS
ELECTROMETALLURGY &
ELECTROPLATING &
PHYSICAL CHEMISTRY

ELECTROCUTION
USE ELECTRIC SHOCK

ELECTRODEPOSITION
UF ELECTROFORMING
BT ELECTROMETALLURGY &
RT CATHODES
CATHODE SPUTTERING
COATING
ELECTROCHEMISTRY
ELECTROLYSIS
ELECTROLYTES
ELECTROLYTIC ANALYSIS
ELECTROLYTIC CELLS
ELECTROPHORESIS
ELECTROPLATING &
ELECTROWINNING
OXIDATION
PLATING
REDUCTION (CHEMICAL)
STARTING SHEETS

ELECTRODE POTENTIALS
UF ELECTROMOTIVE FORCE SERIES
ELECTROMOTIVE SERIES
HYDROGEN POTENTIAL
BT ELECTRICAL PHENOMENA
RT CONTACT POTENTIALS
ELECTRIC POTENTIAL
GALVANIC CORROSION

ELECTRODES &
NT ANODES
CATHODES
COATED ELECTRODES
GRIDS (TUBE COMPONENTS) #
PHOTOCATHODES
WELDING ELECTRODES
WELDING RODS
RT ELECTROCHEMISTRY
ELECTROLYSIS
ELECTROMETALLURGY &
ELECTROPLATING &
ELECTROREFINING
ELECTROWINNING

ELECTROHYDRODYNAMICS
USE MAGNETOHYDRODYNAMICS

ELECTROLESS PLATES
BT COATINGS
RT ELECTROLESS PLATING

ELECTROLESS PLATING
UF BARREL FINISHING
BT COATING
PLATING
RT ELECTROLESS PLATES
ELECTROPLATING &
VAPOR DEPOSITION

ELECTROLUMINESCENCE
BT LUMINESCENCE
RT ELECTROLUMINESCENT LAMPS

ELECTROLUMINESCENT LAMPS
BT ELECTRIC LAMPS
LAMPS &
RT GISCHARGE LAMPS
ELECTROLUMINESCENCE
INCANDESCENT LAMPS
PANELS
PHOSPHORS

ELECTROLYSIS
RT CORROSION
CURRENT DENSITY
DECOMPOSITION REACTIONS
ELECTROCHEMISTRY
ELECTRODEPOSITION
ELECTRODES &
ELECTROLYTES
ELECTROLYTIC CELLS
ELECTROPLATING &
IONIC MOBILITY
OXIDATION
POLARIZATION (ELECTRODES)
REDUCTION (CHEMICAL)

ELECTROLYTES
NT ANOLYTES
CATHOLYTES
BT ELECTRIC CONDUCTORS (MATERIALS)
RT ELECTROCHEMISTRY
ELECTRODEPOSITION
ELECTROLYSIS
ELECTROLYTIC CELLS
ELECTROMETALLURGY &
ELECTROPLATING &
ELECTROREFINING
ELECTROWINNING
FUSED SALTS
IONS

ELECTROLYTIC ANALYSIS
BT CHEMICAL ANALYSIS &
CHEMICAL TESTS
MATERIALS TESTING

PAIR PRODUCTION
PHOTONUCLEAR REACTIONS
RADIATION SHIELDING
RESONANT FREQUENCY
TRANSLUCENCE
TRANSMISSION
TRANSMITTANCE
TRANSPARENCE
WAVE PROPAGATION

ELECTROMAGNETIC FIELDS
RT ELECTRIC FIELDS
ELECTROMAGNETIC THEORY
ELECTROMAGNETIC WAVES
ELECTROMAGNETISM
ELECTROSTATICS
FIELD STRENGTH
MAGNETIC FIELDS
MAGNETO OPTICS

ELECTROMAGNETIC INDUCTION
UF INDUCTION (ELECTROMAGNETIC)
RT COULOMB FRICTION
INDUCTANCE
INDUCTION HEATING
INDUCTIVE REACTANCE
MAGNETIC INDUCTION
ROTATING MACHINES &

ELECTROMAGNETIC ISOTOPE SEPARATION
USE ISOTOPE SEPARATION

ELECTROMAGNETIC PUMPS
(LIMITED TO PUMPS FOR FLUIDS--
EXCLUDES OPTICAL PUMPING)
BT PUMPS
RT OPTICAL PUMPING

ELECTROMAGNETIC RADIATION
USE ELECTROMAGNETIC WAVES

ELECTROMAGNETIC THEORY
RT ELECTROMAGNETIC FIELDS
ELECTROMAGNETIC WAVES
ELECTROSTATICS
MAGNETISM
MAGNETO OPTICS
MAGNETOSTATICS

ELECTROMAGNETIC WAVE FILTERS
NT INFRARED FILTERS
OPTICAL FILTERS
PHOTOGRAPHIC FILTERS
ULTRAVIOLET FILTERS
WAVEGUIDE FILTERS
WRATTEN FILTERS
RT ANALYZERS (ELECTRIC)
BANDPASS FILTERS
DETECTORS
ELECTRIC COILS
ELECTRIC FILTERS
HIGH-PASS FILTERS
LOW-PASS FILTERS

**FIG. 4 EXCERPT FROM THE THESAURUS OF THE ENGINEERS' JOINT COUNCIL**

# NUMBER SYSTEMS

In all civilized countries, computation is based on the decimal (or decadic) system, which utilizes the ten cardinal numbers 0, 1, 2, 3, 4, 5, 6, 7, 8 and 9 for the representation of any number. Numbers larger than 9 are formed by combination of two or more of these digits. Thus the number coming after 9 is formed by the combination of 1 and 0, that is, 10. The number 10 is also the base of the decimal system. The numbers that follow 10 are obtained by successively replacing the 0 by all the other digits of the decimal system, in other words, 1 to 9. Thus we obtain the numbers 11, 12, 13, 14, 15, 16, 17, 18 and 19. Next, the digit 2 is substituted for the 1, thus giving the numbers from 20 to 29. Thereafter the first digit is successively replaced by 3, 4, 5, 6, 7, 8 and 9, so that finally the highest two-digit number is obtained: 99. For the next number, three digits are required: 1 followed by two zeros: 100.

When we write the number 666, we write the same numeral 6 three times, but its significance differs according to the place, or position, it occupies in the number: In the last (third) place it has the value 6, in the penultimate (second) position it has the value 60, and in the first position it has the value 600. The value therefore increases tenfold for each position that it is shifted to the left. The last (extreme right) digit of a number in the decimal system thus represents units, the digit preceding it represents tens, the next digit on the left represents hundreds, and so on. The number denoted by 6804 thus comprises 6 thousands, 8 hundreds, 0 tens and 4 units (Fig. 1). Since 1000 can be represented by $10^3$ (ten to the power three), 100 by $10^2$ (ten to the power two), 10 by $10^1$ (ten to the power one) and 1 by $10^0$ (ten to the power nought), the number 6804 is equivalent to $6 \times 10^3 + 8 \times 10^2 + 0 \times 10^1 + 4 \times 10^0$. The decimal notation is a universally accepted convention for expressing this in a simplified form, by writing only the 6, 8, 0 and 4. In general, a digit occupying the $n$th place (or position) from the right will correspond to that digit multiplied by $10^{n-1}$ that is, the value of its place—its "place value"—is $10^{n-1}$.

Number systems with a base other than 10 are also conceivable. For example, what would a number system with base 7 look like? In that case we have only the seven digits, 0, 1, 2, 3, 4, 5 and 6 for representing any particular number. The base number seven would, in this system, itself have to be represented by a combination of two digits, namely, 1 and 0. The base seven is thus written as 10 (read: one-zero). The number that follows seven —that is, eight—is written as 11 (read: one-one); nine becomes 12 (one-two), and so on up to 16 (one-six). With 6 as the highest numeral in the number system with base seven all the possibilities for the last place have then been "used up," so that for the next number in the scale, the combination 20 (two-zero) will have to be used. From the table on page 129, it appears that this expression 20 in the base-seven system corresponds to 14 in the decimal system. In the base-seven system, the number 20 is followed by the combinations 21 to 26, which correspond to the numbers 15 to 20 in the decimal system. After these come combinations starting with 3, and so on, until the highest two-digit number in the base-seven system is reached: 66 (six-six). Beyond this a third place becomes necessary: the first digit becomes 1, followed by two zeros. Consider, for example, the number 652 in the base-seven system. It must be borne in mind that here, too, just as in the decimal system, each digit has a particular value associated with its position in the number. The last (extreme right) position is always occupied by the units. When a digit is shifted one place to the left, its value increases sevenfold, since the base of the system is seven. A shift of two places to the left corresponds to

$7 \times 7$-fold increase. Thus, in the base-seven system, the place value of a digit (from right to left) is successively $7^0 (= 1)$, $7^1 (= 7)$, $7^2 (= 7 \times 7 = 49)$, $7^3 (= 7 \times 7 \times 7 = 343)$, and so on. In general, a digit occupying the $n$th position from the right corresponds to that digit multiplied by $7^{n-1}$, that is, its place value $7^{n-1}$. Therefore in the base-seven system the number 652 signifies $6 \times 7^2 + 5 \times 7^1 + 2 \times 7^0$, of which again only the 6, 5 and 2 are actually written. This number corresponds to $6 \times 49 + 5 \times 7 + 2 \times 1 = 294 + 35 + 2 = 331$ in the decimal system. In order to indicate what number system is being used, that is, what base has been adopted, the number is printed in parentheses, followed by the base as a subscript. For example, $(583)_{10}$ signifies 583 in the decimal system, with the value $5 \times 10^2 + 8 \times 10^1 + 3 \times 10^0 = 500 + 80 + 3 = 583$. Similarly, $(583)_9$ signifies 583 in the base-nine system, corresponding to $5 \times 9^2 + 8 \times 9^1 + 3 \times 9^0 = 5 \times 81 + 8 \times 9 + 3 \times 1 = 405 + 72 + 3 = 480$; thus we can write $(583)_9 = (480)_{10}$. An expression such as $(4687)_6$ has no real meaning, since the base-six system has only six numerals: 0, 1, 2, 3, 4 and 5. On the other hand, $(4201)_8$ is the equivalent of $4 \times 8^3 + 2 \times 8^2 + 0 \times 8^1 + 1 \times 8^0 = 4 \times 512 + 2 \times 64 + 0 \times 8 + 1 \times 1 = 2048 + 128 + 0 + 1 = 2177$ in the decimal system; therefore $(4201)_8 = (2177)_{10}$. Numbers in a duodecimal (base-twelve) system are also conceivable. Besides 0, this system must comprise eleven other numerals. Since our conventional (decimal) numerals do not go beyond 9, it becomes necessary to introduce a single numeral for "ten," and "eleven," respectively; any convenient symbols may be adopted for these; for example, letters of the alphabet may be employed. For instance, let "a" denote "ten," and "b" denote "eleven." Then the expression $(2ab4)_{12}$ signifies $2 \times 12^3 + 10 \times 12^2 + 11 \times 12^1 + 4 \times 12^0 = 2 \times 1728 + 10 \times 144 + 11 \times 12 + 4 \times 1 = 3456 + 1440 + 132 + 4 = 5032$ in the decimal system, that is, $(2ab4)_{12} = (5032)_{10}$.

place

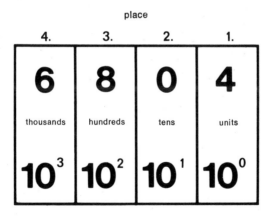

**FIG. 1**

# THE BINARY SYSTEM

Among all possible number systems, a special position is occupied by the binary system, that is, the number system with base 2. The two digits (or "bits") used in this system are 0 and 1, or 0 and L, as the letter L is frequently used in lieu of the numeral 1 in order to emphasize the difference with other number systems; this notation has been adopted in this book. As already explained on page 10, the term "bit" is a commonly used abbreviation of "binary digit." Binary numbers can conveniently be represented by electrical pulses (see page 140). The processing and interlinking of such information-carrying pulse trains in automatic computer equipment requires a knowledge of the rules of computation with the binary digits 0 and L. With these two characters, the largest single-place number that can be represented in the binary system is the number one (L). The next number, two, must already be written as a combination of two digits, L0 (read: one-oh). The number three then becomes LL (one-one). The number four must already be a three-digit combination: L00 (one-oh-oh). In accordance with the definitions relating to number systems in general (page 126), the place value of the $n$th digit from the right in a number in the binary system is $2^{n-1}$. In the expression LL0L0L, the first L occupies the sixth position from the right ($n = 6$), and its place value is therefore $2^{n-1} = 2^{6-1} = 2^5 = 2 \times 2 \times 2 \times 2 \times 2 = 32$. Thus LL0L0L signifies $1 \times 2^5 + 1 \times 2^4 + 0 \times 2^3 + 1 \times 2^2 + 0 \times 2^1 + 1 \times 2^0 = 1 \times 32 + 1 \times 16 + 0 \times 8 + 1 \times 4 + 0 \times 2 + 1 \times 1 = 32 + 16 + 4 + 1 = 53$ in the decimal system, so that $(LL0L0L)_2 = (53)_{10}$.

The great advantage of the binary system is that every number is composed of a succession of "yes-no" decisions, that is, it is coded in binary form. For example, the number LL0L0L could be represented by means of a series of six lamps, each of which is associated with a particular place (or position) in this six-place number. The first, second, fourth and sixth lamp are switched on (corresponding to L), while the third and fifth are off (corresponding to 0). With six lamps there are $2^6$, or 64 possible switch combinations (including the case where all the lamps are off). Thus with six possible yes-no decisions (L-0 decisions), it is possible to represent 64 numbers (actually, 63 numbers and 0). In general, with $n$ yes-no decisions, there are $2^n$ switching possibilities, that is, there are $2^n - 1$ numbers besides 0. In the accompanying table (Fig. 1) the decimal expressions for the numbers zero to thirty-one and their binary equivalents are given. In this case five lamps suffice to represent the yes-no, or on-off, conditions. For the number thirteen $(13)_{10}$, which is written as $(LL0L)_2$ in the binary system (or as 0LL0L when represented in five places, as in the table), the first and fourth lamp must be off, and the second, third and fifth must be on (Fig. 2).

| number | decimal system | seven-base system | binary system |
|---|---|---|---|
| zero | 0 | 0 | O O O O O |
| one | 1 | 1 | O O O O L |
| two | 2 | 2 | O O O L O |
| three | 3 | 3 | O O O L L |
| four | 4 | 4 | O O L O O |
| five | 5 | 5 | O O L O L |
| six | 6 | 6 | O O L L O |
| seven | 7 | 10 | O O L L L |
| eight | 8 | 11 | O L O O O |
| nine | 9 | 12 | O L O O L |
| ten | 10 | 13 | O L O L O |
| eleven | 11 | 14 | O L O L L |
| twelve | 12 | 15 | O L L O O |
| thirteen | 13 | 16 | O L L O L |
| fourteen | 14 | 20 | O L L L O |
| fifteen | 15 | 21 | O L L L L |
| sixteen | 16 | 22 | L O O O O |
| ⋮ | ⋮ | ⋮ | ⋮ |
| thirty-one | 31 | 43 | L L L L L |

FIG. 1

O L L O L

$0 \times 2^4 \quad 1 \times 2^3 \quad 1 \times 2^2 \quad 0 \times 2^1 \quad 1 \times 2^0$

$$0 + 8 + 4 + 0 + 1 = 13$$

FIG. 2

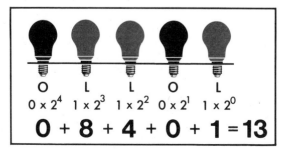

# BINARY ARITHMETIC

An interesting and frequently recurring problem is the conversion of a numerical expression in the decimal system into a numerical expression in the binary system. There is a simple procedure for this: we need merely ascertain which powers of two (1, 2, 4, 8, 16, 32, . . .) compose the number. For example, consider the number 25. It must contain the summand 16, as all the lower powers of two together give only 15. Since $16 = 2^4$, the fifth place from the right in the binary number must be occupied by an L (that is, one), for here is located the 16. Subtracting this from 25, we obtain 9 as the remainder. This contains the summand $8 = 2^3$. Thus the fourth place from the right must also be occupied by an L. On subtracting 8 from 9 we are left with 1. This does not contain 4 or 2, but only the summand 1. Hence the second and third places from the right are each occupied by an 0, while the last (extreme right) place is occupied by an L. The binary expression for 25 is therefore LL00L (see Fig. 1, page 129). For numbers exceeding 32 we must, of course, make use of higher powers than $2^4$. For example, 57 can be conceived as being composed of $1 \times 32 + 1 \times 16 + 1 \times 8 + 0 \times 4 + 0 \times 2 + 1 \times 1$, so that its binary expression is LLL00L. The procedure presented in Fig. 1 is simpler: To convert a decimal number (in this example: 57) into a binary number, first divide it by 2. Then, write down the remainder, and divide the quotient again by 2. Repeat this procedure until you obtain as a quotient 0, with remainder 1. On reading the remainders from last to first, you obtain the binary number LLL00L.

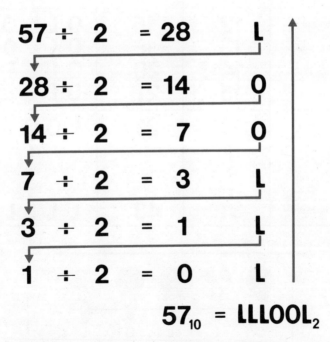

$$57 \div 2 = 28 \quad L$$

$$28 \div 2 = 14 \quad 0$$

$$14 \div 2 = 7 \quad 0$$

$$7 \div 2 = 3 \quad L$$

$$3 \div 2 = 1 \quad L$$

$$1 \div 2 = 0 \quad L$$

$$57_{10} = LLL00L_2$$

**FIG. 1  CONVERSION OF A NUMBER IN THE DECIMAL SYSTEM INTO ITS EQUIVALENT IN THE BINARY SYSTEM**

logical connections
for additions

| | | | |
|---|---|---|---|
| 0 | + 0 | = | 0 |
| 0 | + L | = | L |
| L | + 0 | = | L |
| L | + L | = | LO |

FIG. 2

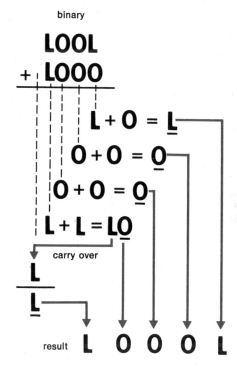

decimal

9
+ 8
17

binary

LOOL
+ LOOO

L + 0 = L
0 + 0 = O
0 + 0 = O
L + L = LO

carry over

L

L

result  L 0 0 0 L

FIG. 3

For the addition of binary numbers, the logical connections indicated in Fig. 2 are utilized. The first three lines of these are self-evident. In the last line the sum L + L must, of course, be equal to 2, which in binary notation is written as LO (one-oh). The addition of the numbers nine and eight, and the corresponding binary numbers LOOL and LOOO, is shown in Fig. 3. The addition commences at the last (extreme right) place of the binary number. Up to the third place from the right all goes smoothly. In the fourth place we have one plus one, giving two; however, since the binary notation for two is LO, the 0 remains in the fourth place, while the L is transferred to the fifth place from the right. When, for example, the numbers fifteen and seven are added, cor-

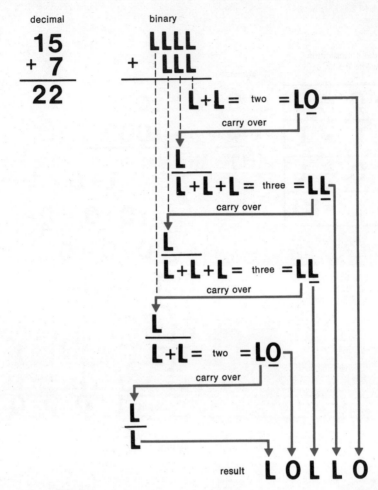

**FIG. 4**

responding to the binary numbers LLLL and LLL (Fig. 4), we obtain in the extreme right place $L + L = L0$. The 0 is written down and the one (L) is carried over to the second place from the right. In the third place from the right, we now obtain $L + L + L = $ three $= LL$ in binary notation. The final L of this number is set down as the result in the second place from the right, while the foremost L is carried over to the third place. In the third place we have again $L + L + L = $ three $= LL$. The final L is set down as the result in the third place, while the foremost L goes to the fourth place, where we must now perform the addition $L + L = L0$. The final 0 is put in the fourth place, while the foremost L is carried over to the fifth place from the right. We have thus arrived at the overall result of the addition: L0LL0.

Multiplication of binary numbers is usually performed as repeated addition (Fig. 5). It utilizes the logical connections indicated in Fig. 6. The multiplication of six times three as a true multiplication is presented in Fig. 7.

```
  LLO
  LLO
+ LLO
-----
LOOLO
```

FIG. 5

logical connections
for multiplication

$$0 \cdot 0 = 0$$
$$0 \cdot L = 0$$
$$L \cdot 0 = 0$$
$$L \cdot L = L$$

FIG. 6

```
LLO · LL
--------
  LLO
+  LLO
--------
 LOOLO
```

FIG. 7

By means of a simple trick, the subtraction of binary numbers can be carried out as addition. For this purpose the so-called complement is required. This principle will first be demonstrated by means of an example in the decimal system. Thus the complement of 46059 in the decimal system (Fig. 8) is 53940. It is obtained by seeking for each digit of the given number 46059 the value which complements that digit to produce 9 (the highest numeral of the decimal system). The complement of 1 is 8, the complement of 2 is 7, the complement of 3 is 6, and so on.

complement to number **46059** in decimal system

is **53940** each digit of this number

complements each digit of number above to give 9

```
check    46059
       + 53940
       -------
         99999
```

FIG. 8

To subtract one number from another, we may, alternatively, add the complement of the number that we wish to subtract. The only requirement is that, before doing this, we must prefix extra zeros, where necessary, so as to give both numbers the same number of digit places. If we then delete the leading 1 in the result and add a 1 in the last place, the result thus finally obtained will be the correct result of the subtraction. As an example, the subtraction 867 − 394 is performed in Fig. 9. The procedure is as follows: to 867 we add 605, which is the complement of 394. The result is 1472. We now delete the leading 1 and add a 1 in the last place, to the 2, giving as the final result: 472 + 1 = 473.

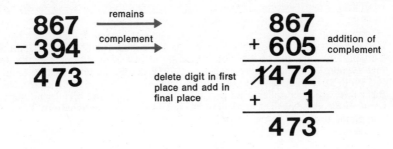

**FIG. 9**

In the case of binary numbers the complement is easy to find. Since the highest numeral in this system is the one (L), finding the complement consists in replacing every 0 by L and every L by 0 in the original number (Fig. 10). To subtract thirteen (= LL0L) from twenty-eight (= LLL00) in the binary system, we first put an extra zero in front of the thirteen to turn it into a five-place number, thus: 0LL0L. We next determine its complement−that is, L00L0−which is now added to LLL00. As Fig. 11 shows, this gives L0LLL0. The first L is deleted and an extra L is added to the last (right-hand) place of this number, so that the final result is 0LLLL.

number **L L O L O L**

complement **O O L O L O**

check **L L L L L L** =

decimal system

**28**
**−13**
**15**

binary system

**L L L O O**
**− L L O L**

FIG. 11

complete this to a five-place number

**L L L O O**
**− O L L O L** ⟶ complement

delete digit in first
place and add in final
place

**L L L O O**
**+ L O O L O**
**̶L O L L L O**
**+          L**
**O L L L L**

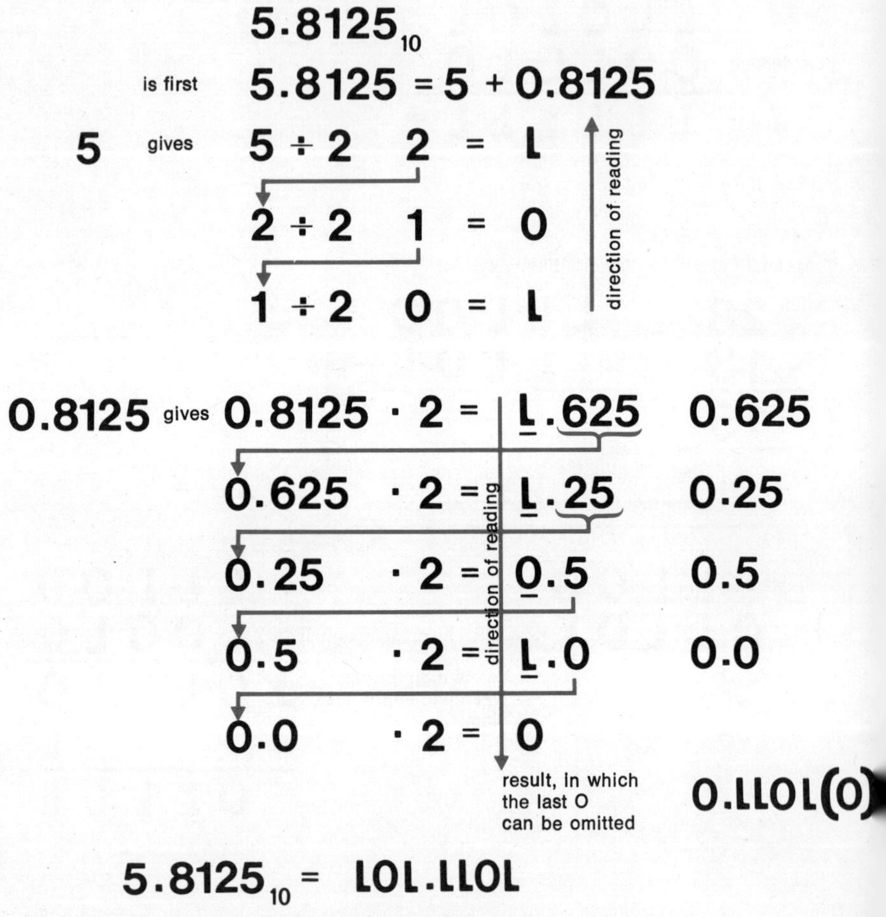

$$5.8125_{10}$$

is first $\quad 5.8125 = 5 + 0.8125$

$5 \quad$ gives $\quad 5 \div 2 \quad 2 \quad = \quad L$

$2 \div 2 \quad 1 \quad = \quad O$

$1 \div 2 \quad 0 \quad = \quad L$

direction of reading

$0.8125$ gives $0.8125 \cdot 2 = \underline{L}.625 \qquad 0.625$

$0.625 \quad \cdot 2 = \underline{L}.25 \qquad 0.25$

$0.25 \quad \cdot 2 = \underline{0}.5 \qquad 0.5$

$0.5 \quad \cdot 2 = \underline{L}.0 \qquad 0.0$

$0.0 \quad \cdot 2 = \phantom{x}0$

direction of reading

result, in which
the last O
can be omitted $\qquad$ 0.LLOL(O)

$$5.8125_{10} = LOL.LLOL$$

FIG. 12 CONVERSION OF A NUMBER IN THE DECIMAL SYSTEM
INTO ITS EQUIVALENT IN THE BINARY SYSTEM

To conclude this discussion of binary arithmetic, the significance of digits after the decimal point in a number system will be explained. When a digit is shifted one place to the left in the decimal system, its place value is increased by a factor ten. Similarly, a shift of one place to the right produces a tenfold decrease in the place value. Thus, in the decimal system, the first decimal place (that is, the first to the right of the decimal point) has the place value $10^{-1} = 1/10$, the second decimal place has the place value $10^{-2} = 1/100$, and so on; the $n$th decimal place correspondingly has the place value $10^{-n} = 1/10^n$. Hence the expression 52.37 has the value $5 \times 10^1 + 2 \times 10^0 + 3 \times 10^{-1} + 7 \times 10^{-2}$. The expression L0L.LL0L in the binary system similarly signifies $1 \times 2^2 + 0 \times 2^1 + 1 \times 2^0 + 1 \times 2^{-1} + 1 \times 2^{-2} + 0 \times 2^{-3} + 1 \times 2^{-4} = 4 + 1 + 0.5 + 0.25 + 0.0625 = 5.8125$ in the decimal system. To convert the expression 5.8125 into a binary number (Fig. 12), we first convert the 5 preceding the decimal point into the binary expression L0L. The next step consists in repeated multiplication of the decimal fraction 0.8125 by 2. Each time, the calculation is continued only with the value that occurs after the decimal point in the product, that is, if the multiplication results in the appearance of an L before the decimal point, then, for the purpose of further calculation, this L must be replaced by 0. Of course, the conversion of a decimal number into a binary number can be accomplished completely — without being left with a remainder — only if it consists of a sum of powers of 2. In all other cases the result will be an infinite succession of digits coming after the decimal point; these may repeat themselves periodically (Fig. 13).

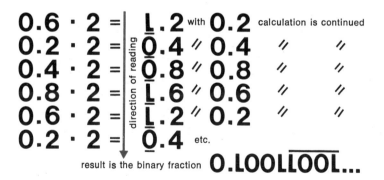

FIG. 13  CONVERSION OF THE DECIMAL NUMBER 0.6
INTO ITS BINARY EQUIVALENT

# LOGICAL OPERATIONS

As the mathematician George Boole showed in 1848, any instruction for dealing with information presented in binary form can be expressed with the aid of three logical operations: AND, OR, and NOT. In 1938 C. E. Shannon pointed out that the operations of Boolean algebra can be performed by means of a suitable arrangement of electrical switches (see page 140 et seq.). The three above-mentioned logical operations are illustrated in Fig. 1. The first two columns, designated by $x$ and $y$, contain the binary digits; of the next three columns, the first contains the connection established by the AND operator ($\wedge$), namely, $x \wedge y$; then follows a column containing the connection established by the OR operator ($\vee$), namely, $x \vee y$; and the last column indicates the negation, symbolized by $\neg$, namely, $\neg x$.

| x | y | AND<br>x∧y | OR<br>x∨y | NOT<br>¬x |
|---|---|---|---|---|
| O | O | O | O | L |
| O | L | O | L | L |
| L | O | O | L | O |
| L | L | L | L | O |

FIG. 1

If the binary digits in the $x$ and $y$ columns are equal, the AND operation yields the same binary digit; if the digits in the $x$ and $y$ columns differ, the result of this operation is always 0. The OR operation yields the value L if at least one of the two digits in the $x$ and $y$ columns is an L. Finally, the NOT operation applied to a binary digit changes it into the other digit of the binary system, that is, 0 becomes L and L becomes 0 (this is called inversion).

The representation of binary addition with the aid of Boolean algebra appears inconvenient and complicated, but it has the advantage that its operational steps can readily be simulated by technical means. For this purpose the addition of two binary numbers can advantageously be split up into two steps:

$$(62) \qquad s_n = (\neg c_n \wedge s'_n) \vee (c_n \wedge \neg s'_n)$$

$$(63) \qquad s'_n = (\neg a_n \wedge b_n) \vee (a_n \wedge \neg b_n)$$

$$(64) \qquad u_n = u'_n \vee (c_n \wedge s'_n)$$

$$(65) \qquad u'_n = a_n \wedge b_n$$

In these equations the symbols have the following meanings:

$s_n$ = the $n$th binary place of the sum;
$s'_n$ = the subtotal of the $n$th binary place;
$c_n$ = the binary carry-over produced in the $(n-1)$th place;
$u_n$ = the binary carry-over produced in the $n$th binary place;
$a_n$ and $b_n$ = the $n$th binary places of the two numbers to be added.

Without wishing, at this point, to go into the technical realization of these operations, it should be noted that the electronic circuit elements whereby the three basic logical operations (AND, OR, NOT) are performed are represented schematically in Fig. 2. With the aid of these circuit elements we shall first simulate equation (63). It is the so-called half-adder, as shown in Fig. 3. To begin with, the sum $s'_n$ is formed (equation 63): the AND operator is applied to $\neg a_n$ and $b_n$, and to $a_n$ and $\neg b_n$; the OR operator is applied to the results, as specified by the equation. The result obtained is $s'_n$. At the same time, the sum $u'_n$ is obtained by applying the AND operator to $a_n$ and $b_n$, as indicated in equation (65). The calculation of $s_n$ and $u_n$ according to

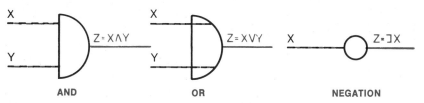

**FIG. 2**

equations (62) and (65) requires a second half-adder and also an OR operator (Fig. 4, digital adder). As the pulses corresponding to the binary digits follow one another at time intervals $\Delta t$, a further circuit element will have to be included, which appropriately delays the carry by storing it until the addition of the next digit place is performed. (The "carry" is the digit added to the next higher digit place, when the sum of the digits in the lower place exceeds the base number, that is, more particularly when it exceeds the value 2.)

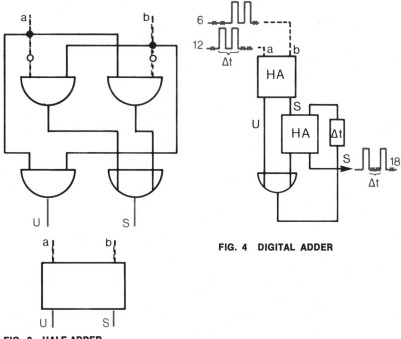

**FIG. 4   DIGITAL ADDER**

**FIG. 3   HALF-ADDER**

139

# ELECTROMAGNETIC SWITCHES

The processing of binary pulse trains will depend on how, in particular, the AND, OR, and NOT, or NOR, operations can be technically accomplished and how the individual operations can be composed of simple switches, which simulate the binary digits 0 and L by the "off" and "on" switch positions. As appears from Fig. 1, the series connection of two contacts represents the AND operation, and the parallel connection of two contacts represents the OR operation. These are normally-open contacts, in other words, they are open so long as the switching element is not actuated. For the negation (NOT) we furthermore require normally-closed contacts, that is, contacts which are closed so long as the switching element is not actuated. Then the negation, which consists in reversing the binary variables (0 becomes L, and L becomes 0), can be accomplished by letting a contact actuated by a switching element "a" function as a normally-closed contact and so affect a second switching element that when open, it causes to be closed a normally-open contact. The two switching elements needed for accomplishing the negation will then always have opposite settings: the binary digit L, which operates on the one switching element, will always produce the binary digit 0 in the other switching element, and vice versa. We see that for the construction of binary switching elements, we can utilize processes that have two stable states with which the binary digits can be associated. It is of no consequence whether the switching elements function electrically, mechanically or, indeed, hydraulically. In the case of electrical switching elements a distinction must be made between electromagnetic switches and electronic switches. The former category comprises many types of relays. The operation of electronic switches (see page 144 et seq.) is based on the special behavior characteristics of semiconductors, superconductors and photoconductors. Hydromechanical and pneumatic switches are the principal mechanically operated types.

First the electromagnetic switches—relays—will be considered. A relay is a switching device comprising one or more contacts which open or close circuits. A relay is actuated by an electromagnet that attracts or releases a

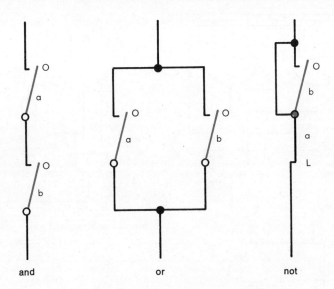

and            or            not

**FIG. 1 PERFORMING THE THREE BASIC LOGICAL OPERATIONS BY MEANS OF SIMPLE SWITCHES**

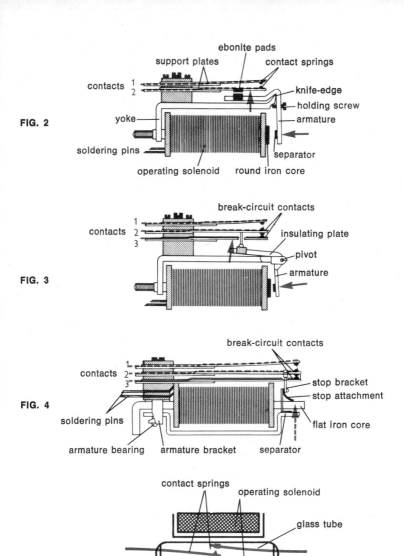

FIG. 2

FIG. 3

FIG. 4

FIG. 5  REED RELAY

movable armature. The latter brings the contacts together or allows them to separate. Four types of relay, which differ in the design of the armature and in other details, are illustrated in Figs. 2–5. The first three types each have an electromagnetic coil with an iron core and an iron yoke (or a long armature, as in Fig. 4), which carries the movable part of the armature and gives the latter the magnetic polarity of the rear part of the core, so that the attraction of different poles acts between the armature and the front of the core. In order to prevent the armature from sticking to the core in consequence of residual magnetism (that is, the magnetism that remains in the iron after the energizing current through the coil has been switched off), a narrow gap between the armature and the core is maintained by means of a separator consisting of a non-magnetic material, for example, brass, so that the armature is certain to be released by the core when the coil is de-energized. The resilient tension of the contact springs causes the armature to swing away from the core.

The electrical connections to the relay coil and the contacts are formed by so-called soldering pins. In the first relay (Fig. 2) the "make" circuit, which includes the contacts 1 and 2, is interrupted when the relay is at rest, that is, when no current is flowing through the electromagnetic coil. When the coil is energized, the armature is attracted and presses the lower spring contact against the upper one, thus closing the circuit. The relays shown in Figs. 3 and 4 are equipped with several sets of contacts, which are simultaneously actuated when the armature is attracted. They include contacts that are closed when the relay is at rest, that is, current which is then flowing through those circuits is interrupted when the electromagnetic coil is energized ("break" circuits). Fig. 5 shows a different type of relay, the so-called reed relay, which takes up much less space than the others. In this relay the magnetic field in the interior of the coil acts directly upon the contact springs, which are made of magnetic material and sealed into a small glass tube. The latter fits inside the coil and is filled with an inert protective gas to prevent oxidation of the contacts. With reed relays it is important to ensure that the mechanical oscillation period of the short reed contacts does not coincide with the oscillation period of the electrical circuits formed as a result of incidental switching operations, which may establish connection between the relay and other circuit elements, such as capacitors and self-inductance circuits. These phenomena can be obviated by the interposition, in series, of a resistor of suitable magnitude, which suppresses the occurrence of electrical oscillations (Fig. 6). The reed relay can be used as a switching element for digital data processing wherever the existence of two stable states, characterized by the actual interruption of the electrical circuit in one of the states (the "off" state), is required. As a rule, however, this requirement of 100% interruption of the circuit is not essential. For most digital data processing purposes, the "on" position has a low resistance and the "off" position has a high resistance (not a complete break of the circuit). Early data processing machines were equipped with electromagnetic switches (relays), which performed the requisite logical operations (Fig. 7). The relatively large amount of space occupied by these devices, and the high current consumption required for actuating the contacts, made such machines very bulky. They not only consumed much current, but also generated a great deal of heat, which made special air-conditioning necessary. Designers therefore soon sought other solutions, as were more particularly offered by the use of electron tubes and electronic switches.

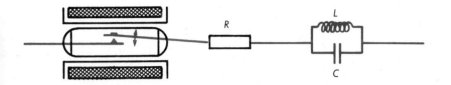

FIG. 6 PREVENTION OF RESONANCE BETWEEN MECHANICAL OSCILLATION
OF THE CONTACTS AND ELECTROMAGNETIC OSCILLATION OF THE
CIRCUIT WITH SELF-INDUCTANCE *L* AND
CAPACITANCE *C* BY MEANS OF THE DAMPING RESISTOR *R*

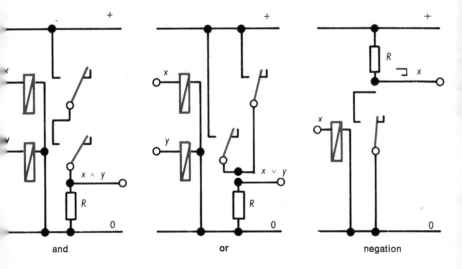

FIG. 7 PERFORMING THE THREE BASIC LOGICAL OPERATIONS
BY MEANS OF SIMPLE SWITCHES

# ELECTRON TUBES

An electron tube (or thermionic valve) is a switching device in which electrons emitted from an incandescent negative electrode (cathode) into an evacuated space flow to a positive electrode (anode), thus producing the anode current. In its two-electrode form the electron tube is called a diode. With a third electrode in the form of a grid interposed between the cathode and anode, the tube is referred to as a triode and, as such, can function as a virtually inertialess switch. The electrons emitted from the cathode can pass through holes in the grid and thus reach the anode. However, when a high negative voltage (negative grid bias) is applied to the grid, the electron stream is suppressed, so that no current then flows through the tube, which is now, if thought of as a switch, in the "off" condition. On the other hand, with a positive grid bias a large amount of current will flow because the electron stream from the cathode to the anode is enhanced; the tube is now in the "on" condition, corresponding to the binary digit L (Figs. 1a and b).

The relation between the grid voltage $U_g$ and the anode current $I_a$ is represented by the characteristic curve in Fig. 2. This curve shows that from the "off" condition (1) there is an almost linear transition to the "on" condition (II), when the maximum current flows through the tube. The transition region (III) is of no importance when the electron tube is used as a switch, but in amplifier circuits it has an important function because of its linear character. The order of magnitude of the anode current is a few milliamps. The very small current that still flows through the grid circuit when the tube is "off" is of the order of $10^{-9}$ amp. A minor proportion of this grid current is produced by electrons, of which only a very small number can pass through the negatively charged grid (only those which happen to possess very high thermal velocities); the greater part of the current in this condition is due to positive ions formed by the residual gas atoms present in the tube. The vacuum in an electron tube is of the order of $10^{-6}$ torr. This low value is attained with the aid of a so-called "getter," a substance (such as barium or magnesium) with a strong affinity for gases, which is vaporized inside the tube, after the latter has been sealed, to remove residual gas. Even so, there are still about $10^9$ gas molecules per cubic centimeter in the tube. Under these conditions the electrons travelling through this highly rarefied gas have a mean free path of about 10 meters; nevertheless, a certain number of collisions between electrons and gas molecules will occur, resulting in the formation of gas ions (positively charged gas molecules), which produce a weak grid current. This current is proportional to the number of residual gas molecules present per cubic centimeter and therefore proportional to the gas pressure in the tube. Thus the grid current provides a measure for the vacuum; special high-vacuum gauges (ionization gauges) based on this principle have been developed.

All combinations of switching elements that can be formed with electro-mechanical relays can also be formed with electron tubes. The advantage of the latter lies more particularly in their higher switching speeds and the smaller amount of space they occupy. A further advantage is the unipolar conductivity of the electron tube. There is, however, a disadvantage in that the hot cathode consumes much current and generates so much heat as to necessitate air-conditioning the room in which the machine is installed.

The unipolarity of the electron tube is due to the fact that the carriers of the electric charge, the electrons, are emitted by only one of the three electrodes, the cathode, by incandescence—that is, by a process resembling evaporation of the electrons from the cathode material. The electron stream can travel in only one direction, from the cathode to the anode. The electric current, conventionally defined, flows in the opposite direction, corresponding

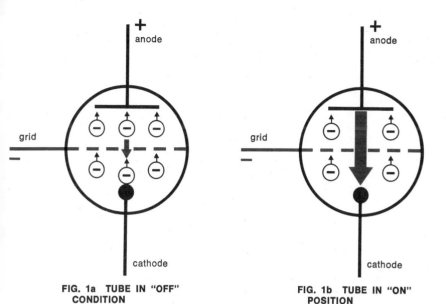

**FIG. 1a  TUBE IN "OFF" CONDITION**

**FIG. 1b  TUBE IN "ON" POSITION**

(electrons move towards anode, current conventionally flows from anode to cathode)

to the arrows in Fig. 1. As appears from the characteristic curve in Fig. 2, the current-blocking effect of the tube diminishes when the grid voltage is first increased (in the positive sense), however, a sufficient number of electrons are still slowed down and produce a negative space charge between the grid and the cathode. This space charge is formed by electrons which fail to

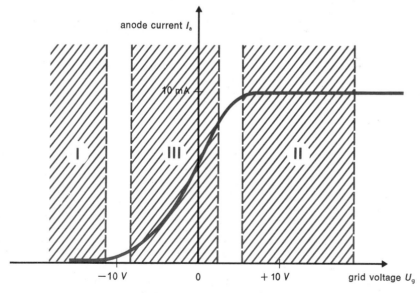

**FIG. 2  CHARACTERISTIC CURVE OF THERMIONIC TUBE, WITH "OFF" REGION (I) AND "ON" REGION (II)**

overcome the counteracting electric field of the grid, and thus fail to pass through the grid and reach the anode. The space charge, being electrically negative, tends to suppress the emission of other electrons from the cathode. With increasing (positive) voltage on the grid, however, the negative space charge between the grid and the cathode is reduced; the anode current increases until all the electrons emitted by the cathode get through to the anode: the so-called saturation current has then been reached (the curve passes from zone III to zone II). The intensity of the saturation current is determined only by the electron-emitting capacity of the cathode, in other words, it is determined primarily by the temperature of the latter. The emission of electrons from the cathode conforms to an exponential function of temperature (Fig. 3, current values 1, 2). The functional relationship in the so-called space charge region (III) is represented by Schottky's space charge law ($U^{3/2}$ law, Fig. 4):

$$(66) \qquad i_a = aU_c^{3/2}$$

where $U_c$ denotes the control voltage, which is the sum of the grid voltage and the anode voltage:

$$(67) \qquad U_c = U_g + DU_a$$

In this expression, $D$ represents the "grid transparency," a term which denotes that fraction of the anode voltage, which is still effective on the side of the grid facing the cathode. This phenomenon may be conceived as in Fig. 5: The greater part of the lines of force extending from the anode towards the cathode are intercepted by the grid and only a fraction of them pass through the grid apertures. This fraction is of the order of 5%, and it is this percentage of the anode voltage that must be added to the grid voltage, as expressed by equation (67).

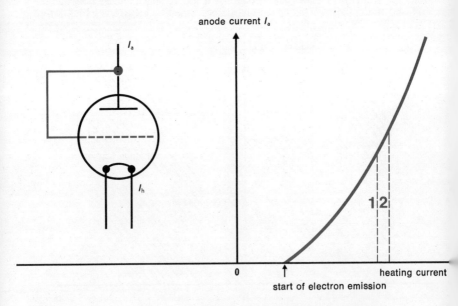

**FIG. 3  ANODE CURRENT AS A FUNCTION OF CATHODE TEMPERATURE**

Nowadays, however, electron tubes have, in their turn, been largely superseded by electronic switching devices based on the use of semiconductors. These devices take up very little space and are characterized by low power consumption and low losses. In the context of data processing systems, they are referred to as logic(al) elements, these being the smallest building blocks whose function corresponds to the logical operators AND, OR, NOT, and NOR.

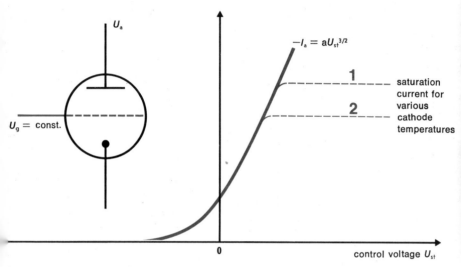

**FIG. 4    SCHOTTKY EFFECT** ($U^{3/2}$ Law)

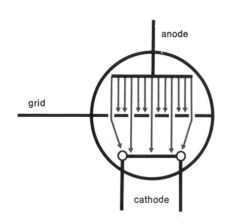

**FIG. 5   GRID TRANSPARENCY EFFECT**

# SEMICONDUCTOR LOGIC ELEMENTS

A semiconductor is a substance whose electrical resistivity is intermediate between that of metals and that of insulators—that is, at ordinary temperatures, there are only relatively few free electrons available for the conduction of electric current in such a substance, whereas in a metal there is an abundance of such electrons. Typical semiconductors are found in the fourth column of the periodic table of the chemical elements (see page 57), which is the column headed by carbon. Germanium and silicon resemble carbon in being chemically tetravalent and in having the same crystal lattice system, composed of tetrahedral assemblies of atoms (Fig. 1a). As shown by Fig. 1b, which represents a plane projection of a portion of this space lattice, each atom has four neighbors, to each of which it is linked by a covalent bond. As the bond energy of this covalent bond is of the order of magnitude of 1 eV (electron-volt, that quantity of energy gained by one electron in passing through a potential difference of 1 volt), the concentration of electrons per cubic centimeter in the semiconductor is about $10^8$ times lower than in a metal, namely, $10^{15}$ electrons/cm³ as against $10^{23}$ electrons/cm³.

The conductivity of semiconductors can, however, be varied within wide limits by the incorporation of higher-valency or lower-valency foreign atoms, which act as points of disturbance in the crystal lattice. For example, if atoms of elements in the fifth column of the periodic table (for example, arsenic or antimony) are thus incorporated, the fifth electron—the valency electron, which determines the valency of their chemical bond properties—is so loosely bound in the germanium or silicon lattice that it is released by the thermal energy of the environment at ordinary temperatures and is available as a quasi-free electron for the conduction of electricity (Fig. 2a). The term "quasi-free" denotes that the individual electron is always in interaction with the crystal lattice. The number of surplus electrons depends on the number of foreign atoms incorporated into the semiconductor. These surplus electrons produce electrical conductivity which, on account of the negative charge of the conduction electrons involved, is referred to as n-type conductivity. The foreign atoms that provide these surplus electrons are called donors.

If atoms of elements in the third column of the periodic table (for example, gallium or indium) are incorporated into a semiconductor, a deficiency of electrons occurs because one covalent bond in the lattice remains unsaturated. As a result, one of the semiconductor atoms retains a surplus positive charge. This charge strives to achieve saturation by capturing one of the quasi-free electrons that are flying about in the crystal (Fig. 2b). If this succeeds, however, there will be an electron vacancy at some other point, and the positive charge will thus have, in effect, moved along to that point. This charge can thus be conceived as a mobile vacancy and it is therefore called a "hole." The current associated with the transfer of holes as positive charge carriers is called the hole current. Added foreign substances (impurities), whose atoms attract electrons (hole electrons) from the atoms in the crystal lattice and so create holes, are called acceptors. The addition of impurities to semiconductors to control their conduction properties is termed "doping." The addition of an acceptor impurity causes positive conduction associated with holes (p-type conductivity), whereas a donor impurity supplies free electrons for negative conduction (n-type conductivity).

The energy level diagram (Fig. 3) represents the energy states in a semiconductor crystal of infinite extent. The region designated as the valence band is the range of energy levels of electrons in which the latter are still bound to the atom, that is, still within the attraction of the positive charge of

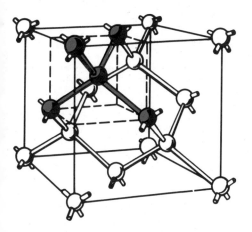

**FIG. 1a  CRYSTAL STRUCTURE OF GERMANIUM AND SILICON**

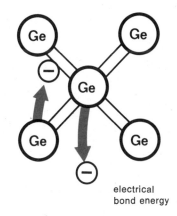

electrical bond energy

**FIG. 1b  PLANE PROJECTION OF CRYSTAL LATTICE**

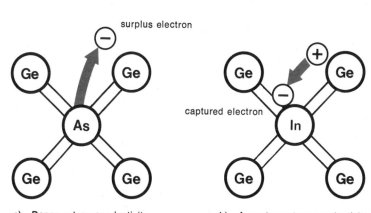

surplus electron

captured electron

a)  Donor, n-type conductivity

b)  Acceptor, p-type conductivity

**FIG. 2  HOW N-TYPE AND P-TYPE CONDUCTIVITY ARE PRODUCED BY INCORPORATION OF FOREIGN ATOMS**

As = arsenic        In = indium        Ge = germanium

the nucleus. The forbidden band comprises those energy levels which are of the order of magnitude of the bond energy between the individual atoms. This energy, corresponding to the width $\Delta E$ of the forbidden band, has to be overcome in order to release the electrons or, in other words, to give them so much energy that they are able to move about as quasi-free electrons within the crystal lattice. They have then arrived in the so-called conduction band.

Donor impurities are able to introduce electrons into the conduction band at ordinary temperatures. The energy levels of these substances in the energy level diagram must therefore be close below the lower limit of the conduction band. Conversely, the energy levels of acceptor impurities must be close above the upper limit of the valence band, since these substances are able, at ordinary temperatures, to capture electrons from that band and thus cause holes which give rise to positive conduction. It is these two different types of conductivity that make semiconductors suitable for use as electronic switching elements, more particularly in circumstances where, in one and the same crystal, a region of p-type conductivity is adjacent to a region of n-type conductivity, thus giving the semiconductor a unipolar conductive character. The surface at which a positively and a negatively conducting region meet each other is referred to as a p-n boundary.

In a semiconductor crystal in which one half is doped with an acceptor and the other half with a donor impurity there is such a p-n boundary. At this boundary the positive charges of the positively conducting region — that is, the semiconductor ions that have not yet managed to capture free electrons in that region — combine with electrons from the negatively conducting region. As a result, positive charges remain behind in the latter region, whereas a surplus of negative charge is accumulated in the positively conducting region. In this way a narrow space charge layer is formed, which acquires a negative charge on the side adjacent to the positively conducting region and a positive charge on the side adjacent to the negatively conducting region. The potential difference associated with this space charge eventually inhibits the continuation of the recombination process, and a state of equilibrium is reached in which two parts of the crystal with different conductivity types are separated from each other by a potential difference at the boundary (Fig. 4). Thus, the positively conducting region is separated from the negatively conducting region by a barrier of high electric resistance, in which there is a low concentration of charge carriers (barrier layer).

If a voltage is connected across such a crystal in such a manner that the negative pole is applied to the positively conducting, and the positive pole is applied to the negatively conducting region, then the charge carriers in each of these regions will be attracted to the respective poles, with the result that the barrier layer becomes wider (Fig. 5). But if the poles are reversed, the charge carriers will be pushed back into the barrier layer, where they rapidly recombine, so that this layer becomes narrower (Fig. 6). Since the barrier layer with its reduced concentration of charge carriers has a high resistance, the overall resistance of the semiconductor crystal in the first case will be higher (wide barrier layer), and in the second case will be lower (narrow barrier layer), than in the condition where no voltage is applied across the crystal. The resistance is therefore dependent on the direction of the current through the crystal. It is this that causes the unipolar conductivity of the semiconductor crystals which comprise a p-n boundary.

Such semiconductor circuit elements are referred to as crystal diodes. They are characterized by having a high-resistance and a low-resistance direction. When an alternating current is applied to the crystal diode, the diode will function as a rectifier. The width of the barrier layer varies with the frequency of the current. Because of their unipolar conductivity, crystal

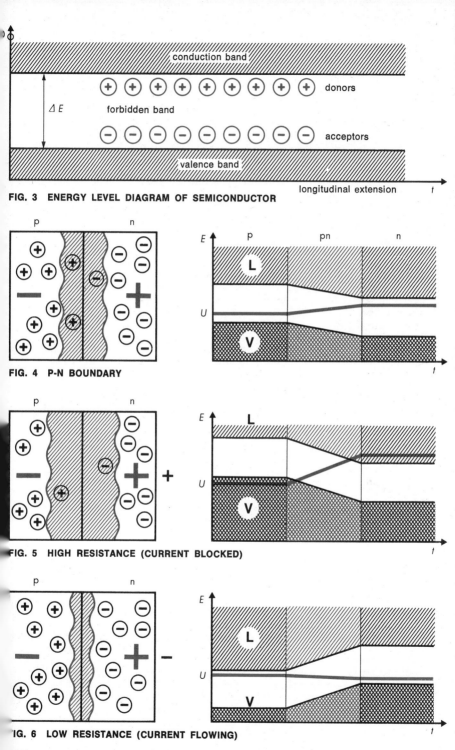

**FIG. 3 ENERGY LEVEL DIAGRAM OF SEMICONDUCTOR**

conduction band

$+$ donors

$\Delta E$ forbidden band

$-$ acceptors

valence band

longitudinal extension $t$

**FIG. 4 P-N BOUNDARY**

p    n

**FIG. 5 HIGH RESISTANCE (CURRENT BLOCKED)**

p    n

**FIG. 6 LOW RESISTANCE (CURRENT FLOWING)**

p    n

= barrier layer

diodes can be employed as electronic switches (Fig. 7) and more particularly as "logic elements" (see page 147) in data processing systems. Usually, however, a device with three electrodes, known as a transistor (in effect, a crystal triode), is used for the purpose. It comprises two barrier layers. Thus the p-n-p transistor consists of a thin slice of n-type semiconductor sandwiched between two pieces of p-type semiconductor. In the n-p-n transistor, the situation is reversed. The p-n-p transistor is illustrated schematically in Fig. 8, which also shows the corresponding energy level diagram. If a transistor is cut in the middle, we see that it really consists of two crystal diodes joined together. For the transistor to function effectively, the middle region must be so narrow that charge carriers can, by their thermal velocities, diffuse through this region, for only in this way is it possible for processes in the p-type semiconductor on one side of the middle region to affect processes in the p-type semiconductor on the other side thereof. In fact, the functioning of a triode consists in the control of one electric circuit by another.

In the transistor the electrode called the emitter corresponds to the cathode in the electron tube, while the collector is the electrode that corresponds to the anode (Fig. 8a). The middle part, which separates the emitter region from the collector region, corresponds to the grid and is called the base. The thickness of the base must not exceed about 50 microns, this being the dimension corresponding approximately to the diffusion path of the charge carriers. In comparison with the triode, the transistor offers a number of advantages. For one thing, it does not require any input of energy to liberate the electrons: In the semiconductor, the electrons attain quasi-free mobility as a result of the thermal energy of the environment, even at ordinary temperatures. Thus the high current consumption and the attendant objectionable heat evolution that are associated with other types of switching devices do not arise with transistors. Besides, the transistor is very much smaller. A disadvantage is that in the symmetrical transistor, the electrons can travel through the base only at "thermal" velocities—about $10^5$ cm/sec. Hence they are unable to keep pace with voltages whose frequencies exceed $10^5$ Hertz. This means that above about $10^4$ Hertz the functioning of the transistor becomes frequency-dependent. This undesirable effect can be obviated by incorporating a resistivity gradient in the base (by appropriate doping), which has the effect of accelerating the charge carriers towards the collector. Such a transistor is referred to as a drift transistor. The energy level diagrams corresponding to these two transistor types—the symmetrical and the drift—are shown in Figs. 8a and 8b. In the symmetrical transistor there is no potential gradient within the base. This means that variations in the voltage of the collector in no way affect the emitter-base circuit. In the electron tube this can be achieved, with regard to the anode voltage, only by the introduction of several grids, that is, by reducing the "grid transparency" (pentode).

Like electron tubes, transistors can be utilized as electronic switches. In a so-called grounded-emitter circuit, the emitter (which corresponds to the cathode of the electron tube) is at zero potential; the base thus functions as the grid. Two switch positions can be produced, in which the current in the emitter-collector circuit ($I_{CE}$) either disappears or takes on a value of several milliamps, corresponding to the "off" (blocked) and "on" (conducting) condition of the transistor respectively. See Fig. 9.

Before entering into a discussion of the various switching devices, we must once again note that a coded information flow always consists of a sequence of binary digits (bits). In general, the time interval $\Delta t$ between successive bits should be kept as small as possible, the attainable shortness of this interval being dependent on the operating time of the electronic switches employed. With semiconductors, as well as with electron tubes, the operating times can be reduced to as little as 1 nanosecond ($10^{-9}$ second). The two

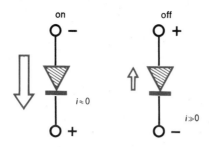

**FIG. 7   SEMICONDUCTOR DIODE AS ELECTRONIC SWITCH**

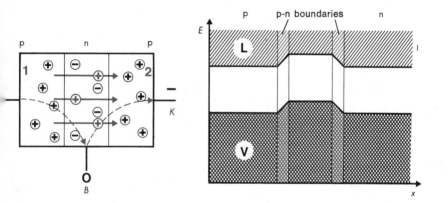

**FIG. 8a   MODE OF FUNCTIONING OF THE SYMMETRICAL TRANSISTORS**

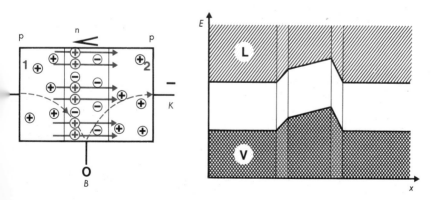

**FIG. 8b   MODE OF FUNCTIONING OF THE DRIFT TRANSISTOR**

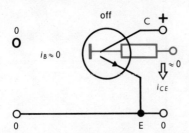
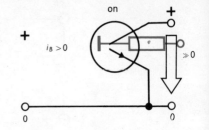

**FIG. 9 p-n-p TRANSISTOR AS ELECTRONIC SWITCH**

binary digits 0 and L can be represented in two ways by the switching operation (Figs. 10a and b). Either the voltage $U(0)$ or $U(L)$ is maintained during a full time interval $\Delta t$ or, alternatively, the binary digit L is represented by a voltage pulse whose duration $\tau$ is less than $\Delta t$, while the binary digit 0 is represented by the absence of any pulse. The former case is referred to as static technique, the latter as pulse technique.

The simulation of the three basic logical operations by electronic switches (logic elements) will now be further discussed. The AND operation performed by three types of electronic switch (electron tube, crystal diode, transistor) is indicated in Figs. 11a, b, c. With the electron tube or the transistor used as an AND element, the output voltage $U(0)$ occurs when no current is flowing through the resistance $R$. This is always the case when one or both electronic switches continue to block the circuit; they allow current to flow only when a higher voltage $U(L)$ is applied to both inputs $(x, y)$. Then the internal resistance of the two switches is less than $R$, so that the anode voltage or the collector voltage $U(L)$ is applied to $R$. In the case of the diode circuit, in accordance with the definition of the operation, the voltage $U(L)$ will be applied to the output when no current flows through $R$. This is the case only when the voltage $U(L)$ is likewise applied to both outputs. If the voltage $U(0)$ is applied to one input, then the corresponding diode is switched "on," in the direction of flow; its internal resistance is there-

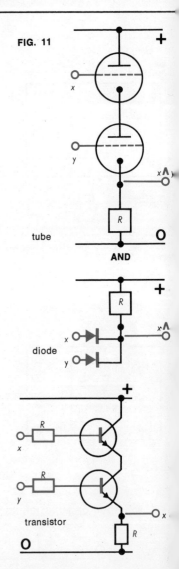

FIG. 11

tube

AND

diode

transistor

154

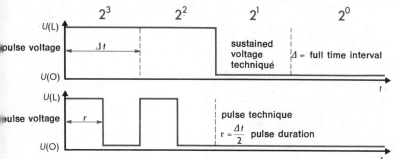

FIG. 10  BINARY REPRESENTATION OF THE NUMBER 12

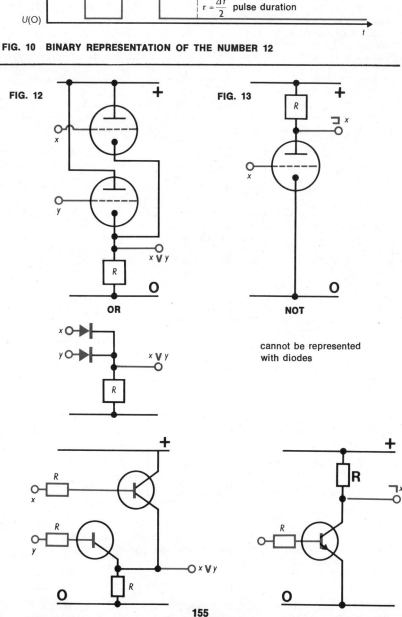

155

fore substantially lower than $R$, so that $U(0)$ occurs at the output. For performing the OR operation (Figs. 12a, b, c) by electron tubes or transistors the two electronic switches required are connected in parallel, so that the voltage $U(L)$ always occurs at the output when $U(L)$ is applied to one of the inputs. Only when both inputs have the voltage $U(0)$ is the output connected to the voltage $U(0)$ through $R$. If diodes are used, the voltage $U(0)$ will be applied to the output, when this voltage is applied to both inputs. If $U(L)$ is applied to one of the inputs $(x,y)$, then $U(L)$ will occur at the output, because the diode resistance in the direction of flow is significantly lower than $R$. The NOT operation is represented in Fig. 13 on page 155. If this switching operation is performed by means of an electron tube or a transistor, blocking of the tube or transistor by the input voltage $U(0)$ will cause the voltage $U(L)$ to occur at the output, as no current then flows through $R$. However, if the tube or transistor is made conductive by an input voltage $U(L)$, then the internal resistance $W$ of the electronic switch is much lower than $R$, so that the voltage $U(0)$ will then occur at the output. A negation circuit cannot be formed with diodes, as these are not reversible.

Because of the finite propagation velocity of electromagnetic energy in circuits, time lags are liable to occur between pulse trains arriving at the input through circuits differing in length within an electronic computer, so that the problem of synchronization arises (see page 158). If these lags affect only some of the incoming signals, the unretarded signals will have to be specially slowed down if the two groups of signals are subsequently to be combined (Fig. 14). The so-called "flip-flop circuit" is particularly suitable for switching elements that produce such retardation. It is a bistable device, that is, it comprises two stable states and two input terminals corresponding to those states; in use, it remains in either state until the application of a signal causes it to change to the other state. Therefore a flip-flop can be regarded as a storage device that is able to store information equivalent to one bit. Its mode of functioning is illustrated in Fig. 15a, which more particularly shows the circuit arrangement first devised by Eccles and Jordan in 1919. By means of an external stimulus (triggering), this device can be switched back and forth from one stable state to the other, that is, it can vibrate between the two. Hence it is sometimes referred to as a bistable multivibrator; the circuit, as such, is also known as a "trigger circuit" or Eccles-Jordan circuit. In Fig. 15a it has electron tubes, in Fig. 15b it has thyratrons (the thyratron is a hot-cathode gas tube, usually a triode, in which a control electrode initiates the anode current but does not limit it), and in Fig. 15c it has transistors as its electronic elements.

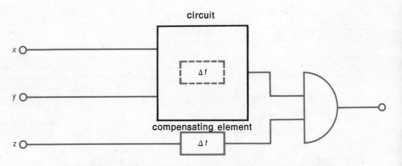

**FIG. 14 COMPENSATION OF TIME LAGS DUE TO ELECTRICAL CIRCUITS**

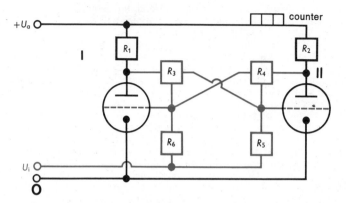

**FIG. 15a   BISTABLE MULTIVIBRATOR WITH ELECTRON TUBES (ECCLES-JORDAN TRIGGER CIRCUIT)**

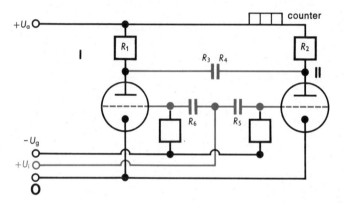

**FIG. 15b   BISTABLE STEP-DOWN CIRCUIT WITH THYRATRONS**

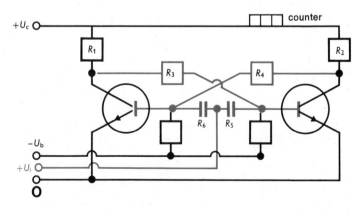

**FIG. 15c   FLIP-FLOP CIRCUIT WITH TRANSISTORS**

A circuit of this kind is basically symmetrical, but when it is switched on, minor asymmetry in the components (for example) will cause it to pass into one of the two stable states. In either state, one of the two electronic switches (tube or transistor) is conductive (I) while the other is blocked (II). The current flowing through the electronic switch I causes a voltage drop in the resistance $R_1$, so that, through the resistance $R_3$, an anode voltage (or collector voltage), which is reduced by the amount of this voltage drop, is applied to the grid (or the base) of the blocked switch II. On the other hand, no current flows through the blocked switch, so that the full anode voltage (or collector voltage) of this switch is applied, through the resistances $R_1$ and $R_2$, to the grid (or the base) of the conductive switch I, thus maintaining it in this state. Now if, through the resistance $R_2$, a negative voltage pulse (trigger pulse) is applied to the grid (or the base) of the conductive switch I, the flow of current through it will stop. Then the grid (or the base) of the hitherto blocked switch II receives, through the resistances $R_1$ and $R_3$, the full anode voltage (or collector voltage), so that a current now flows through this switch. As a result, a voltage drop occurs in the resistance $R_2$, which now maintains the blocked state of the initially conductive switch I, which has meanwhile become the blocked switch. Thus, in consequence of a negative trigger pulse, the flip-flop has passed from one stable state to the other.

If one input is connected through two capacitors to the two grids (or bases) of the corresponding electronic switches, and if the output is connected to one of the anodes (or collectors) of these switches, as shown in Fig. 15, or, alternatively, if a counting device is incorporated in one of the supply leads to the anode (or collector), then, when a pulse train LLLL is applied to the input, the pulse train at the output will oscillate between L and 0 (0L0L), that is, one bit is stored each time. At every alternate bit, an L occurs at the output. The two stable states that correspond to "conductive" and "blocked" are technically termed "set" and "reset" respectively. A high voltage at the output corresponds to the binary digit L, a low voltage corresponds to the binary digit 0.

A flip-flop can be conceived as a step-down device with a step-down ratio of 1:2. A series circuit comprising $n$ flip-flops will thus provide a step-down ratio of $1:2^n$. The flip-flop arrangement with thyratrons, shown in Fig. 15b, serves to reduce the pulse train frequency of the trigger voltage. It was devised by C. E. Wynn-Williams in 1931. His problem was to count high pulse sequence frequencies in connection with the counting of particles, which were detected by means of Geiger-type tubes. As the then-available mechanical counting devices were unable to keep pace with these frequencies, it was necessary to reduce the number of pulses arriving at the input of those devices. This was accomplished with the aid of thyratron flip-flop circuits in the ratio of $1:2^n$.

In general, flip-flops can be used for synchronizing the pulses that arrive simultaneously at the input of a sequential system comprising several circuits and take different lengths of time to traverse these circuits. This is achieved with the aid of timing pulses which simultaneously release the pulses that arrive, with slight time differences, at various flip-flops (Fig. 16). Let the time intervals between the timing pulses be $\Delta t$. A second timing sequence with the same pulse frequency, but displaced by an amount $\frac{1}{2}\Delta t$ in relation to the first, is produced. In this way the signals are made to pass from one circuit to another immediately after the time $\frac{1}{2}\Delta t$ — that is, within the sequential system, the pulses are delayed only by amounts $\frac{1}{2}\Delta t$ on passing from circuit to circuit. This is necessary because the circuit in question must be freed for the reception of pulses from the preceding circuit (Fig. 17).

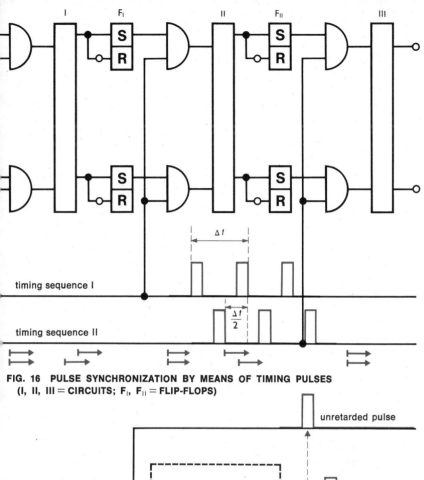

FIG. 16  PULSE SYNCHRONIZATION BY MEANS OF TIMING PULSES
(I, II, III = CIRCUITS; $F_I$, $F_{II}$ = FLIP-FLOPS)

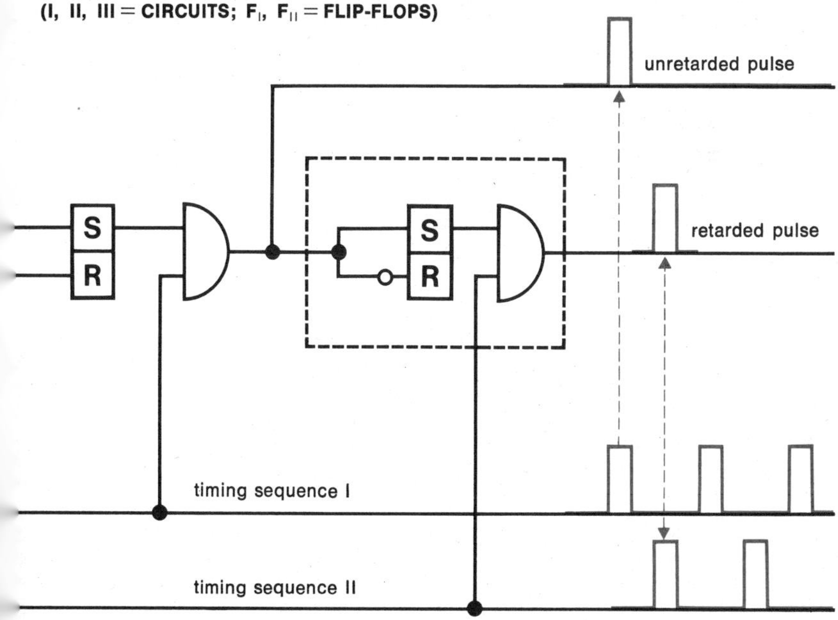

FIG. 17  MODE OF FUNCTIONING OF A SINGLE DELAY ELEMENT

# PHOTO-ELECTRIC LOGIC ELEMENTS

Besides electronic switches, in which the charge carriers that produce the electric current flowing through them are controlled by an additional electrode, there also exist logic elements in which the current is controlled by light. The operation of such photo-electric switches is based primarily on the photo-electric effect, that is, on the fact that the radiation energy of light can serve to liberate electrons from atoms and thus produce a photo-electron current. The photo-electric effect may, in appropriate circumstances, occur on the surface, or in the interior of a substance, or in the vicinity of a boundary layer; it is correspondingly referred to as the photo-emissive, the photo-conductive, and the photo-voltaic effect, respectively.

The energy balance of the photo-emissive effect conforms to a relationship discovered by Einstein, which states that the energy of a radiation quantum is:

(68) $\quad E = h\nu$

where $h$ is Planck's constant (elementary quantum of action: $h = 6.45 \times 10^{-28}$ erg/sec.) and $\nu$ is the frequency of the incident radiation. This energy is imparted to an electron within the solid, and enables this electron (in the case of the photo-emissive effect) to emerge from the surface of the solid and utilize the rest of the energy (not consumed in effecting its escape from the solid) as kinetic energy for its further motion. The energy balance of the photo-emissive effect is represented by Einstein's equation:

(69) $\quad h\nu = \frac{1}{2}m_\epsilon v^2 + A = \epsilon U + h\nu_0$

In this expression $A$ denotes the so-called photo-electric work function; $\frac{1}{2}m_\epsilon v^2$ is the kinetic energy of the emitted electron; $h\nu_0$ is that radiation quantum (of frequency $\nu_0$) which is just sufficient to enable the electron to break through the surface, but which leaves no surplus of kinetic energy, so that we can put $A = h\nu_0$; $\epsilon U$ denotes that amount of potential energy which remains available to the electron as kinetic energy when $h\nu > h\nu_0$ ($U$ is the symbol representing a potential; $\epsilon$ is the elementary electric charge). From Einstein's equation (69) it follows that the energy of the electron is greater according as the frequency of the incident light is higher.

Fig. 1 illustrates the principle of a photo-electric cell (or photocell). It consists essentially of a collecting electrode (anode) and a photo-electrically sensitive cathode onto which the light beam is directed and from which photo-emission of electrons occurs as a surface effect. Fig. 2 is a skeleton view of a device called a photomultiplier. In this the primarily produced photo-electric current is multiplied by secondary emission of electrons, so that separate amplification is unnecessary. This multiplication by a factor of about 10 is effected at two parallel electrodes between which the electrons are accelerated. In principle, every material is photo-electrically sensitive. Most materials, however, respond only to irradiation with ultraviolet light. For practical purposes this is a drawback, and for this reason, photo-cathodes have been developed which respond to visible light. Photo-cathodes made of alkali metals are very suitable for this purpose, particularly those in which the element cesium is incorporated.

As a rule, photo-cathodes constructed as shown in Fig. 3 are used. By means of oxidation, an exceedingly thin film of silver oxide is deposited on a silver plate, which is then exposed to cesium vapor, so that the silver oxide becomes covered with a very thin coating of cesium oxide, in the surface of which cesium atoms are embedded. Such coatings are highly photo-sensitive over almost the whole range of visible light, including the red end of the spectrum.

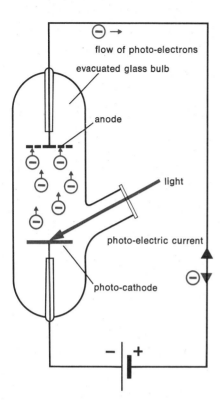

flow of photo-electrons

evacuated glass bulb

anode

light

photo-electric current

photo-cathode

− +

**FIG. 1  DIAGRAM SHOWING MAIN FEATURES OF A PHOTO-ELECTRIC CELL AND HOW IT WORKS**

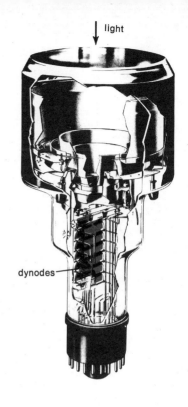

light

dynodes

**FIG. 2  PHOTOMULTIPLIER WITH CURRENT AMPLIFICATION BY MEANS OF SECONDARY-EMISSION ELECTRODES (DYNODES)**

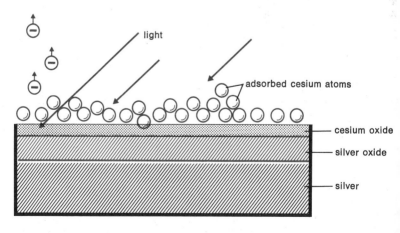

light

adsorbed cesium atoms

cesium oxide

silver oxide

silver

**FIG. 3  DIAGRAM OF A CESIUM PHOTO-CATHODE**

The photo-electric current is proportional to the intensity of the light that enters the photo-electric cell (Fig. 4). Its response to variations in light intensity is practically inertialess and instant, so that it can readily be modulated. A well known application of the photo-electric cell is in the reproduction of sound from optical sound tracks of films. The variations in blackening of the film cause light intensity variations, which in turn control the strength of the photo-electric current. These current variations are amplified and fed to loudspeakers. When the photo-electric cell is employed as a switch, the condition where no light is entering the cell (binary digit 0) corresponds to the state of very high electrical resistance, so that no current flows (the switch is "off"). When light is admitted (binary digit L), a photo-electric current flows and can be used to actuate electrical circuits (the switch is "on"). The photo-electric cell described in the foregoing does not need to have an accelerating voltage applied to it. However, with an appropriately constructed and evacuated photo-electric cell, it is possible to apply such a voltage; the advantage is that all the electrons then reach the anode (there is no interposed grid as in the electron tube), and no space charges are formed. In a cell filled with an inert gas at low pressure, the application of an accelerating voltage additionally produces a phenomenon called "gas amplification," that is, the photo-electrons form ions, which intensify the photo-electric current by a factor ranging from 25 to 125, depending on the geometric arrangement of the components. With the aid of such photo-electric cells, which are also known as photo-diodes, it is possible to perform the three basic logical operations. For this it is merely necessary to replace the circuit breaker contacts of the relays, illustrated on pages 141 and 143, by photo-diodes and to actuate the contacts, not by electromagnetic forces, but in this case by light beams.

If the liberation of electrons occurs in the interior of the material, rather than in the vicinity of the surface, or if the energy of the electrons is not sufficient to eject them from the surface of the material (usually a semiconductor), the electrons will, nevertheless, become quasi-free in the interior of the material and thus increase its electrical conductivity (photo-conductive effect). The earliest known photo-conductive material was selenium, whose properties in this respect have been known for more than a hundred years, although it was not until about fifty years later that it began to find technical application, more particularly, for so-called light barriers, which were used in burglar alarms, counting devices for packages on belt conveyors or people on escalators, devices for automatically opening and closing doors, and so on. All these devices operated on the principle that when a beam of light is shining into a selenium photo-electric cell, the resistance of the latter is low, so that a current flows through it; but when the beam is interrupted, the sudden great increase in the resistance of the selenium (by a factor in the region of $10^3$ to $10^4$) breaks the electrical circuit, thereby actuating a relay which in turn sets off an alarm, energizes a counting device (Fig. 5), and so on.

Nowadays cadmium sulphide, or cadmium selenide, is preferred for photo-conductive cells. These substances have light-to-dark photo-current ratios of the order of $10^9:1$. Such cells can also be utilized as logic elements, that is, as components for performing logical operations, in which the condition of high resistance (no light entering the cell) corresponds to the binary digit 0, and the condition of low resistance (light entering) corresponds to the binary digit L. In this case control is effected by light pulses.

Finally, the photo-voltaic effect can also be utilized for the operation of switching elements. In these devices, an electromotive force is generated by allowing light to fall on the boundary between dissimilar materials, for ex-

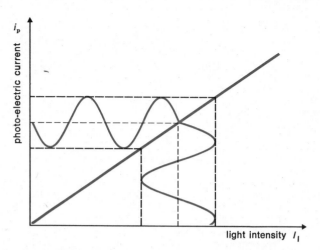

**FIG. 4 PHOTO-ELECTRIC CURRENT AS A FUNCTION OF INCIDENT LIGHT INTENSITY, WITH INDICATION OF MODULATION RESPONSE**

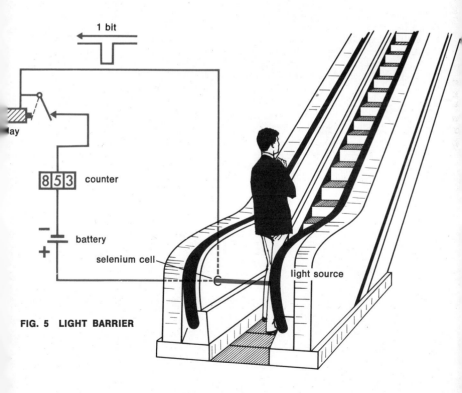

**FIG. 5 LIGHT BARRIER**

163

ample, the boundary between a metal and a semiconductor, or a p-n boundary (see page 150 et seq.). As a result, a potential difference is produced across the boundary. The layers to be traversed by the incident light in order to reach the boundary must, of course, be suitably thin and transparent (Figs. 6, 7 and 8). Photo-voltaic cells can thus directly transform light energy into electrical energy. They are used as solar batteries for the supply of power to artificial satellites and spacecraft. The photo-sensitive material preferred for such purposes is silicon, a semiconductor that can generate a relatively high photo-voltage (in excess of 1 volt).

When a photo-voltaic cell is used as an electronic switch, this in itself low voltage must suffice to represent the binary digit L. The only way to obtain a higher voltage is by connecting a number of such cells in series. The importance of these devices lies, more particularly, in a special field of data processing, namely, character recognition (see page 206). In these semiconductor photocells, too, the primary photo-electric effect consists in dislodging electrons, or (positive) holes, from the atoms within the material. If this occurs in the vicinity of the boundary, the photo-voltaic effect is produced.

A feature common to all electronic switches is that they can be operated with super-high-frequency control pulses, in other words, it is possible to use trigger frequencies up to the order of magnitude of $10^9$ Hertz. Semiconductors used in such electronic switches have to be highly doped in order to achieve a sufficiently high velocity of the charge carriers — approaching the velocity of light — which is needed for coping with such high frequencies. Such very high switching speeds are not always necessary, however. Instead, other requirements may be more important, for example, the device must be unaffected by temperature or be insensitive to bombardment by atomic particles. Such conditions are encountered, for example, in the case of logic elements installed in artificial satellites and spacecraft, which are exposed to the very low temperatures of outer space, and to bombardment by photons, electrons and gamma rays (especially when traversing the Van Allen belts). Under such conditions it may be preferable to use so-called fluidic devices.

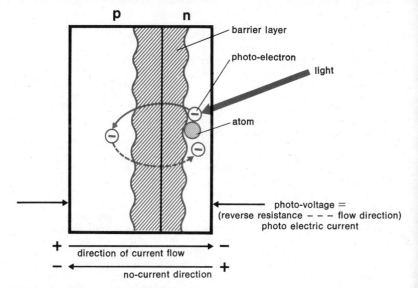

**FIG. 6   HOW A PHOTO-VOLTAGE IS PRODUCED
AT A p-n BOUNDARY IN A SEMICONDUCTOR**

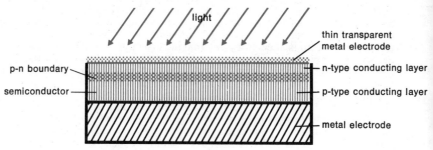

**FIG. 7   DIAGRAM OF A PHOTO-VOLTAIC CELL
(THE TRANSPARENT METAL FILM IS DEPOSITED BY VAPORIZATION)**

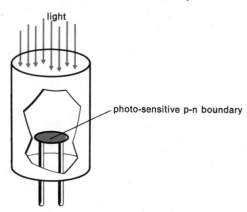

**FIG. 8   PHOTO-DIODE**

# FLUIDIC SWITCHES

The term "fluidics" (as the counterpart of "electronics") refers to the use of jets of liquid, or gas, to actuate mechanical flip-flop logic elements, which have been developed to provide a system of control logic, and power amplification, in the adverse environment of space. Compressed air, water, or oil may be used for the actuation of such switches. The binary digits O and L may be represented by the static pressure of the working fluid (comparable to the electric voltage in electronics) or by the volumetric rate of flow (comparable to electric current). A fluidic switch consists essentially of a piston whose movement produces an on-off switching operation. A simple arrangement is illustrated in Fig. 1a. Above the double piston acts a pressure whose mean value is $p_m$. The system has three inputs ($N$, $M$ and $A$) and one output ($x$). When a pressure $p_A > p_m$ is applied to the input $A$ (corresponding to the binary digit L), the piston rises; a pressure $p_A < p_m$, applied to $A$, will cause the piston to descend to the position shown in the drawing. In combination with the other two inputs, it is thus possible, with this simple fluidic element, to perform the three basic logical operations. Furthermore, input and output may be interchanged, so that the output can be connected direct to other switching elements of the same type. Fig. 2 shows a fluidic switching element which has two stable states; in this respect, it functionally corresponds to the electronic flip-flop (see page 157). The use of a fluid actuating medium does, however, impose limitations upon the speed of transmission. Besides, the various quantities, such as flow rates and pressure differences, cannot be measured so easily and conveniently as voltages and currents. Two other adverse factors that may affect fluidic switches are turbulence and corrosion. A new type of switch has, however, been designed to take advantage of turbulence and utilize it as a functional feature. A jet of fluid having a turbulent outer layer is disturbed if its turbulence pattern is affected by external intervention. This may, for example, be achieved by injecting fluid into the turbulent layer or by extracting fluid from it. It may also be achieved by the so-called Koanda effect, which consists in influencing the turbulence on one or the other side of a fluid jet, thus deflecting it in a desired direction. A fluidic switch based on this principle is shown in Fig. 3. In the power amplification element in Fig. 3b, the fluid power supply entering through the input channel is discharged equally through the two diverging channels $A_1$ and $A_2$ when no fluid is injected through the control nozzles (Fig. 3b, left). A weak control jet introduced on the left causes a greater proportion of the fluid to be discharged through $A_2$ (infinitely-variable control). The device in Fig. 3a is a fluidic flip-flop: Turning on the fluid in the control nozzle on the same side causes the power supply to flip to the opposite output channel.

Such fluidic elements can be made of metal, plastics or ceramic materials, so that they are highly resistant to mechanical actions, or extremes of temperature, or both. Also, they are unaffected by radiation, bombardment by nuclear particles, and so on. On the other hand, they are highly sensitive to leaks and to the presence of dirt particles, which are liable to cause jamming of the pistons or disturbance of the jet movements.

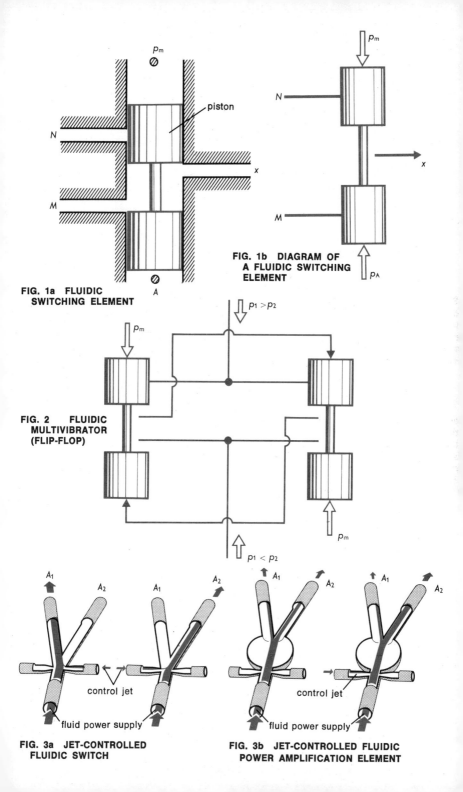

FIG. 1a FLUIDIC
SWITCHING ELEMENT

FIG. 1b DIAGRAM OF
A FLUIDIC SWITCHING
ELEMENT

FIG. 2 FLUIDIC
MULTIVIBRATOR
(FLIP-FLOP)

FIG. 3a JET-CONTROLLED
FLUIDIC SWITCH

FIG. 3b JET-CONTROLLED FLUIDIC
POWER AMPLIFICATION ELEMENT

# MECHANICAL STORAGE DEVICES

The flip-flop is a storage device which is able to store one bit for any desired length of time. Devices of this sort may be used for the synchronization of electrical pulses which have travelled through different circuits and have thus been subjected to time lags. The flip-flop is a bistable switching element, that is, it has two stable states which, respectively, characterize the binary digits L and O. In general, processes with bistable states are suitable as components for storage devices.

The simplest method of storing information in the form of the binary digits L and O is by means of index cards that are subdivided into squares. When the binary digit L occurs, the corresponding square is filled in with ink, whereas it is left blank when the binary digit O occurs. Alternatively, the L may be characterized by a punched hole (punched cards). The magnetizing and demagnetizing of iron, or ferrites, provides two stable states, which can likewise be utilized for information storage. Another possibility is the displacement of the superconductive transition temperature, under the influence of a magnetic field. (For certain metals the electrical resistance becomes vanishingly small at a temperature a few degrees above absolute zero. This phenomenon is termed superconductivity, and the temperature at which it occurs is the transition temperature). In a case where storage is required only for a brief period, it is possible to make use of the propagation time of acoustic waves and other time-lag phenomena, such as the delay in the actuation of a relay brought about by a brass jacket. Magnetic storage methods have acquired considerable practical importance in recent years (see page 170 et seq.).

Punched cards as a mechanical method of data storage have been in use since 1880, when H. Hollerith, an American engineer, designed and constructed a successful sorting machine. The usual punched cards (Fig. 1) are divided into 80 columns comprising lines which correspond to the digits 1 to 9. For example, if the number 1224 has to be recorded in the first four columns of a card, this is done by punching, in the first column the line 1, in the second the line 2, in the third the line 2, and in the fourth the line 4. A large mass of numerical data can be stored on the card in this way. By punching holes in additional rows not corresponding to digits it is possible to record supplementary information, for example, whether the punched digits are to be understood as alphabetical characters (according to a particular code) instead of numerical data. The top left-hand corner of each card is cut away, so that in a stack of cards, any card that happens to be the wrong way up is at once detected. The simplest mechanical method of sorting those punched cards having the same distinctive data from a stack is illustrated in Fig. 2. In the selecting device, the requisite selecting pins are inserted through the stack. Certain distinctive portions on the cards are marked by perforations in the form of slots instead of round holes. When the pins have been inserted, the device is rotated 180 degrees, so that all those cards which have slots instead of holes around the inserted pins will drop a certain distance corresponding to the length of a slot (6 mm) and can thus easily be picked out.

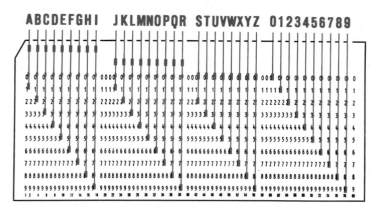

**FIG. 1  PUNCH CARD WITH NUMBER AND LETTER CODING**

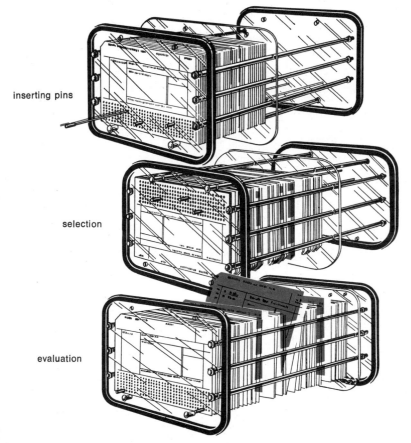

inserting pins

selection

evaluation

**FIG. 2  SORTING DEVICE FOR SLOTTED CARDS**

# MAGNETIC STORAGE DEVICES

All magnetic storage devices make use of the two stable directions of magnetization, which can be reversed so as to store the binary digits L and O respectively. There are four main types of magnetic store (or magnetic memory), based on the use of magnetic tapes, drums, discs or cores. Before dealing with these in further detail, we shall first consider the principles of magnetization and the physical properties of magnetic materials.

An atom (diameter about $10^{-8}$ cm) is conceived as consisting of a positively charged nucleus (diameter about $10^{-12}$ cm) surrounded by a cloud of electrons (electronic envelope) containing a number of electrons, each carrying a negative elementary charge, equal to the number of positive elementary charges in the nucleus of the atom (this latter number is termed the nuclear charge number). The electrons revolve around the nucleus in specific elliptical orbits (quantum orbits), in the manner of planets orbiting around the sun. Their charge completely compensates the positive charge in the nucleus, so that, externally, the atom is electrically neutral.

This conception of the atom, which is known as the Bohr-Sommerfeld atomic model, fits in with Ampère's classical theory of magnetism, which states that a magnetic field is produced as the cumulative overall effect of a multitude of small circular electric currents. Each orbiting, negatively charged electron forms a circular current that produces an orbital magnetic moment; in addition, the electron has a magnetic moment of its own (spin moment), which is due to the spin of the electron about its own axis. As a rule the orbital moments of the various electrons in the atom compensate one another, whereas the spin moments — especially if the atom has an odd number of electrons — produce a resultant magnetic moment (Fig. 1).

In what are known as ferromagnetic materials (which include the metals iron, nickel and cobalt), the atoms have a resultant magnetic moment, which is due to the spin of those electrons in not fully occupied inner electron shells. They differ from other materials in that there is a relatively powerful mutual action of a special kind (so-called exchange forces) between these magnetic moments, which assists the atomic magnetic moments to arrange themselves parallel to one another. This occurs over comparatively large regions of the material (Weiss's domains), which thus become spontaneously magnetized (Fig. 2). Outwardly, however, the material appears non-magnetic because the spontaneous magnetization of the various domains is totally disordered as regards its direction and intensity, so that they cancel one another. But in a magnetic field these domains undergo reorientation and arrange themselves parallel to the direction of the field, this effect being more pronounced in proportion as the external magnetic field is of higher intensity. The resulting magnetization of the ferromagnetic material is a great many times more powerful than that of a non-ferromagnetic material in the same magnetic field.

The earliest known mineral substance in which magnetization was observed is magnetite (magnetic iron ore), which is composed of the oxides of divalent and trivalent iron; its chemical formula is $FeO \cdot Fe_2O_3$, usually written simply as $Fe_3O_4$. In 1909 S. Hilbert discovered that magnetic material can also be obtained by replacing the divalent iron oxide ($FeO$) by the oxides of other divalent metals. Ceramic ferromagnetic compounds of this kind are known as ferrites. Such compounds possess three valuable properties: high permeability (that is, they are easily magnetizable), low eddy-current losses (that is, low heat evolution on magnetization) and high electrical resistance (so that wire windings can be applied directly to these materials without any special insulation).

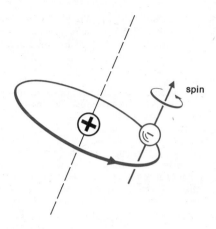

spin

**FIG. 1   MAGNETIC MOMENT OF AN ATOM ILLUSTRATED BY THE HYDROGEN ATOM**

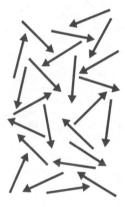

a) spin orientation in paramagnetic and . . .

b) ferromagnetic material

**FIG. 2**

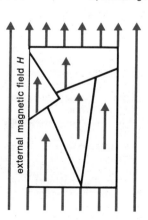

external magnetic field *H*

c) ferromagnetic saturation: all the Weiss domains are oriented parallel to the external magnetic field

The crystal lattice of a ferrite has a spinel structure based on a cubic fundamental lattice in which tetrahedrons and octahedrons are embedded (Fig. 3). A ferrite is manufactured by fusion of a divalent metallic oxide with the trivalent iron oxide ($Fe_2O_3$), with the aid of a small quantity of a fluxing agent. The constituent oxides are ground to a fine powder and mixed together, wet or dry, in certain proportions. This mixture is fired at a high temperature – but not so high as to cause sintering (partial fusion) – so as to bring about the formation of the ferrite compound. When the material has cooled, it is ground again and then molded to the desired shapes by pressing or casting. Then follows a further burning process, lasting several hours, at a temperature of between $1100°$ and $1400°$ C. When this process is performed in a neutral atmosphere – that is, such that the hot gases to which the material is exposed exercise neither a reducing nor an oxidizing action – a ferrite is obtained whose magnetic reversal takes place abruptly, whereas otherwise this transition is effected smoothly. The mechanical properties, particularly the hardness, are also influenced by the manufacturing process.

For data storage purposes, it is undoubtedly advantageous if the storage elements employed can perform the transition from one stable state to the other as quickly as possible. It is, therefore, desirable that the direction of magnetization be able to change suddenly, almost instantly, when required to do so. Such properties can best be demonstrated by measuring the magnetization of the material as a function of the direction and intensity of the externally applied magnetic field. In this way a magnetization curve is obtained whose behavior is dependent on the direction of the magnetic field; it is known as the hysteresis curve (Fig. 4). The abscissae represent the intensity $H$ of the magnetic field, while the ordinates represent the magnetization $M$ of the material. The virgin ferrite, that is, the ferrite not yet influenced by any external magnetic field, has no magnetism of its own. When an external magnetic field is applied, the virgin curve first starts from the origin of the co-ordinates. The magnetic field intensity induced in the ferrite increases with the external magnetic field up to the value $H_s$ of that field; all the Weiss domains have then become oriented parallel to one another, and the magnetization of the material has attained its saturation value $M_s$. Further intensification of the magnetizing field produces no change in magnetization. When the magnetizing field intensity is reduced again, the Weiss domains do not revert to their original disordered state, but retain their parallel orientation over fairly large regions. Because of this, the ferrite has residual magnetism (remanence) corresponding to the ordinate $M_r$ when the magnetizing field is zero.

In order to get rid of this residual magnetism, that is, to make the Weiss domains revert to their disordered state, a magnetizing field acting in the opposite direction must be applied. When this field reaches an intensity of $-H_c$ (termed the coercive force), the intensity of magnetization of the ferrite becomes zero. The Weiss domains have now already become oriented in the opposite direction. The magnetism of the ferrite can thus be reversed, and when the magnetizing field intensity reaches the value $-H_s$, the magnetization of the ferrite reaches its saturation value $-M_s$. The area within the hysteresis curve (representing the magnetization intensity plotted against the magnetizing field intensity, Fig. 4) is proportional to the energy necessary for effecting the transition of the ferrite from one stable state of magnetization to the other (reversed) state.

More particularly suitable for the storage of binary data are ferrites having a hysteresis curve presenting as nearly rectangular a shape as possible, so that the transition from one state to the other is achieved suddenly and change-over times are therefore short. Furthermore, high values for the residual magnetism ($M_r$) are advantageous for the storage of powerful impulses, while low values

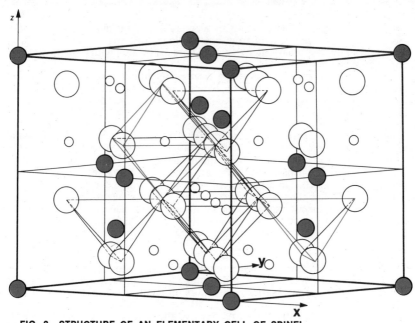

**FIG. 3  STRUCTURE OF AN ELEMENTARY CELL OF SPINEL**

◯ = $O^2$ -ions    O = $Fe^3$ -ions    ● = $Zn^2$ -ions

geometric arrangement:

◯: tetrahedral

O: tetrahedral

●: cubic face-centered

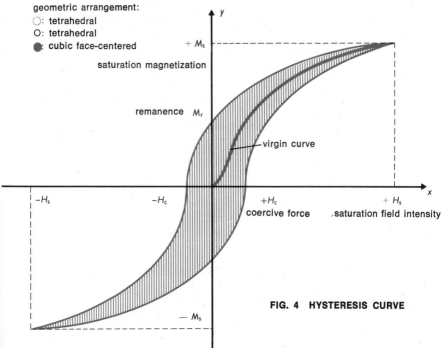

saturation magnetization

remanence  $M_r$

virgin curve

coercive force

saturation field intensity

**FIG. 4  HYSTERESIS CURVE**

of the coercive force ($H_c$) are advantageous for minimizing the energy needed for effecting the change-over from one stable state to the other (Fig. 5a). Fig. 5b shows how the binary digits L and O are associated with the two states of magnetization $+M_r$ and $-M_r$.

A magnetic core is a small ring of ferrite (Fig. 6) that is capable of assuming two states, so that it can serve as a switching device or a storage medium. The storage of information in a magnetic core is accomplished as follows: The core is magnetized by means of two wires passing through it. Through each wire a current pulse of intensity $\frac{1}{2} I_s$ (half-current) is passed. The sum $I_s$ of the two pulses corresponds to the current intensity that produces the saturation value $H_s$ of the magnetic field strength. The duration of these current pulses must be longer than the change-over time of the magnetic core. In effecting the change-over, the right-hand part of the hysteresis curve is traversed, up to the magnetization value $M_s$. On removal of the pulse, this value decreases to $M_r$. The binary digit L has thus been stored. When current pulses whose total value is $-I_s$ are passed through the wires, a saturation field intensity $-H_s$ is produced, causing the core to change over to its other stable state (Fig. 7). As a result, a voltage pulse is produced (this is the reading operation). Division of the pulses into equal parts, $+\frac{1}{2}I_s$ and $-\frac{1}{2}I_s$, is done for reasons of so-called coincidence storage.

As a magnetic core can store only one bit of information at a time, a very large number of cores are required, strung together on wires to form a matrix, which can function as a high-capacity store (or memory). The storage of a word of medium length requires as many as 50 bits. Storage capacities of some tens of thousands of words, therefore, involve the use of correspondingly large numbers of cores. In order to retrieve a particular bit of information from the store, that is, to "read," or "sense," the setting of one particular core from among the tens of thousands, the two currents $\frac{1}{2}I_s$ are applied to that column and to that row of the store matrix, which intersect at the core in question. Then all the cores that are located in the same column and all those in the same row are traversed by the inducing pulse $\frac{1}{2}I_s$; but, on account of the rectangular shape of the hysteresis curve of the ferrite, this half-current is not sufficient to initiate the change-over of the core to its other stable state. However, at the intersection of that particular row and that particular column, in other words, at the core with which we are specifically concerned, the two half-currents are added together to give the intensity $I_s$ that produces the saturation field intensity $H_s$.

If the binary digit O is put in as the detecting pulse, the core (magnetic ferrite ring) responds by changing over if it contains the information L. This change-over produces a reading (or sensing) pulse in the sensing wire which passes diagonally through the cores (Fig. 8). But if the binary digit O is stored in that core, no reading pulse is emitted. In the reading process, the stored information is extracted and is, at the same time, also destroyed. If it is necessary to retain the information in the store, it must be regenerated. With magnetic core storage, the operations of reading and regeneration are performed not simultaneously, but successively. The time that this takes up, which is of the order of one microsecond, is determined by the time taken to effect the magnetic reversal. The cycle of reading and regeneration is called the memory cycle. "Read access time" in a magnetic core memory is the time required to read the core, but not including the time required to regenerate it.

In spite of various precautions, the half-currents $\frac{1}{2}I_s$ cause relatively high disturbing signals in the sensing wire. The auxiliary equipment must therefore be able to distinguish sharply between working signals and disturbing signals. For this reason, too, it is advantageous to have high values for the residual magnetism $M_r$ and low values for the coercive force $H_c$. A helpful feature of

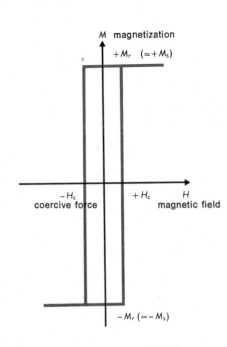

FIG. 5a IDEALIZED RECTANGULAR
HYSTERESIS CURVE

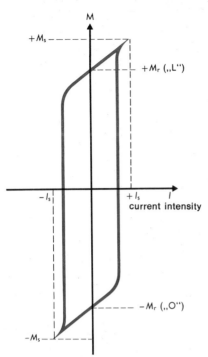

FIG. 5b BINARY DIGITS L AND O
ASSOCIATED WITH THE REMANENCE
VALUES $+M_r$ AND $-M_r$ ($I$ = CURRENT
INTENSITY FOR PRODUCING
THE MAGNETIC FIELD $H$)

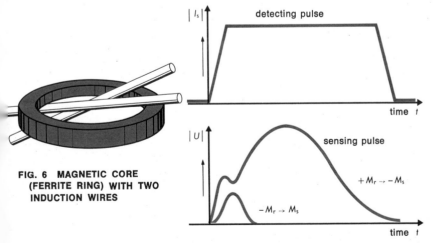

FIG. 6 MAGNETIC CORE
(FERRITE RING) WITH TWO
INDUCTION WIRES

FIG. 7 SHAPE OF DETECTING PULSE
AND SENSING PULSE

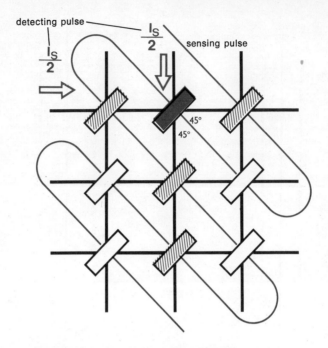

**FIG. 8   SCHEMATIC OF A MAGNETIC CORE MEMORY**

binary data storage systems is that it is not necessary to transmit the pulses accurately in their original form. It is, instead, quite sufficient for practical purposes so to distinguish between working pulses and disturbing pulses that the former can trigger a flip-flop circuit, that is, produce a switching pulse. A flip-flop can operate with a much degenerated input pulse and yet in turn emit a fully regenerated and amplified rectangular pulse.

Advantages of the magnetic core memory are its short switching time and therefore its short access time to the stored information, and also its construction, based on all-electric operation with no mechanical moving parts. A drawback is that this type of storage system is very expensive, mainly because it is composed of a vast number of ferrite rings, 1 to 2 mm in diameter, which have to be laboriously threaded on to wires.

Another form of magnetic storage for the binary digits is the magnetic drum store. It is a combined electromechanical system. The device comprises a rotating cylinder provided with a magnetizable ferrite surface, which is divided into approximately 300 circumferential channels (or tracks), on each of which approximately 1000 individual pulses can be recorded. During one revolution of the cylinder, each channel passes under a set of electromagnetic write heads and read heads. During recording, a write head converts incoming pulses into magnetized spots, each occupying a so-called storage location; each spot, or absence of a spot, represents one bit. The arrival of bits at the write head is synchronized with the rotation of the cylinder, so as to place the spots at their designated locations. The speed of rotation is about 10,000 r.p.m., and the access time is of the order of 0.1 to 1 microsecond. As the magnetized spot passes under the read head, the reading electromagnet receives an electric

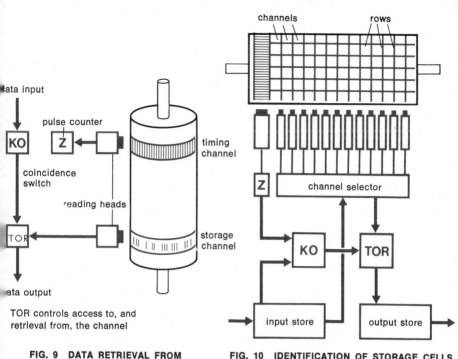

**FIG. 9  DATA RETRIEVAL FROM
A MAGNETIC DRUM STORE**

**FIG. 10  IDENTIFICATION OF STORAGE CELLS
BY CHANNEL AND ROW**

pulse; each of these pulses is interpreted as the binary digit L; the absence of a pulse is interpreted as the binary digit O. The magnetic spot remains unchanged on passing under the read head. Consequently, no regeneration is necessary. The information is not destroyed, but can be read over and over again; this is an important advantage of this storage method. Finding the individual storage locations is effected by means of timing channels; these supply successive pulses at a uniform rate corresponding to the spacing of the locations. These pulses are compared with the read pulses coming in at the same rate, and when there is coincidence, the output of the stored pulse is released (Figs. 9 and 10).

The simplest method of magnetic information storage is by means of magnetic tape. Between 10 and 20 pulses can be recorded on a length of 1 mm; thus a tape with a length of, say, 100 m has a storage capacity of about 200,000 bits. This high capacity, obtained at relatively low cost, makes tape the obvious choice for information storage in all cases where rapid access is not essential. To retrieve a particular item of information, it may be necessary to run through the whole tape, so that access times may be several seconds.

Another type of magnetic store is the rotating disc (Fig. 11). This storage device comprises up to 50 flat circular plates coated on both surfaces with a magnetizable material. About $10^9$ bits can be stored in such a device. The information is stored on recording tracks, being read from or written onto these by means of read/write heads. The latter can read or write at rates of between $10^5$ and $10^6$ bits per second. The access time about 0.15 second, is relatively long, as the speed of the discs is substantially lower than that of a magnetic drum.

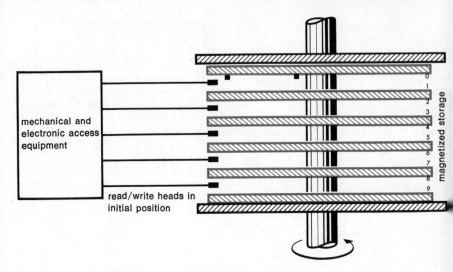

mechanical and electronic access equipment

magnetized storage

read/write heads in initial position

**FIG. 11   ROTATING DISC STORE WITH ACCESS EQUIPMENT**

The storage methods discussed in the foregoing are suited specially to the requirements of digital technique, that is, for processing by means of electronic circuits that distinguish between the two binary states L and O by bistable behavior. Information storage based on this principle therefore requires a coding of the information in the form of binary variables. This involves breaking down the data into pulse trains. Undoubtedly this is advantageous for further processing in an electronic computer, but it is doubtful whether this kind of storage offers similar advantages when it comes to storing sense data as a totality, as is necessary, for example, for purposes of documentation. For this, an entirely different form of storage can suitably be used, which does not break down the information into pulse trains, but stores it as a totality, more particularly, an optical storage method based on microphotographic techniques. In that case the information need merely be filed in accordance with a suitable system of classification, so that any particular document can be retrieved from the store with the aid of a mechanical sorting device. In one such technique, for example, the document is reduced in size by optical means, copied on to 16 mm x 23 mm standard film, and coupled to a second film, which is optically coded with a classification number and other data by means of a coarse-mesh half-tone screen (Fig. 12). The microphotographic records are stored in boxes. A million of these records can be stored in a space of one cubic meter. If each microphotographic record is estimated to comprise 1000 bits of information, a cubic meter can thus hold about $10^9$ (one thousand million) bits. The records are retrieved from the store by means of an optical sorting machine. In principle, the operation of selecting a record from the store is performed by a photoelectric cell, as shown schematically in Fig. 13. Of course, the microphotographic record may also be combined with a punched card, so that selection can then be done by means of a punched card sorting machine (Fig. 14). On weighing the advantages and disadvantages of magnetic (digital) and optical storage, respectively, it can be said that the magnetic method is preferable for the storage of variable data intended for processing in a computer, whereas the optical (photographic) method is preferable in cases where printed information or drawings have to be stored as complete units.

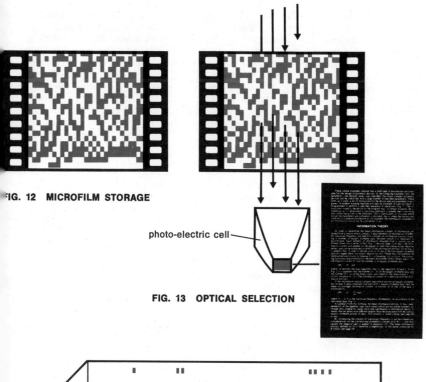

FIG. 12   MICROFILM STORAGE

photo-electric cell

FIG. 13   OPTICAL SELECTION

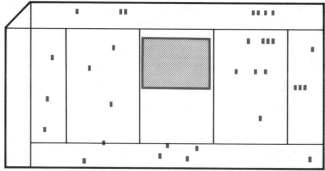

FIG. 14   PUNCH CARD COMBINED WITH MICROFILM

# ACOUSTIC DATA STORAGE SYSTEMS

The function of the flip-flop circuit as a storage device consists in compensating for time lags in the switching circuits and thus synchronizing the various bit sequences. Acoustic storage devices are also used for this purpose sometimes. The storage time in such a device is determined by the transit time of waves in an elastic medium (for example, sound waves in a liquid). A metal tube, 1 to 2 cm in diameter and between 50 and 100 cm in length, filled with liquid mercury, is closed at one end by a piezoelectric sound transmitter and at the other end by a pickup device (receiver) (Fig. 1). The train of incoming pulses is fed through the piezoelectric sound transmitter to a quartz crystal, which converts the electric pulses into a sequence of pressure pulses of the same frequency. These pressure pulses (sound vibrations), applied to the

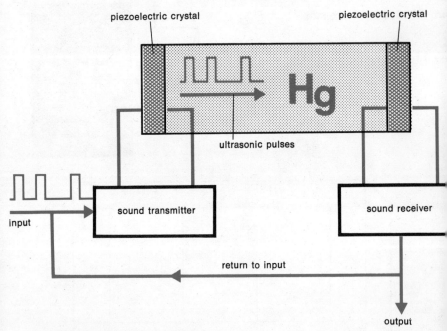

**FIG. 1 ACOUSTIC DATA STORAGE**

mercury, are propagated through it, taking about 1 millisecond to travel the distance from one end of the tube to the other, where they are picked up by the receiver. The receiver then converts them back into electric pulses. If it is desired to store the pulse train for a greater length of time, the pulses are returned from the receiver to the sound transmitter. The cycle can thus be repeated, so that multiples of the "single" retention time are obtainable. The access time, after which the pulse train becomes available again, depends on the transit time of the pulses through the tube.

# THIN-FILM STORAGE DEVICES

Information storage devices differ in their access time, which ranges from several seconds (magnetic tapes) to approximately one microsecond (magnetic cores). The processes in electronic circuits can, however, operate a thousand times faster than the shortest access time of the fastest of the storage systems described. It is therefore of interest to describe devices which, though not yet in general use in the memories of electronic computers, have been tested experimentally. These are termed "thin-film memories." A device of this type consists of a very thin film ($10^{-4}$ to $10^{-3}$ cm thick) of magnetic substance deposited—by evaporation—on a plate of non-magnetizable material, such as glass. The film can be magnetically polarized for the storage of digital information. A magnetic substance used for the purpose is, for example, Permalloy, a high-permeability alloy of nickel (81%) and iron (19%). The magnetization phenomena associated with the thin-film device are represented by a hysteresis curve in the shape of an astroid (Fig. 1). The magnetic reversal process is

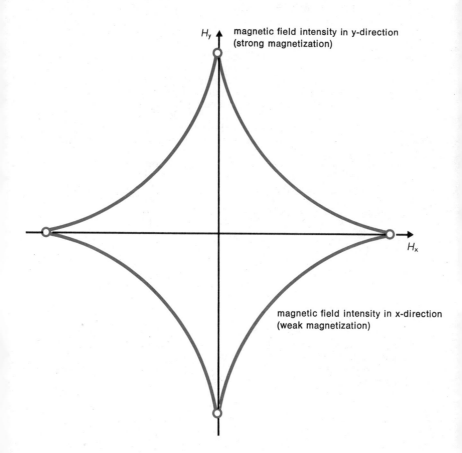

$H_y$ — magnetic field intensity in y-direction (strong magnetization)

$H_x$

magnetic field intensity in x-direction (weak magnetization)

**FIG. 1  MAGNETIZATION CURVE FOR THIN MAGNETIC FILM**

achieved in 1 nanosecond (one thousand millionth of a second, which is 1 milli-microsecond). This reversal is readily accomplished in one direction (x-direction, minimum potential energy), but difficult to accomplish in the direction perpendicular thereto (y-direction, maximum potential energy).

The thin-film storage device, like the magnetic core storage device, is operated by three wires: the control wire, the information wire and the sensing wire (Fig. 2). The construction of a memory matrix composed of thin-film components is shown schematically in Fig. 3.

Another type of thin-film storage device utilizes the ability of a magnetic field to be able, at very low temperatures, to transform a metal from its normal conductive condition to a condition of superconductivity, which is the phenomenon wherein the resistance of the metal becomes zero or very nearly zero. The magnetic field which accomplishes this may be produced by an electric current flowing in the superconductor itself. The cryotron is a device whose function is based on this principle. It is essentially a normally resistive element that can be maintained at the threshold of superconductivity by surrounding it with a powerful magnetic field. The cryotron is used in memory and switching devices in computer systems. It is composed of two conductors of different metals whose transition from the normally conductive to the superconductive state, and vice versa, occurs at different temperatures. For example, the control conductor may consist of lead (transition temperature $7.2°$ $K = -265.9° C$), which remains constantly superconductive at the low operating temperature. The information conductor, on the other hand, consists of a metal with a lower transition temperature, such as tin (transition temperature $3.6° K = -269.6° C$). The state of conductivity of the information conductor can be influenced by means of the magnetic field of the control conductor. In Fig. 4 the curves represent the relation between the transition temperature (in degrees Kelvin, °K) and the magnetic field intensity (in Oersted) for various metals. One form of construction for such a storage element is exemplified in Fig. 5 (Crowe cell).

In this last-mentioned device, the storing film consists of tin. It is magnetically coupled to the control conductor and the sensing conductor, which are located above and below the tin film, respectively. Suppose that in the initial state the control conductor carries no current, while in the film a supercurrent is circulating clockwise, this current being associated with the binary digit L. Now if the control conductor receives a current pulse, another current pulse, of equal magnitude, is induced in the film as a result of the magnetic coupling between the two circuits. Consequently, the current in the film exceeds the critical intensity, that is, it generates its own magnetic field, which causes the tin film to revert to its normal conductive condition, so that an ohmic resistance develops. The intensity of the current in the film then decreases, and heat is evolved. This in turn causes the film to become superconductive, so that the current retains the value it has reached. If no more pulses are transmitted to the control conductor, the current in the film undergoes a further decrease and may thus attain negative values. Then the current pattern in the film is as shown for the state O in Fig. 6. The two stable superconductive states, corresponding to opposite directions of flow of the current, are therefore suitable for storing the binary digits L and O. These storage cells have access times of 10–15 nanoseconds. Their practical application is still in its infancy.

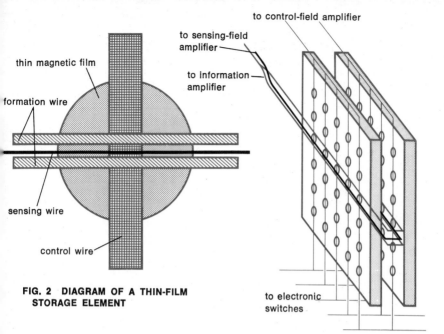

thin magnetic film

formation wire

sensing wire

control wire

**FIG. 2  DIAGRAM OF A THIN-FILM STORAGE ELEMENT**

to control-field amplifier

to sensing-field amplifier

to information amplifier

to electronic switches

**FIG. 3  SCHEMATIC OF A MEMORY MATRIX FOR THIN FILM**

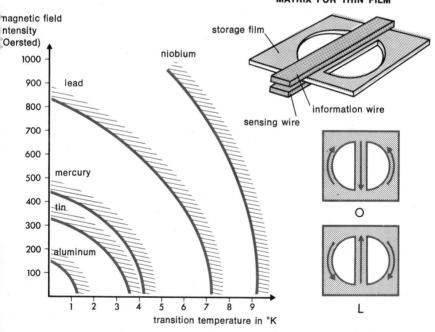

magnetic field intensity (Oersted)

niobium

lead

mercury

tin

aluminum

transition temperature in °K

**FIG. 4  RELATION BETWEEN TRANSITION TEMPERATURE AND MAGNETIC FIELD INTENSITY (for each metal the region of normal conductivity is on the right of the curve)**

storage film

information wire

sensing wire

O

L

**FIG. 5  CROWE CELL, A SPECIAL FORM OF CRYOTRON**

# ANALOG COMPUTATION PRINCIPLES

Digital computation techniques based on the use of binary variables have been discussed in the foregoing chapters of this book, and there can be no doubt that the future will bring a considerable further extension of their use. This does not in any way detract from the value of analog methods. These can, briefly, be defined as the representation and measurement of numerical quantities by means of continuously variable physical quantities such as voltages, currents, and so on. More particularly, they represent functional behavior patterns as a whole instead of breaking them down into individual steps as in digital methods. Thus, analog computation is always advantageous in cases where a variable quantity occurs as a function of time and can be represented by, for example, an electrical analogy in which the magnitude of a voltage or current is directly proportional to the variable.

Although it is possible, in principle, to resolve any functional behavior pattern into digital steps, the analog technique has the advantage, in so far as suitable cases are concerned, of providing a technically simpler solution. The circuit elements of electronic analog computers comprise potentiometers, ohmic resistors, low-loss capacitors, and direct-current amplifiers. With such equipment it is possible to perform the four basic arithmetical operations as well as differentiation and integration. In addition, non-linear circuit elements are used: rectifiers, function generators (which accept one or more input variables and provide an output variable based on some mathematical function), and multiplier and comparator circuits. The principal analog circuit elements are indicated schematically in Fig. 1. Each of these comprises a direct-current amplifier, which has to be stabilized, drift-free, and free from grid current. An electron tube amplifier should have an amplitude range of $\pm 100$ volts; for a transistorized amplifier, it should be $\pm 10$ volts. In contrast with digital computation, in which all the numerical quantities are expressed by binary digits that are fed into the circuit elements as voltage or current pulses of uniform intensity, with analog computation, the quantities are expressed in the form of voltage or current pulses. Similarly, for the solving of equations, the mathematical operations are simulated in such a manner that they are interlinked in the construction of the equation.

Multiplication by a constant factor larger than unity is performed by a direct-current amplifier alone. If the factor is smaller than unity, the amplifier input must be combined with a potentiometer (Figs. 1a and b). For addition and subtraction, voltages that are proportional to the corresponding numerical quantities are fed simultaneously through different resistances to the input of the amplifier (Fig. 1c). The amplifier performs the addition or subtraction operations according to the algebraic signs of the numerical quantities and of the voltages associated with them. In Fig. 1c the symbols $U_1$ and $U_2$ denote the input voltages, while $R_1$ and $R_2$ denote the associated input resistances through which the currents $I_1$ and $I_2$ are conducted to the grid. Presupposing that there is no grid current (that is, that $I_g = 0$), the sum of the currents $I_1$ and $I_2$ flows as the coupling current $I_k$ through the coupling resistance $R_k$ to the output, where the voltage $U_a$, which—in the case of an addition—is proportional to the sum of the two input voltages, provided that $R_1$ is equal to $R_2$. The current and voltage pulses are, accordingly, expressed by the following four equations:

$$(70) \quad U_1 - U_g - I_1 R_1 = 0$$
$$U_2 - U_3 - I_2 R_2 = 0$$
$$U_g - U_a - I_k R_k = 0$$
$$I_k = I_1 + I_2$$

| | analog circuit element | symbol and mathematical relationship | circuit |
|---|---|---|---|
| a | amplifier | 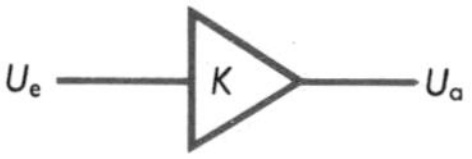 $U_e \longrightarrow \triangleright K \longrightarrow U_a$ <br><br> $U_a = -K\,U_e$ | 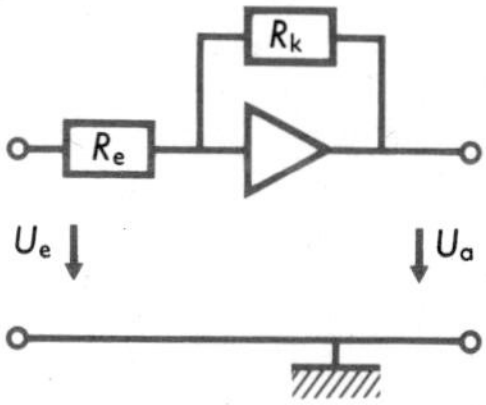 |
| b | sign changer | 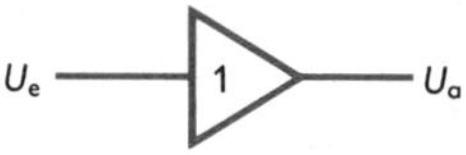 $U_e \longrightarrow \triangleright 1 \longrightarrow U_a$ <br><br> $U_a = -U_e$ | 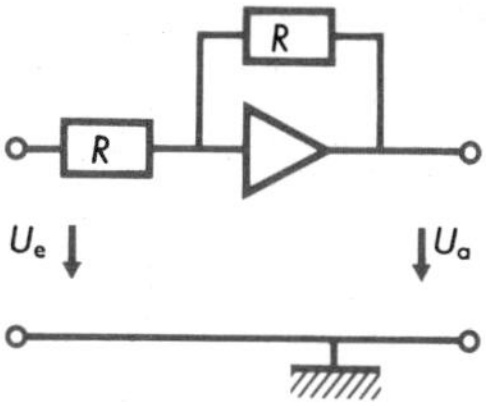 |
| c | summator | 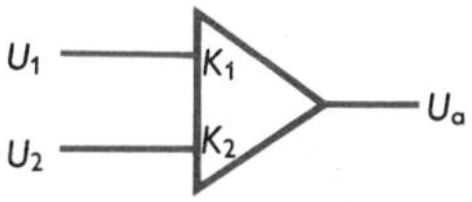 $U_1 \longrightarrow K_1$ <br> $U_2 \longrightarrow K_2 \longrightarrow U_a$ <br><br> $U_a = -\sum_{i=1}^{n} K_i\,U_i$ | 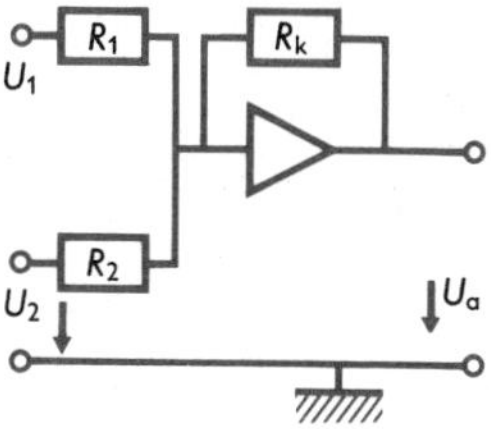 |
| d | differentiator | 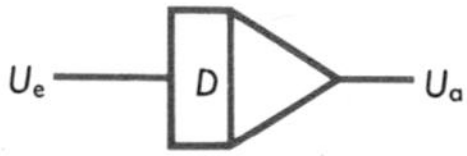 $U_e \longrightarrow \boxed{D} \longrightarrow U_a$ <br><br> $U_a = -\dfrac{d\,U_e}{dt}$ | 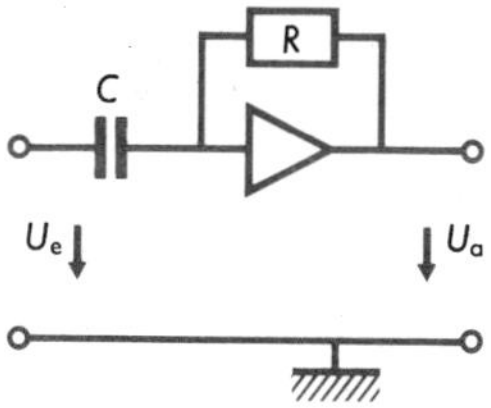 |
| e | integrator | 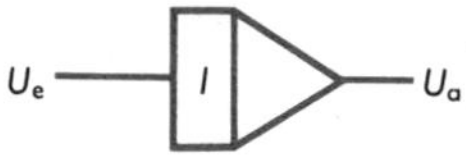 $U_e \longrightarrow \boxed{I} \longrightarrow U_a$ <br><br> $U_a = \left[ \dfrac{1}{RC} \int_0^t U_a\,dt + U_0 \right]$ | 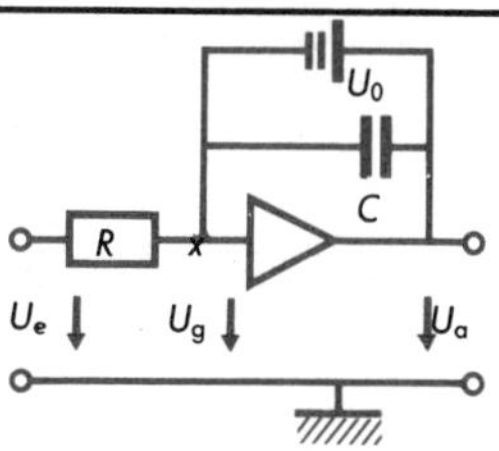 |

FIGS. 1 a–e   THE PRINCIPAL ANALOG CIRCUIT ELEMENTS

On eliminating the currents from these equations we obtain:

(71)     $(U_1 - U_g)/R_1 + (U_2 - U_g)/R_2 = (U_g - U_a)/R_k$

Bearing in mind that, because of the 180° phase displacement between input and output voltage (that is, between $U_a$ and $U_g$), there exists the relation:

(72)     $U_a = -vU_g$

where $v$ denotes the amplification factor, equation (71) yields the relation:

(73)     $U_1/R_1 + U_2/R = -U_a[1/R_k + 1/v(1/R_1 + 1/R_2 + 1/R_k)]$

For very high amplification ($v \to \infty$) this is simplified to:

(74)     $U_a = -((R_k/R_1)U_1 + (R_k/R_2)U_2)$

which can be written in the general form:

(75)     $U_a = -(k_1U_1 + \cdots + k_nU_n)$

where $k_n$ is the ratio of the coupling resistance to the input resistances. If the input resistances are together equal to the coupling resistances, all the quantities $k_n$ will have the value 1.

The circuit diagram for the direct-current amplifier as a differentiator is shown in Fig. 1d. In this case, the input resistance is a reactance with the capacitance $C$ and the value $1/j\omega C$. The coupling resistance will be taken as equal to $R$. For the ratio between input and output voltage, we then have:

(76)     $U_a/U_e = -1/j\omega CR$

whence we obtain for the relation between the output voltage $U_a$ and the input voltage $U_e$:

(77)     $U_a = -[1/CR \int_0^t U_e dt + U_0]$

The output voltage is, therefore, proportional to the differential quotient of the input voltage with respect to time.

Fig. 1e shows the arrangement of a circuit element serving as an integrator with the aid of a direct-current amplifier. In this case a reactance is adopted as the coupling resistance; the following relation then holds:

(78)     $U_a/U_e = -j\omega CR$

From this we obtain the equation expressing the relation between $U_a$ and $U_e$:

(79)     $U_a = -CR(dU_e/dt)$

We thus see that the output voltage is proportional to the time integral of the input voltage; the capacitor voltage for $t = 0$ occurs as the initial condition.

Multiplication and division require the use of non-linear components. Eminently suitable for the purpose are semiconductor diodes with characteristic curves presenting a square shape over a wide range of values. Such multipliers operate in accordance with either of two different principles. In the first place, the multiplication of two functions is reducible to determining the difference between two squares, as appears from the following relation:

(80)     $f(t)g(t) = \frac{1}{4}[\{f(t) + g(t)\}^2 - \{f(t) - g(t)\}^2]$

Secondly, a square-wave voltage of constant period can, in terms of the height and width of the voltage pulses, be varied proportionally to the functions $f(t)$ and $g(t)$ in such a manner that the pulse area is proportional to the product of these two functions.

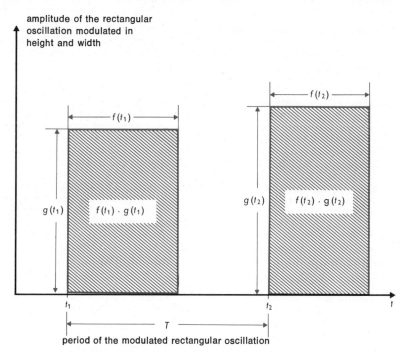

FIG. 2   MODULATION MULTIPLIER (DURING EACH PERIOD OF
THE RECTANGULAR OSCILLATION THE VALUES OF $f(t)$
AND $g(t)$ ARE ALLOWED TO UNDERGO ONLY A NEGLIGIBLE
CHANGE; $T$ SHOULD BE CHOSEN ACCORDINGLY)

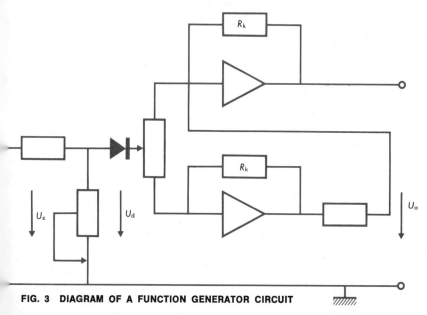

FIG. 3   DIAGRAM OF A FUNCTION GENERATOR CIRCUIT

187

A device utilizing the first-mentioned principle is called a parabolic multiplier, while the second type is called a modulation multiplier (Fig. 2). Functions which cannot be represented in a finite form can be built up piecemeal with the aid of a function generator, corresponding in principle to the approximation of a curve by a series of tangents or chords. For each section of the approximation, a circuit is needed, as shown schematically in Fig. 3. The voltage $U_e$, which varies in accordance with any particular function of time, is applied to the input of such a circuit. Depending on the magnitude of the diode bias voltage $U_d$, the diode becomes conductive only after this voltage has been reached and then supplies a portion of the function's course. A complete diode function generator forms a network consisting of a number of such circuits. In an arrangement of this kind the diodes are oppositely poled in relation to one another in the positive and the negative input voltage range, and the diode bias voltage is also oppositely directed in the two ranges. The graphic symbol for the multiplier is shown in Fig. 4. Division of two functions can be achieved by connecting a multiplier into the reverse feedback branch of an amplifier (Fig. 5). As appears from the circuit diagram, the multiplier gives a quantity which is proportional to the product of the voltages $U_2$ and $U_a$ (proportionality factor $k$). Since the reverse feedback voltage $kU_2U_a$ is fed to the grid circuit simultaneously with the input voltage $U_1$, the grid voltage is:

(81) $\qquad kU_2U_a + U_1 = U_g$

But according to equation (72): $U_g = U_a/v$, where $v$ denotes the amplification factor. As this factor should be made as high as possible, the grid input voltage can be taken as approximately zero. Therefore:

(82) $\qquad kU_2U_a + U_1 = 0$

whence:

(83) $\qquad U_a = -(1/k)(U_1/U_2)$

that is, the output voltage is proportional to the quotient of the input voltages. If the output voltage is caused to control the vertical deflection of the electron beam in a cathode ray tube whose horizontal deflection is proportional to time, the function can be represented directly as a visible curve (Fig. 6).

The advantages of using analog circuit elements are undoubtedly that their construction corresponds to the mathematical linkage of the individual quantities in the problem to be solved and that the results derived from them can readily be presented in a visual form, for example, as a curve appearing on a fluorescent screen.

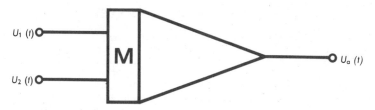

**FIG. 4  SYMBOL REPRESENTING A MULTIPLIER**

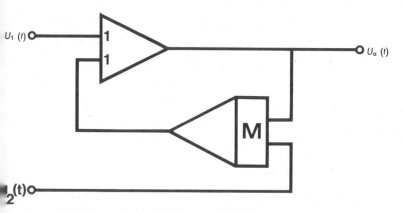

**FIG. 5  CIRCUIT FOR THE DIVISION OF TWO FUNCTIONS BY MEANS OF ANALOG CIRCUIT ELEMENTS**

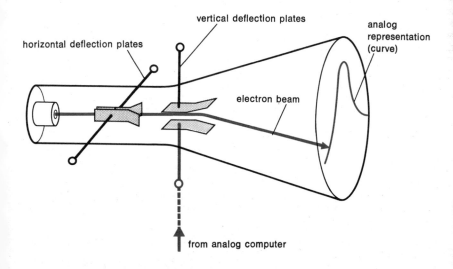

**FIG. 6  CATHODE RAY TUBE PROVIDES AN ANALOG DISPLAY**

# DATA PROCESSING SYSTEMS

The term "data processing" is widely applied to automatic computer installations, more particularly those based on electronic operating principles. A distinction is made between digital and analog computers, while the term "hybrid computer" refers to a mixed computer system in which analog and digital devices are combined. An earlier form of data processing is exemplified by the Hollerith electromechanical tabulating system, which is used for the evaluation of data stored on punched cards. The operation of a Hollerith sorting machine is illustrated in Figs. 1 and 2. The punched cards are stacked in the hopper, from where they are slid forward by a moving blade and thus brought under the feed roller. The card moves along between a scanning spring and a contact roller. Whenever this spring touches the contact roller through a perforation in the card, an electromagnet is energized and attracts an armature on which ten sorting springs are resting. As a result, all those springs whose ends have not been passed by the card at that instant will descend below the level of the card, and the card will be directed into a pocket corresponding to the perforation in question. Cards which have no perforation in the column scanned by the spring will slide under all the sorting springs and be deposited in the pocket for the reception of unperforated cards.

With an electronic computer, vastly higher data processing speeds can be attained (up to about $10^9$ bits per second). Digital computers are classified as special-purpose and general-purpose, respectively, the former being designed to handle one particular type of work as efficiently as possible, whereas the latter may be used for any task that can be handled by a digital computer. The operations involved in data processing fall into three main categories: input of data to be processed; the actual processing of data; and the output of new data resulting from processing. An electronic data processing system comprises the central processor and the necessary input/output equipment. The term "hardware" refers to the physical units of which a computer system is composed; "software" refers to the programs or routines that can be used on a particular computer system.

Fig. 3 schematically shows the main components of a processing system. The central processor can be described as the nerve center, or brain, of the whole system. It is made up of three major components: the control unit, the memory, and the arithmetic unit. The control unit directs the step-by-step operation of the system; it selects instructions from the memory, interprets them and directs their execution; it is itself, to a large extent, under the control of the program. The memory (internal store) is the device in which the data for processing, and the instructions governing the processing, are stored and held in readiness for use. Most of the memory is taken up by instructions. The arithmetic unit performs the actual arithmetical and logical operations indicated by the instructions. Commonly employed input devices are the card reader, the magnetic tape unit, and the paper tape reader; they read the coded data recorded on such media and translate them into electronic pulses, which are passed to the central processor. Output devices are, for example, the card punch, the paper tape punch, the magnetic tape unit, and the printer. The output may thus be obtained in the form of punched cards or tape, magnetic tape, or a printed report. The manual control operations are performed at the console; this component provides a monitoring display of information from the computer (through a typewriter or by means of indicator lights) and facilities for communicating messages to the computer (through a typewriter or by means of control keys). The various units forming the equipment of a typical data processing system are illustrated in Fig. 4.

A program is a set of instructions for solving a given problem by a com-

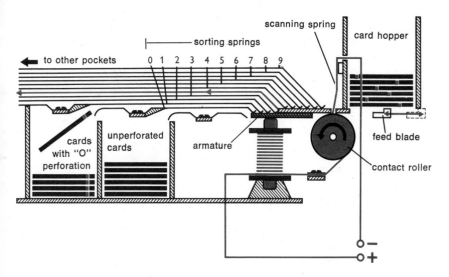

**FIG. 1  HOLLERITH SORTING MACHINE (SCHEMATIC)**

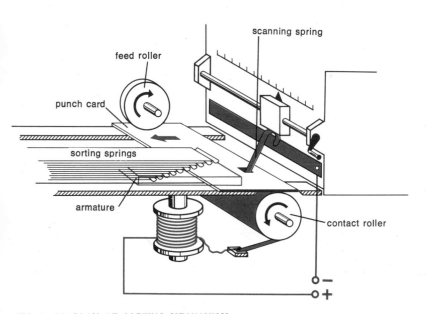

**FIG. 2  DIAGRAM OF SORTING MECHANISM**

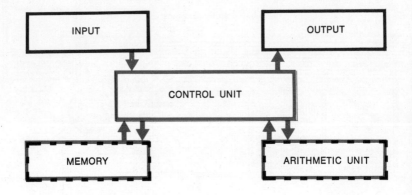

**FIG. 3   MAIN COMPONENTS OF A DATA PROCESSING SYSTEM**

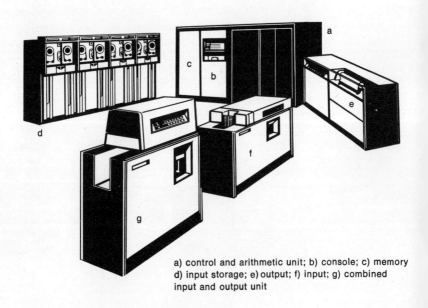

a) control and arithmetic unit; b) console; c) memory
d) input storage; e) output; f) input; g) combined
input and output unit

**FIG. 4   UNIVAC DATA PROCESSING EQUIPMENT**

puter. It tells the machine exactly how to handle the problem and usually comprises alternative routines to take care of variations. Programming denotes the operations involved in producing such a set of instructions: preparing a program flow chart (a diagram representing a sequence of events by means of conventional symbols), or a decision table (representing relationships between certain variables and specifying the required action); preparing instructions in coded form; testing the program; and preparing instructions for using the program. Whether the optimum capabilities of the computer will be utilized will largely depend on the skill and judgment exercised by the programmer. The more expertly the program has been produced, the more rapidly can the computer solve a particular problem.

The data input procedure can be explained with reference to a simple electronic computer, shown schematically in Fig. 5. The input device in this case is a punched tape reader, while the output is performed through a printer. A five-unit code is employed for encoding the external data; a five-unit code is also used for the output. The input and output devices are connected to the control unit (or program controller). The latter comprises — in this instance — a delay line register (AR), an instruction register (or program register, BR), and a control register (or program counter, BZR). The arithmetic unit is here assumed to comprise an adder (addition network), and the memory is in the form of a magnetic drum. In the diagram the addition of a given number $y$ to a stored number $x$ is represented. The delay-line register comprises a series of time-lag circuit elements (see page 159) in which the pulses are slowed down. After traversing the delay network, the pulse train is returned to the input of the network. When the last pulse of a data input sequence has entered, each bit can be retrieved from the appropriate circuit element of the delay network.

The data are passed from the delay line register to the arithmetic unit, where the pulses of the internal pulse train ($x$) are added to the pulses of the external pulse train ($y$), this being done bit by bit, starting with the lowest binary position. The instruction register comprises an operation part, with seven operating instructions, and an address part, with eight binary positions. In the present example, the seven operations denote the following instructions (or commands):

N: clear the delay line register; the circulation of data in this register is interrupted for the duration of one word.

T: the pulse train circulating in the delay line register is recorded in a location ($n$) of the drum store.

S: jump of the computer operation to this location ($n$); the address part is transferred via the switch S to the instruction register.

P: jump to the location ($n$), if the contents of the delay line register are positive.

D: printing teleprinter characters corresponding to the five lowest positions of the delay line register (output).

L: the combination of perforations in the paper tape reader supplies the five lowest positions of the delay line register (input).

A: the control register contains an instruction which, at the position A, comprises a pulse for actuating the electronic switch A. The address part represents the decimal value 75. At the instant when location 75 of the drum store reaches the read/write head, the sector selecting switch (A) closes for the duration of one word, and the stored pulse train, together with the contents till then present in the delay line register, traverses the adder. At the same time the state of the control register is increased by 1 to 149. This instruction is then ready for the next cycle, whereby the instruction of the location 149 P 201 is put into the instruction register. This is followed by the printout cycle, that is, the addition result is printed by the output teleprinter.

In the data processing system described in the foregoing, a printer is employed as the output device, presenting the result in the form of printed characters (letters of the alphabet, numerals 0–9). It is, however, often desirable to obtain the output in analog form, that is, instead of giving the result as a mass of numerical values (which might, for example, have to be plotted in

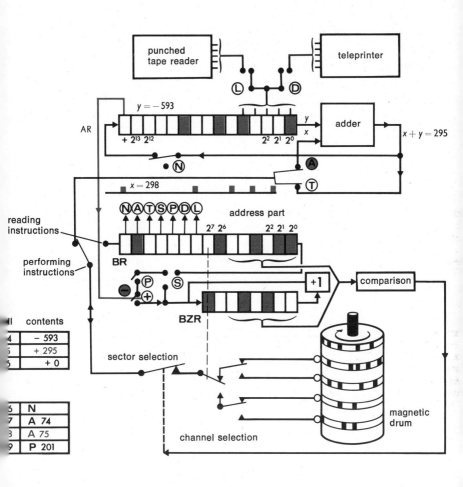

**FIG. 5 SEQUENCE OF OPERATIONS IN A PROGRAM-CONTROLLED DATA PROCESSING SYSTEM**

graph form to make them properly intelligible), they are presented directly in visual form by means of an analog display unit. A cathode ray device may be used for the purpose (digital-analog converter, Fig. 6, below). The vertical deflection plates are not, however, fed with a continuously-variable analog voltage; instead, digital voltage (or current) pulses from the output of a digital computer are supplied and are integrated by means of a capacitor. The resultant charging voltage of the capacitor is then an analog variable with respect to the quantities defined by the binary pulse trains.

Correspondingly, the transition from analog to digital signals can be achieved by means of a digital-analog converter. A device that can be used

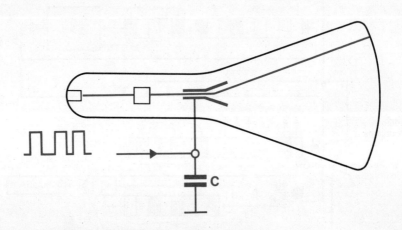

**FIG. 6  DIGITAL-ANALOG CONVERTER: THE CHARGING VOLTAGE OF CAPACITOR C IS ANALOGOUS WITH THE NUMBERS DIGITALLY CODED AS CURRENT PULSES**

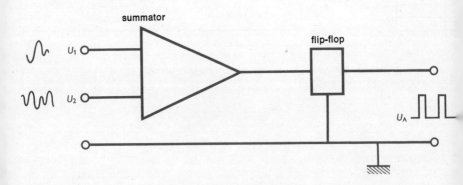

**FIG. 7  ANALOG-DIGITAL CONVERTER (COMPARATOR)**

196

for the purpose is the comparator. In general, this is a device that compares two signals and indicates agreement or disagreement; it produces a signal dependent on the result of the comparison. As indicated schematically in Fig. 7, it comprises a summing unit and a flip-flop (see page 156 et seq.) whose function resembles that of a polarized relay. According as the output voltage of the amplifier is positive or negative, a positive or a zero voltage pulse is emitted from the comparator. The analog function is thus converted into a digital pulse train.

From the foregoing considerations, it emerges that the advantages of the one technique can be combined with those of the other, so as to achieve optimum utilization of the favorable possibilities of both and to minimize their disadvantages. In cases where computer equipment does not have to fulfill stringent requirements of accuracy, an analog system is undoubtedly cheaper to construct than a digital system. With increasing accuracy, however, the cost of the analog equipment rises exponentially. The reason for this is that the very accurate measurement of analog voltages is difficult and requires sophisticated and expensive apparatus. With the digital computer, on the other hand, the cost of the equipment is approximately proportional to the accuracy it can attain, so that, where high accuracy is essential, the digital technique is less expensive than the analog technique (Fig. 8). That digital

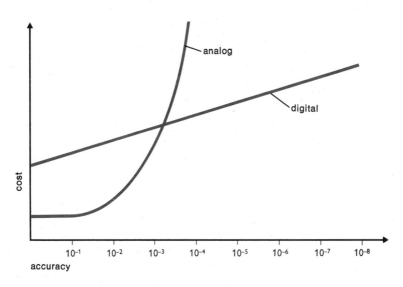

**FIG. 8  RELATIVE COST AND ACCURACY OF ANALOG
AND DIGITAL SYSTEMS**

and analog representations of information are, in themselves, by no means novel developments is illustrated by Fig. 9. The abacus embodies a very simple application of digital computing technique, while the simplest application of the analog principle is provided by the slide rule. In the abacus, each ball represents a digit; in the slide rule, each division corresponds to the logarithm of a number, the length of the scale being the analog variable.

Electronic computers can be designed to perform specific duties. Such machines are referred to as special-purpose computers. This special character is reflected primarily in the design of the computer's memory and the operation codes (which specify the particular operations to be performed) stored in it. More especially, the internal data contained in the magnetic core memory determine the computer's language. This memory unit is composed of magnetic cores (ferrite rings) whose pattern of charges represents the coded data (see page 174 et seq.). The flow of information provided by the external data put into the machine has to be adapted to a particular language in order to issue instructions that will cause the machine to perform meaningful operations. It is up to the programmer to achieve this adaptation, that is, to prepare a "machine-oriented" program. In this context, the term "machine language" refers to instructions written in machine code — the coding system embodied in the design of the computer — which can be directly obeyed by the computer without translation. Alternatively, however, it is possible to apply "problem-oriented" programming. For this purpose, so-called problem-oriented languages have been devised, these being oriented to a particular class of problem — for example, scientific, technical or commercial — rather than to a particular type of computer. Such languages can be used with any computer of suitable capacity.

The development of electronic computers is towards achieving ever-

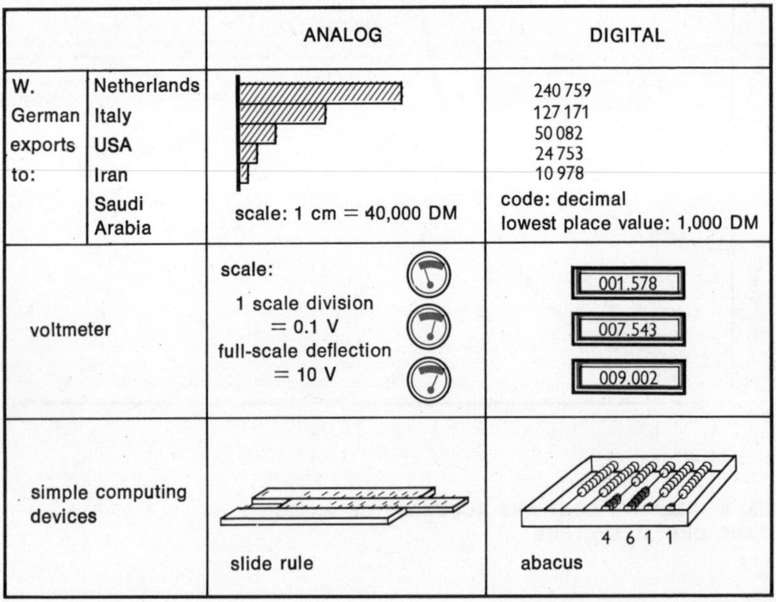

| | | ANALOG | DIGITAL |
|---|---|---|---|
| W. German exports to: | Netherlands Italy USA Iran Saudi Arabia | scale: 1 cm = 40,000 DM | 240 759 127 171 50 082 24 753 10 978 code: decimal lowest place value: 1,000 DM |
| voltmeter | | scale: 1 scale division = 0.1 V full-scale deflection = 10 V | 001.578 007.543 009.002 |
| simple computing devices | | slide rule | abacus 4 6 1 1 |

**FIG. 9  ANALOG AND DIGITAL COMPUTATION PROCEDURES**

higher switching speeds and thus higher computing rates. The so-called first-generation computers, which used electron tubes, achieved switching times of $10^{-3}$ to $10^{-4}$ seconds (that is, of the order of milliseconds); in the second-generation computers, which had transistors, the switching times were reduced to about $10^{-6}$ seconds (of the order of microseconds); the third-generation computers, built with integrated circuits,* attain switching times of $10^{-8}$ to $10^{-9}$ seconds (of the order of nanoseconds) (Fig. 10). With such speeds the problem of transmission enters a new phase, because even with electrical transmission distances of only 30 cm, a pulse time delay of 1 nanosecond occurs. We thus come up against a limit, since the velocity of transmission of the pulses can never exceed the velocity of light ($3 \times 10^{10}$ cm/sec. or $3 \times 10^5$ km/sec. or 186,000 miles/sec.). This makes it the more important to keep the transmission distances as short as possible and to make the circuit elements themselves as small as possible (miniaturization). The success that has been achieved in this field of semiconductor electronics, with its micro-miniaturized components, has been closely bound up with the development of the third-generation computers. However, not only the transmission of data within the computer itself, but also the long-distance transmission of the external data is becoming increasingly important, as it is more economical to install large central data processing facilities and to keep the input and output devices at the point—remote from the computer center—where they are actually required. Time-sharing systems have been evolved for such purposes. The term "time-sharing" refers to the use of a computer for two or more purposes during the same overall time interval, whereby the various sequences are dealt with concurrently by sharing the time of parts of the equipment among them (see also page 218).

* The integrated circuit is a development of micro-electronics, in which a whole circuit is formed chemically and by micro-manipulation on a single chip of semiconductor material, usually silicon. Wire connections between circuit elements are eliminated, and extremely compact construction is achieved.

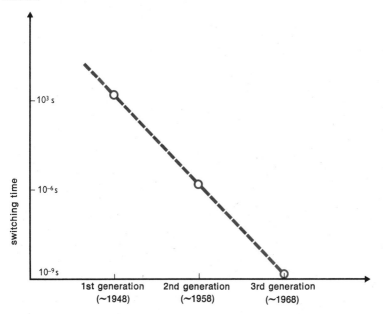

FIG. 10  THREE GENERATIONS OF COMPUTERS AND THEIR OPERATING SPEEDS

# MACHINE LANGUAGES AND SYMBOLIC LANGUAGES

For the processing of information by a computer, it is necessary to put the flow of information in a coded form that the machine can handle, in other words, it has to be presented to the computer in a suitable "machine language." In practical terms this means that we must put our instructions (commands) in such a form that the data processing system is able to understand and perform them. Each type of computer has its own built-in system of accepting and handling the instructions it receives (Fig. 1). Thus, in some machines, the word length or instruction length may be variable; the individual instruction may consist of a single character or several characters. Other machines operate with a fixed word length, in which case each instruction must consist of a specific number of characters or bits. For example, the instruction length of the IBM computer type 1401 varies from one to eight characters. On the other hand, in the Siemens computer S 2002 a constant instruction length of 12 characters is employed.

To illustrate this, consider the instruction: "Go out!" This comprises the command or operation "go" and the further indication "out." Now if, for instance, we allocated the location 400 in the core memory to the word "out," then the instruction expressed in the language of the IBM 1401 would be: B 400, meaning "branch to core memory location 400."* Here B would be the operation part of the instruction, that is, the part which specifies the particular operation to be performed. In the Siemens S 2002, on the other hand, the operation part always comprises three bit positions. However, in the IBM 1401 the single-position operation part may be augmented by a further, single-position indication. In terms of the above example, this would signify "go out, when . . . ," or in the language of this computer: B 400 A, meaning "branch to location 400, when the last punched card in the output is being read." What particular form the coding for the performance of individual operations will have to take for each type of computer will depend on its technical design features. The computer manufacturers give guidance on how their data processing systems should be programmed. This information is issued in the form of instruction codes (listing the characters and symbols forming the rules of a particular computer code or programming language), manuals, and practical training schemes for personnel. As already stated, the operation part of an instruction as employed in the Siemens S 2002 invariably comprises three positions; these are always combinations of digits, for example, "122." In the IBM 1401, the special character / is the single-position operation part for clearing (or erasing) data in the memory.

To facilitate programming and to reduce the risk of errors, the computer manufacturers supply so-called assembly programs. An assembly program (or assembler) is one which operates on symbolic input data to produce appropriate machine instructions; it translates the symbolic language program into a machine language program. The advantage of this procedure is that the symbolic language is simpler to learn and to use than a machine language.

Symbolic programming signifies the use of symbols to represent addresses (designations of locations in a storage device) in order to facilitate programming. More specifically, it refers to writing a program in a source language, this being a programming language which cannot be directly processed by the

---

* The term "branch" (synonymous with "jump") signifies a departure from the normal sequence of program steps, in response to a branch instruction. In performing a program, the computer obeys instructions stored in successive locations of the memory. A branch instruction alters this sequence of operation by directing the program controller (or control unit) to perform a specific series of instructions; it specifies the location of the next instruction to be executed.

|  | Autocoder symbolic language | Machine language | | | |
|---|---|---|---|---|---|
| Instruction | | | | | |
| **1. Arithmetical instructions** | | | | | |
| add | A | A | | | |
| subtract | S | S | | | |
| multiply | M | @ | | | |
| divide | D | % | | | |
| **2. Transfer instructions** | | | | | |
| move characters | MCW | M | | | |
| load character | LCA | L | | | |
| move numerical | MN | D | | | |
| move zone | MZ | Y | | | |
| **3. Comparison instructions** | | | | | |
| compare | C | C | | | |
| branch if indicator on | BIN | B | + | OP- | supplement |
| branch if word mark or zone | BZW | V | + | OP- | supplement |
| **4. Organization instructions** | | | | | |
| branch | B | B | | | |
| modify address | MA | # | | | |
| **5. Special instructions** | | | | | |
| clear storage | CS | / | | | |
| set word mark | SW | , | | | |
| clear word mark | CW | ¤ | | | |
| halt | H | . | | | |
| no operation | NOP | N | | | |

**FIG. 1  INSTRUCTIONS AND THEIR SYMBOLS FOR THE IBM COMPUTER 1401**

computer but first has to be compiled into a so-called object program consisting of instructions in machine language.

A symbolic programming language developed for the IBM 1401 is the SPS code (Symbolic Programming System). For use with subsequent developments of this computer, which were characterized by larger core memory capacity and additional features, a more comprehensive programming language called AUTOCODER was evolved. Fig. 1 shows the principal instructions for the IBM 1401 written in this symbolic language; the corresponding commands, expressed in the actual machine language for this computer, are also shown. To each memory location is allocated an address; thus the address part of an instruction states where the characters to which the instruction refers are located. For example, for the IBM 1401 computer, MCW 405,505 denotes: "move characters from 405 to 505" (see Fig. 1, page 201).

AUTOCODER is a machine-oriented language, that is, it is designed for use with a specific computer. On the other hand, a problem-oriented language is a source language (see above) oriented to the description of a particular class of problems, for example, mathematical, scientific, technical or commercial. It is independent of the actual computer and has the advantage that the user can write statements in a form with which he is familiar (for example, in mathematical notation or in English) and concentrate his programming on the actual problem, without having to concern himself with the particular features of the computer. For use by the computer, such a language requires translation into the appropriate machine language, that is, into instructions written in machine code, which can be directly performed by the computer. This process of translation is carried out with the aid of a special program (called the compiler) that converts the problem-oriented language instructions into machine language for the particular type of computer to be used. This conversion produces a so-called object program, which can be read and acted upon by the computer.

Well known examples of problem-oriented languages are the mathematical languages ALGOL and FORTRAN and the business language COBOL. For instance, with FORTRAN (an acronym for FORmula TRANslation), the source program is composed of standardized combinations of mathematical formulas and English statements. Thus the formula $V = \frac{4}{3}\pi r^3$, for the volume of a sphere, is written as V = (4.0/3.0)*PI*(R**3), where / denotes division, * denotes multiplication and ** denotes exponentiation. Similarly, the expression $c = \sqrt{a^2 + b^2}$ would appear as follows in the FORTRAN notation: C = SQRT (A**2 + B**2), where SQRT is the abbreviation of "square root," that is, the function provided for calculating square roots.

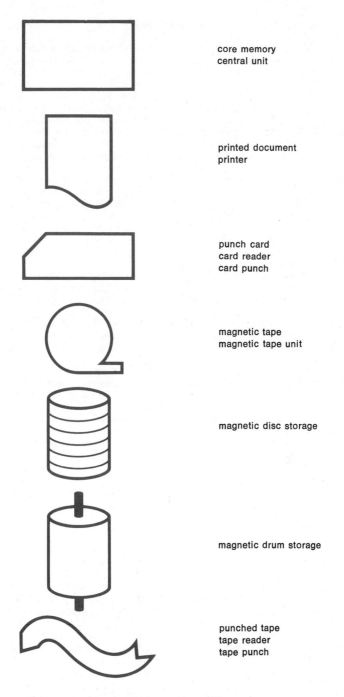

core memory
central unit

printed document
printer

punch card
card reader
card punch

magnetic tape
magnetic tape unit

magnetic disc storage

magnetic drum storage

punched tape
tape reader
tape punch

**FIG. 2   SYSTEM FLOW-CHARTING SYMBOLS**

# PROGRAMMING

Programming consists in producing a set of instructions for a computer to make it perform a specified task. The instructions ultimately carried out by the computer are those presented to it in the form of an appropriate machine code (or instruction code), which it can obey directly. The first step in programming i; the analysis of the particular problem. This consists in breaking the proble·.ı down into logical steps, which is usually done by preparing a flowchart of the problem. Flowcharting is the operation of producing a diagram showing the interconnected logical steps for solving the problem and therefore the relationship between the various parts of the program. The diagram which indicates the successive program steps is termed a program flowchart. Usually an outline flowchart and a detail flowchart have to be prepared. Standard symbols, each with a specific meaning, are used in flowcharting. Typical symbols for the purpose are illustrated in Fig. 1. These comprise symbols representing the following type of functions: flowlines (showing the transfer of control from one operation to another), process (any kind of processing function), decision (a switching operation to choose between several alternative paths), connector (representing an entry from, or exit to, another part of the program flowchart), terminal (start, stop, halt, or interrupt).

In the program flowchart, the emphasis is on the logical and arithmetical operations that make up a particular procedure. On the other hand, the systems flowchart is a diagrammatic representation of the flow of information through the various components of the data processing system; it shows the logical sequence of events, that is, data collection, data preparation, and the computer runs involved (a "run" is the execution of one program or routine). For these flowcharts standardized symbols are also used, some of which are illustrated on page 203.

The program flowchart provides the basis for coding, that is, translating the logical steps of the flowchart into instructions to the computer. These may be given in machine language or in a symbolic language. The coded instructions must reproduce the logic of the program flowchart as simply and efficiently as possible. In actual practice, programming techniques vary a great deal, depending on the type of computer for which the program is intended and on what type of language is used. Also, there are individual variations between one programmer and another. It is therefore not possible to give general rules for programming.

The program is tested by running it on the computer with test data, that is, sample data covering a wide range of combinations, prepared as input for program testing. The results obtained are compared with results calculated manually from the test data. When a program is tested for the first time, it is almost invariably found to contain errors ("bugs"). Correcting these errors is called debugging the program—an important operation, for which particular techniques have been developed. The errors may arise from incorrect use of the programming language or incorrect application of logic to the solution of the problem. The completed program must be supported by proper documentation, which, in the present context, comprises the necessary operating instructions and other essential information (for example, a detailed flowchart with explanatory text, particulars of the source program, and so on) to enable persons other than the programmer to understand and operate the program correctly. Programs may exist as punched cards or punched paper tape, but are more usually stored on magnetic tape or a direct access file.

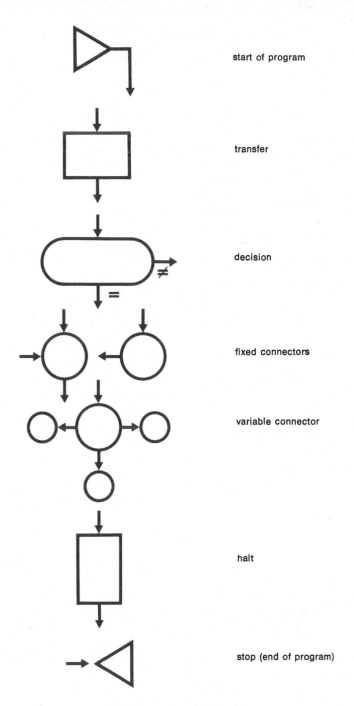

FIG. 1  PROGRAM FLOW-CHARTING SYMBOLS

205

# CHARACTER RECOGNITION

"Electronic" character recognition is primarily a problem of suitable technical preparation of the material for input to a data processing system. Punched tape and punched cards are reliable data-carrying media, but the disadvantages of these forms of input consist in the considerable expenditure of time, manpower and material involved in transferring the information for processing to these media (punching or perforating the tape or cards). A further drawback is that human operators find it difficult to read information stored on tape or cards. To avoid these difficulties, the external data which are fed to the processing system as figures, numbers, typescript, and perhaps handwriting, should be directly convertible into pulse trains that the system can utilize, without necessitating any intermediate stage of data storage in the form of punched tape or cards. This possibility of character recognition and identification is provided by magnetic or optical methods. In the magnetic method, the characters to be identified must be associated with magnetizable material. For this purpose a magnetizable ink (incorporating iron oxide) is used. The optical method is less expensive in that the characters are written, typed, or printed in the ordinary way. The machine responds only to the intensity variations that are manifested by the reflected light when a scanning beam moves across the characters. In order to keep the input equipment as simple and inexpensive as possible, the designers took advantage of the digital properties of existing data processing systems and developed forms of writing in which the characters, though still legible to the human observer, are stylized to such an extent that electronic computers are able to identify them unerringly.

An example of magnetic character recognition is provided by the French digital writing system known as CMC-7, in which each character is represented by seven vertical lines that are separated by four narrow and two wide spaces for figures and by three narrow and three wide spaces for letters of the alphabet. The narrow and wide spaces correspond to the binary digits O and L respectively (Fig. 1). This system is therefore a binary six-unit code, of which 41 bit combinations are used, namely, 26 for the letters, 10 for the figures, and 5 for special characters. The character which we, for example, recognize as "8" is observed by the character reading device as a sequence of seven closely and widely spaced lines and interpreted as a series of voltage pulses (Fig. 2). The method of reading these magnetic characters is shown schematically in Fig. 3. It consists essentially in evaluating the short (O), long (L), and interrupting pulses, the latter being the spaces between the characters. For this it is not even necessary to use a bistable flip-flop circuit (see page 156); instead, a simpler monostable circuit (monoflop), whose quasi-stationary state lasts longer than the short pulse pause but is shorter than a long pause, will suffice for the purpose. In this way the six-unit code for the characters used in the CMC-7 system is stored in a shift register (a device to store information in the form of pulses) and fed into the data processing equipment by means of an AND circuit with six inputs.

Since magnetic character recognition always presupposes the use of magnetic printing or writing devices, it is more expensive and more susceptible to disturbance than optical character recognition. For optical recognition, the International Standardization Organization (ISO) has proposed a set of characters: the OCR-A (Optical Character Recognition, Series A). This alphanumeric system—comprising letters and numbers—is represented in Fig. 4. Optical recognition can be achieved by breaking down the characters

**FIG. 1  CMC-7 MAGNETIC WRITING**

as seen by human eye

as perceived by reading device

converted into rectangular voltage pulses

**FIG. 2**

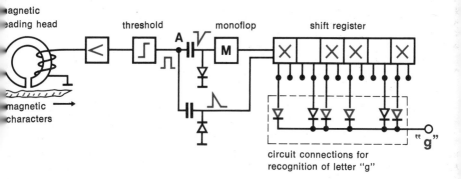

magnetic reading head

threshold

monoflop

shift register

A

M

magnetic characters

circuit connections for recognition of letter "g"

"g"

**FIG. 3  READING SEQUENCE FOR CMC-7 MAGNETIC WRITING**

ABCDEFGHIJKLM
NOPQRSTUVWXYZ
0123456789

**FIG. 4  OCR-A CHARACTERS**

into vertical lines (vertical line analysis, Fig. 5a) or into small squares (matrix method, Fig. 5b). In both cases the character is scanned by a beam of light. The light reflected by the lines composing the character is picked up by photoelectric cells and thus produces a series of voltage variations which correspond to the light and dark areas successively scanned. By triggering flip-flop circuits, these variations are converted into a train of rectangular pulses necessary for input into the electronic data processing system.

In the electromechanical method of optical character recognition, the scanning is performed by means of a slotted disc which rotates at speeds of up to 15,000 r.p.m. (Fig. 6). The light reflected from the character forms an image of the character on the rotating disc. The latter comprises about 30 symmetrically arranged radial slots about 0.25 mm wide. The light that passes through these slots varies in intensity and is made to pass through another slot disposed at right angles to the slots in the rotating disc. As a result, the light reaching the photomultiplier installed behind this slot corresponds only to the area of intersection of a disc slot and the slot behind it. In this way the image is broken down into almost point-shaped elements. The sequence of voltage variations emerging from the photomultiplier is converted into a train of rectangular pulses which are then fed into the data processing system.

In the purely electronic method of optical character recognition, the character is scanned by an electronically controlled light beam emitted by the fluorescent screen of a cathode ray tube (Fig. 7). The point-shaped beam is guided vertically across the characters, which move past at constant speed in such a manner that eight vertical scanning operations are performed for each character. The pulse train emitted by the photomultiplier, which converts the light reflected from the individual points of the character into voltage variations, is next converted into a train of rectangular pulses and

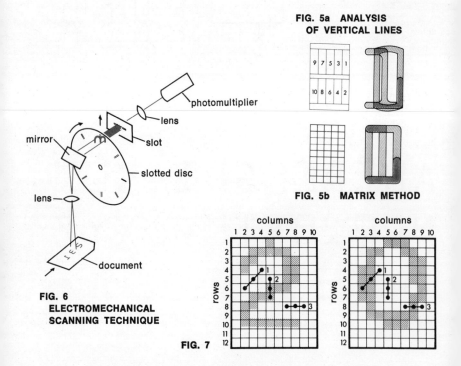

FIG. 5a  ANALYSIS
OF VERTICAL LINES

FIG. 5b  MATRIX METHOD

FIG. 6
ELECTROMECHANICAL
SCANNING TECHNIQUE

FIG. 7

fed to a shift register. The operation of this register is so timed that the scanning area of the character is divided into 20 horizontal scanning lines, so that the whole of this area comprises $8 \times 20 = 160$ elementary areas (matrix elements) of which, on average, 96 are occupied by a character (which only partly fills the scanning area). In this form the character is stored in the shift register, which is composed of 160 flip-flops. If the positions of the flip-flops ("set," "reset," see page 160) are indicated on a panel of lamps corresponding to the elements of the scanning area, the stored characters can be made visible as patterns of lights (Fig. 8).

By using ultraviolet light in addition to visible light the optical character recognition methods can be made largely independent of disturbances, since the usual printing inks appear black in ultraviolet rays. This is more particularly applicable to the use of incandescent lamps in the electromechanical method. Optical methods of reading personal handwriting require very complex scanning systems, and no really satisfactory method has yet been devised for doing this.

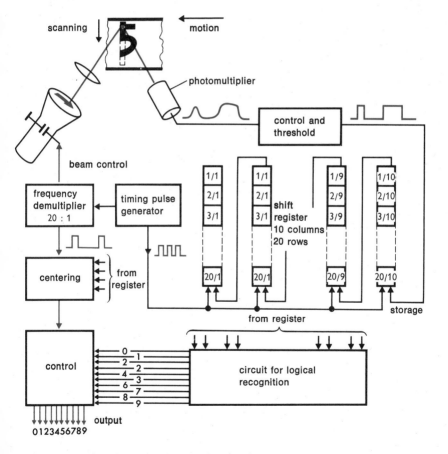

**FIG. 8 ELECTRONIC SCANNING TECHNIQUE USING A CATHODE RAY TUBE**

# HIGH-SPEED PRINTERS AND FILMSETTING TECHNIQUES

High-speed printers have been evolved from the teleprinter. They operate on electromechanical principles, attaining speeds of up to 1300 strokes per second. Fig. 1 is a schematic diagram of the Univac high-speed printer. Its principal feature is a type drum which has 128 bands of printing characters along its length. Each band contains 51 characters around the circumference of the drum. The characters are arranged on the drum in a checkerboard pattern. Opposite each type band is a small type hammer, which strikes from the rear against the paper moving past the drum. In Fig. 1 it is assumed that the information is obtained from a large store (in this case a magnetic drum). Reading is done line by line from the store, the information being stored intermediately. Through the action of the code wheel, which rotates with the type drum, the intermediate store is "informed" when a particular character is located opposite a particular hammer at a particular point. This information, combined with the line-by-line information from the magnetic store, instructs a second store to actuate the appropriate type hammers. All similar characters are printed with one stroke. This high-speed printer attains an average rate of about ten lines per second, each line comprising 128 characters.

Another form of high-speed printer is illustrated in Fig. 2. This machine uses a horizontal type wheel rotating at high speed. Synchronization between type wheel position and hammer action is achieved through a synchronizing pulse generator wheel, which is scanned photo-electrically. Another interesting variant is the IBM 72 machine, which represents the direct further development of a teleprinter, except that the carriage is stationary; instead, a special spherical type head moves rapidly to and fro (Figs. 3a, b). This head, which can rotate and swivel, is controlled by means of a seven-unit code (Fig. 3c).

The filmsetting technique solves the problem arising from the difference in operating speed between a typesetting machine and an electronic data processor. Whereas punched-tape-controlled typesetting machines using conventional lead type cannot exceed about 10 characters per second, the data processor has an output rate of more than 1000 characters per second, that is, the characters are supplied at a rate 100 times higher than the rate with which the conventional typesetting machine can cope. This discrepancy has been overcome by the development of electromechanical and electronic methods of typesetting, comprehensively known as filmsetting.

In electromechanical filmsetting methods, the characters (letters of the alphabet, numerals, and so on) are stored on films in magazines, or in frames with a matrix-like arrangement, or on a rotating disc or drum. The desired kind of type is chosen electromechanically; the lines of type are then formed as a photographic image focused on film by optical means. In the purely electronic methods, on the other hand, the individual character is broken down, by means of an optical screen, into sequences of bits (electric pulses) which are stored electronically. They can then at any time be reproduced visually by means of a picture tube.

One form of electromechanical filmsetting is seen in the Photon (Lumitype) equipment, which uses a rotating disc or drum as the device for storing the characters. The storage disc of the Photon 513 model (Fig. 4) has a diameter of 20 cm. At its outer edge, the disc is provided with marks that serve as a time pulse generator for determining the precise position of the selected letters. Within this are eight circles with a total of 1440 photographically negative characters, comprising 16 alphabets, each with 90 characters (capitals, small letters, special characters and marks, and so on). These can, by optical adjustments to the apparatus, be presented in 12 different sizes. Thus

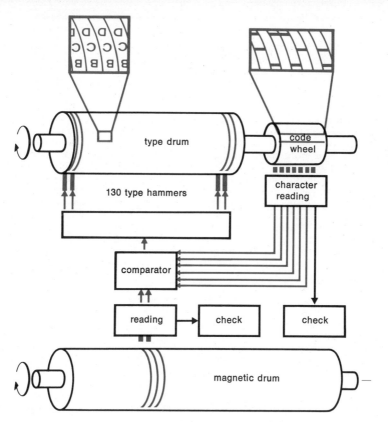

**FIG. 1  UNIVAC HIGH-SPEED PRINTER**

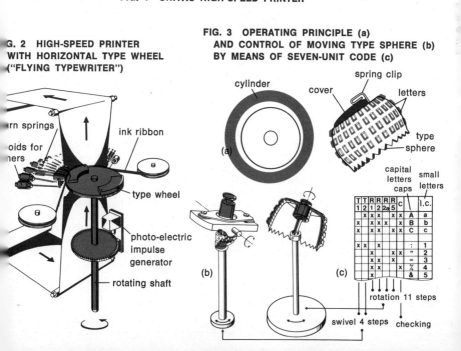

**FIG. 2  HIGH-SPEED PRINTER WITH HORIZONTAL TYPE WHEEL ("FLYING TYPEWRITER")**

**FIG. 3  OPERATING PRINCIPLE (a) AND CONTROL OF MOVING TYPE SPHERE (b) BY MEANS OF SEVEN-UNIT CODE (c)**

a total of 192 type alphabets, with 17,280 characters in all, are available for typesetting. The disc rotates at 600 r.p.m. An electromechanical control system ensures that the selected letter is focused in the desired location on a photographic film. This is achieved by means of an electronic flash, whose action is synchronized with the focusing operation.

The Photon (Lumitype) 713 equipment uses a rotating aluminum drum instead of a disc. This drum carries two film strips with the negatives of the letters (Figs. 5 and 6). Each strip comprises four sets of 96 characters, which in turn can be presented in 12 sizes, so that the drum stores a total of 9246 characters. In a more recent version of the machine there are two drums, so that the storage capacity is doubled (18,492 characters). The functioning principle of a filmsetting machine of this kind is illustrated in Fig. 5. The flash bulbs are disposed inside the drum and form images of the individual characters — by means of an optical system comprising prisms, mirrors and lenses — on the highly sensitive film. The beam of light is guided line by line across the film. Images of different size, as required, are thus produced by appropriate selection of lenses mounted in a rotatable disc. The film is wound; the carriage, comprising the mirror for forming the sequence of character images line by line, is moved along; and the lenses and diaphragms (not shown) are adjusted by precision mechanisms driven by stepping motors (electric motors which operate in steps). The setting rate attainable with this machine is of the order of 80,000 characters per hour.

The Lino-Quick machine uses frames that comprise negatives of the characters and are interposed in the beam emitted by a constant source of light. The light flashes are produced by means of a revolving shutter. Each frame contains 184 characters, and a setting rate of about 40,000 characters per hour can be attained. The Linotron 505 forms a transition to the purely electronic methods. In this machine, optical scanning is performed by light from the image spots of a cathode ray tube. The scanning operation breaks down the characters (stored as negatives) into a series of screen dots, which in turn are converted into pulse trains by a photomultiplier and fed to a recording tube.

With electronic filmsetting techniques, the output equipment comprises a cathode ray tube serving as an analog converter (see page 184 et seq.). Controlled by the pulses of the characters coded in binary digital form, the electron beam in this tube inscribes each individual character on a fluorescent screen from which the text is then photographed line by line. Fig. 7 is a schematic diagram of a filmsetting machine originally developed by Rudolf Hell. Named Digiset, it can be connected direct to an electronic data processing system. It comprises a central control unit, a core memory and a recording device whose output element is the cathode ray tube. The characters (letters of the alphabet, figures, special marks, and so on) are stored as internal data in the core memory. The image area for each character is broken down by means of an optical screen into about 400 pulses per square millimeter (Fig. 8). In common with electronic methods generally, the images of the characters are stored electronically (in the form of bit sequences in storage units).

If an elementary area (square) of the grid is entirely covered by a character, the pulses corresponding to that area have the binary digit value L. If the elementary square is not, or is only partly, covered by a character, it is represented by the binary digit O. As a rule, 1000 bits are sufficient for the storage of one character. With punched tape input it is possible to feed 256 characters and setting instructions into the device at one and the same time. This would necessitate a core memory storage capacity of 256,000 bits.

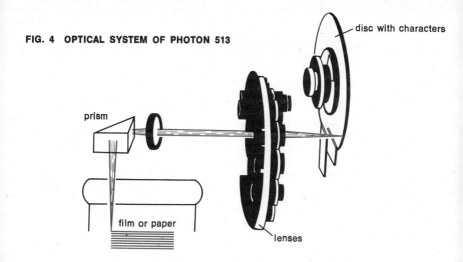

**FIG. 4 OPTICAL SYSTEM OF PHOTON 513**

disc with characters

prism

film or paper

lenses

**FIG. 5 OPTICAL SYSTEM OF PHOTON 713**

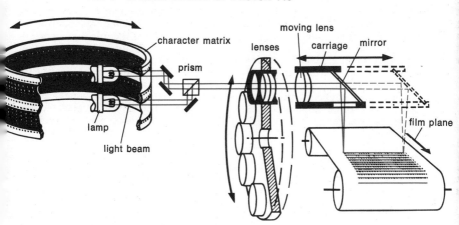

character matrix

moving lens

carriage

mirror

lenses

prism

lamp

light beam

film plane

**FIG. 6**

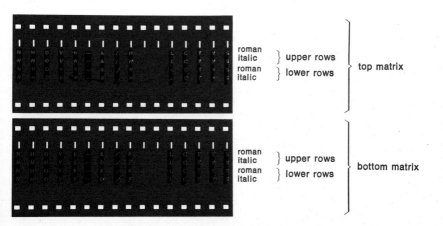

roman
italic } upper rows
roman
italic } lower rows
} top matrix

roman
italic } upper rows
roman
italic } lower rows
bottom matrix

For practical purposes, however, 192,000 bits is an adequate capacity. Interrogation of the characters from the memory is effected by means of an input code, which is supplied either direct from the output of a data processor or from a punched tape reader. If the character scanning area is subdivided into 400 pulses per mm$^2$, the recording electron beam in the cathode ray tube must have a diameter of 0.05 mm, corresponding to a cross-sectional area of 0.0025 mm$^2$.

The core memory of the Digiset is "charged" with a certain kind of lettering. If a change of lettering style is desired, the memory is recharged with different lettering by means of punched tape, for which an eight-track tape is usually employed. The 1000 bits for each character require about 130 rows of perforations in this tape. Depending on the nature and the scanning screen of the characters in question, varying lengths of punched tape (generally about 80 m) are required for programming the machine. At a reading rate of 1000 characters per second it takes only about half a minute to read this amount of tape into the memory. One and the same kind of lettering can, moreover, be altered in various ways by simple electronic manipulations. For example, the letters may be made narrower and set closer together. Alternatively, they may be set farther apart, or slantwise to give italics (Fig. 9). The size of the characters can furthermore be varied between 4 and 32 typographical points (one point corresponds to a height of 0.376 mm). These possibilities of variation dispense with the whole range of type magazines that are required in conjunction with conventional, punched-tape-controlled, lead typesetting machines. Fig. 10 is a specimen of text recorded on a portion of the photographic film. The lines are numbered to facilitate the pinpointing of typographic errors. To rectify such errors it is necessary to reset the line.

Fig. 11 schematizes the whole process of setting a document in print by means of the Digiset system. The typewritten manuscript is edited and is then copied on a keyboard perforator, which records the text on punched tape and at the same time produces a typed copy. The latter is corrected for typographical errors and spelling. The corrected text is then again recorded on punched tape by means of a perforator. The typed copy which this machine produces (together with the punched tape) is then subjected to a second proofreading.

The original punched tape and the second punched tape are simultaneously fed into two tape reading devices, which convert the coded characters into electrical pulses. The pulses from the two tapes are fed into a special computer (Digicom), which interpolates the corrections into the original text and passes the corrected, coded characters (in the form of pulse trains) to a tape punch, which then produces the punched tape that will serve to control the Digiset filmsetting machine. The latter converts the control pulses from this tape into suitable pulses for producing the printed characters and, additionally, gives out another punched tape, which is used for checking purposes. At the same time, the characters become visible on the fluorescent screen of the cathode ray tube and are photographed on to film, which then passes through a developing system, so that finally the text, permanently recorded on film, is obtained, as shown in Fig. 10. Copies are produced from this film, as required, and are fed into a special apparatus (Starsettograph) for further processing, for instance, the addition of titles (by optical projection), or rearrangement into two columns of text for further reproduction by photomechanical methods. The high processing rate of up to 3000 characters per second cannot be fully utilized for the actual typesetting, as a great many additional instructions also have to be fed in at the same time. These relate to the actual setting of the characters, variations in their size or style (roman,

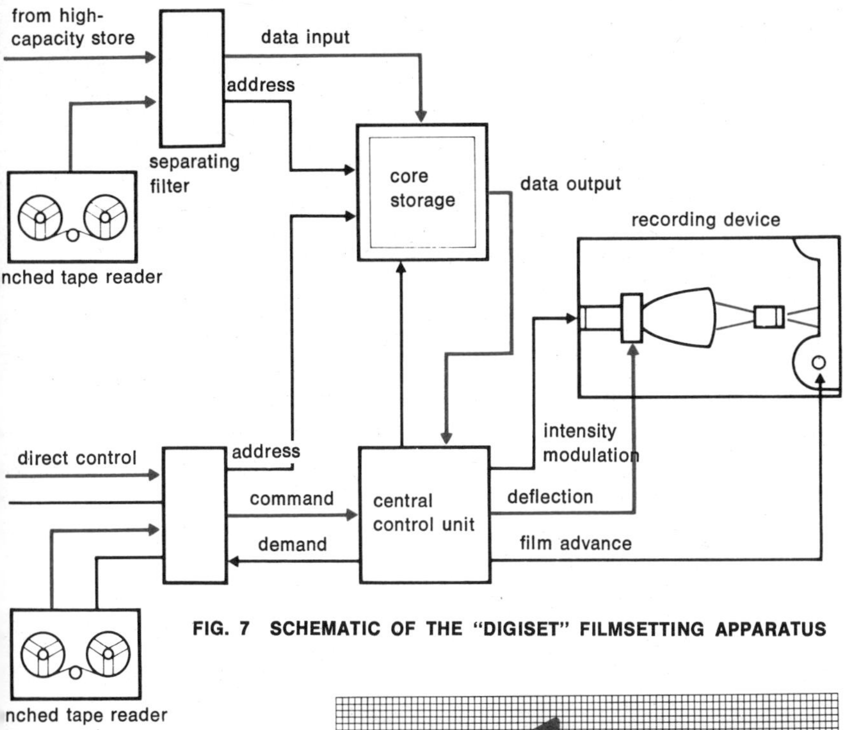

from high-
capacity store
data input
address
separating
filter
core
storage
data output
recording device
nched tape reader
intensity
modulation
direct control
address
command
central
control unit
deflection
demand
film advance
nched tape reader


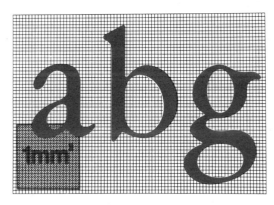

**FIG. 7 SCHEMATIC OF THE "DIGISET" FILMSETTING APPARATUS**

abg
1mm²


**FIG. 8 CHARACTER SCANNING SCREEN (400 SQUARES PER mm²)**

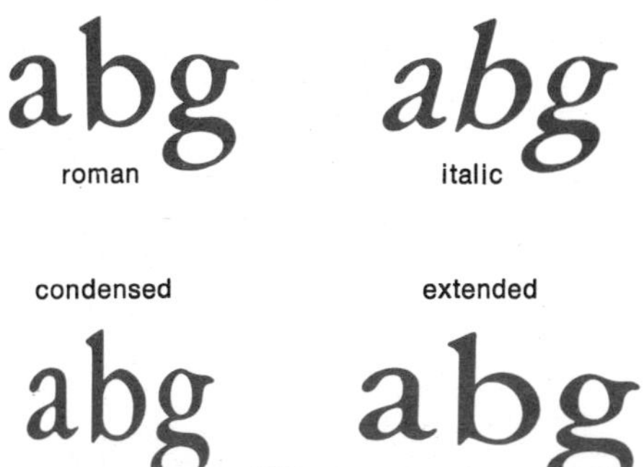

abg
roman
abg
italic
condensed
extended
abg
abg


**FIG. 9**

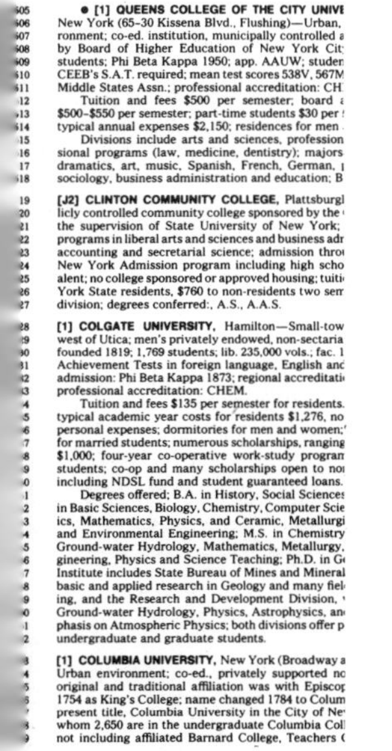

• **[1] QUEENS COLLEGE OF THE CITY UNIVE**
New York (65–30 Kissena Blvd., Flushing)—Urban,
ronment; co-ed. institution, municipally controlled a
by Board of Higher Education of New York Cit
students; Phi Beta Kappa 1950; app. AAUW; studer
CEEB's S.A.T. required; mean test scores 538V, 567M
Middle States Assn.; professional accreditation: CH
Tuition and fees $500 per semester; board a
$500–$550 per semester; part-time students $30 per
typical annual expenses $2,150; residences for men
Divisions include arts and sciences, profession
sional programs (law, medicine, dentistry); majors
dramatics, art, music, Spanish, French, German,
sociology, business administration and education; B

**[J2] CLINTON COMMUNITY COLLEGE,** Plattsburgl
licly controlled community college sponsored by the
the supervision of State University of New York;
programs in liberal arts and sciences and business adr
accounting and secretarial science; admission thro
New York Admission program including high scho
alent; no college sponsored or approved housing; tuiti
York State residents, $760 to non-residents two sem
division; degrees conferred:, A.S., A.A.S.

**[1] COLGATE UNIVERSITY,** Hamilton—Small-tow
west of Utica; men's privately endowed, non-sectaria
founded 1819; 1,769 students; lib. 235,000 vols.; fac. 1
Achievement Tests in foreign language, English anc
admission: Phi Beta Kappa 1873; regional accreditati
professional accreditation: CHEM.
Tuition and fees $135 per semester for residents.
typical academic year costs for residents $1,276, no
personal expenses; dormitories for men and women;
for married students; numerous scholarships, ranging
$1,000; four-year co-operative work-study progran
students; co-op and many scholarships open to no
including NDSL fund and student guaranteed loans.
Degrees offered; B.A. in History, Social Sciences
in Basic Sciences, Biology, Chemistry, Computer Scie
ics, Mathematics, Physics, and Ceramic, Metallurgi
and Environmental Engineering; M.S. in Chemistry
Ground-water Hydrology, Mathematics, Metallurgy,
gineering, Physics and Science Teaching; Ph.D. in G
Institute includes State Bureau of Mines and Mineral
basic and applied research in Geology and many fiel
ing, and the Research and Development Division,
Ground-water Hydrology, Physics, Astrophysics, an
phasis on Atmospheric Physics; both divisions offer p
undergraduate and graduate students.

**[1] COLUMBIA UNIVERSITY,** New York (Broadway a
Urban environment; co-ed., privately supported nc
original and traditional affiliation was with Episcop
1754 as King's College; name changed 1784 to Colum
present title, Columbia University in the City of Ne
whom 2,650 are in the undergraduate Columbia Col
not including affiliated Barnard College, Teachers

**FIG. 10 SAMPLE OF DIGISET FILMSETTING**

italic), punctuation marks, and so on. For practical purposes the effective setting speed is about 400 characters per second (but even this is equivalent to about 1.5 million characters per hour!).

The versatility and speed of the filmsetting techniques have obviated the discrepancy in operating rate that used to exist between electronic data processing systems and typesetting equipment, so that now the speeds of the output devices are suitably geared to one another. They attain performance rates of the order of one megabit (one million bits) per second. But with these electronic typesetting and printing devices, we are still faced with the practical problem of manual input of the text from the original manuscript. Therefore, the high operating rates of filmsetting equipment combined with a data processing system can be fully utilized only if the input is held in readiness in electronically stored form. Even if the input material is available on punched tape, only about one-tenth of the attainable speed is utilized, since the paper tape punch can cope with at most about 100 characters per second. In recent years, input has been effected by means of a magnetic tape reader (a device for sensing data recorded as magnetized spots on magnetic tape), with additional electronic equipment comprising a buffer store (for temporary storage of data). With such systems it is possible to attain speeds of up to 28,000 characters per second.

FIG. 11 SEQUENCE OF OPERATION
WITH DIGISET EQUIPMENT
(according to R. Hell)

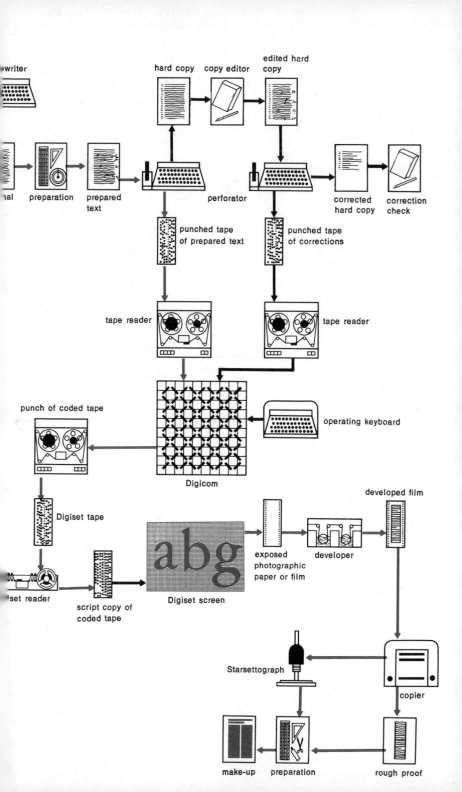

# TIME-SHARING SYSTEMS

With the filmsetting technique it becomes possible to operate a central computer (for example, with the Digiset system) by means of punched paper tape or magnetic tape from a transmitting device, which may be remote from the computer and connected to it by means of long-distance data transmission lines. The term "time-sharing" is applied to the operation of such installations comprising a central data processor (computer) and several terminal units (input/output devices) located at some considerable distance from it, with which it can communicate. Such systems are used for special purposes, for example, information and travel reservation services, monitoring and control of industrial processes, teaching machine link-ups, and so on. Time-sharing systems differ from one another in the nature of the functions they perform, but in general time-sharing can be defined as a technique in which a number of terminal units can concurrently use a central data processor for input, processing and output functions. Multi-programming is a technique whereby a computer can handle numerous programs simultaneously by overlapping or interleaving their execution. Thus, in a multiprogramming computer, several programs may be processed simultaneously by switching from one to another in a fixed sequence, so that a certain number of instructions can be performed each time. Alternatively, the users at their respective terminal units may each be allotted a certain amount of computer time in succession. A system based on this latter principle is illustrated schematically in Fig. 1. A dynamic time-sharing allocator is a program which co-ordinates the operation of a time-sharing computer, including the automatic switching from one program to another in a multiprogramming sequence. It also controls the input and output functions, so that several peripheral units (input, output and storage devices associated with the computer) can operate concurrently while data processing is performed in the central processor. In order to achieve maximum time-sharing efficiency, most of the peripheral units of the computer — magnetic character readers, high-speed line printers, card readers, card punches, and so on — have an automatic interrupt device. These units may interrupt, be reactivated, and continue their operation independently; thus the computer can coordinate the operation of a number of peripheral units, each performing its input, output or storage operations at its own speed.

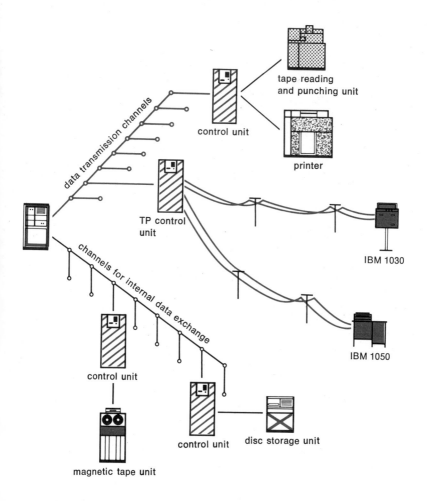

tape reading
and punching unit

control unit

printer

data transmission channels

TP control
unit

IBM 1030

channels for internal data exchange

IBM 1050

control unit

control unit

disc storage unit

magnetic tape unit

**FIG. 1   DIAGRAM OF A TIME-SHARING NETWORK**

# DATA TRANSMISSION

Data transmission differs from conventional telecommunication in that the information is represented in digital instead of analog form (as in telephony). How can existing telecommunication networks, designed essentially for analog representation, be properly utilized also for digital data transmission? The analogy between the flow of electricity in a wire and the flow of a liquid through a pipeline is only a very approximate one. In reality, an electrical conductor is surrounded by electric and magnetic fields of force, which play an important part, more particularly, when they undergo rapid variations. In that case adjacent conductors influence one another in consequence of the displacement current caused by the varying electric field and inductively in consequence of the induced voltage caused by the varying magnetic field. For example, in telephony the sound vibrations in the frequency range from 300 to 3600 cycles/sec. give rise to amplitude modified direct currents, that is, variable currents, by means of which the speech is transmitted.

In the early days of telephony these currents were transmitted entirely through overhead wires (Fig. 1), whereas nowadays this form of transmission has become the exception rather than the rule. The two wires forming a telephonly circuit are relatively far apart in the case of overhead telephone lines, so that capacitive and inductive interactions are too slight to cause any really significant amount of disturbance. Within the range of speech frequencies used in telephony, there is also very little disturbance when the pairs of wires for the various circuits are—for reasons of economy and for protection against external influences—combined into cables that are installed underground (Fig. 2). The cable core is composed of so-called quads. Each quad comprises four separately insulated conductors twisted together, that is, two pairs of conductors corresponding to two circuits. Every five of these quads are grouped together in a primary bundle, and every five or ten of such primary bundles are in turn combined into main bundles.

Capacitive and inductive influences become critical only when currents of higher frequency have to be transmitted, as is, for example, necessary in radio communication. Electromagnetic energy is propagated through space without the benefit of a metallic conductor when, in consequence of the high frequency of the current concerned, the displacement current predominates over the conductor current. High-frequency radio waves can be concentrated into a beam, like light rays, and be modulated with speech frequency (Fig. 3). These high-frequency waves serve as the carrier for the much lower-frequency speech modulation. Such modulation may be of three kinds: amplitude modulation, frequency modulation and phase modulation. In amplitude modulation, the amplitude of the carrier (of constant frequency) is varied proportionally to the amplitude of the signal. In frequency modulation, the frequency of the carrier (whose amplitude remains constant) is varied proportionally to the amplitude of the signal. In phase modulation, the phase of the carrier is advanced and retarded proportionally to the frequency of the modulating signal, the phase shift being proportional to the amplitude of the latter. See Fig. 4.

The possibility of thus superimposing relatively low-frequency signals upon high-frequency alternating currents provides the means for the multiple utilization of transmission paths. In one and the same transmission path, a number of so-called channels can be operated simultaneously, each of which is characterized by a certain frequency range. The frequency spacing of 700 cycles/sec. between channels ensures proper separation and thus eliminates the objectionable phenomenon of cross-talk, that is, disturbance due to speech sounds from neighboring channels.

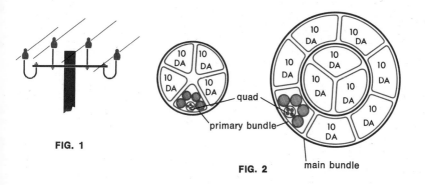

**FIG. 1**

quad

primary bundle

main bundle

**FIG. 2**

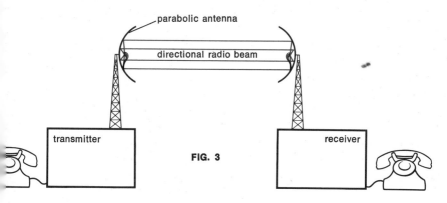

parabolic antenna

directional radio beam

transmitter

**FIG. 3**

receiver

**FIGS. 1–3  TRANSMISSION TECHNIQUES IN TELEPHONY**

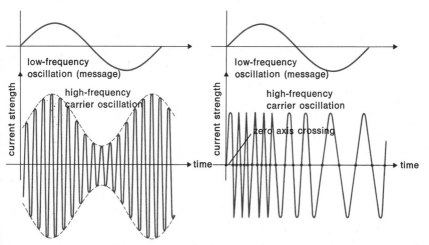

low-frequency
oscillation (message)

high-frequency
carrier oscillation

current strength

time

**FIG. 4a  AMPLITUDE MODULATION**

low-frequency
oscillation (message)

high-frequency
carrier oscillation

zero axis crossing

current strength

time

**FIG. 4b  FREQUENCY MODULATION**

The multiple utilization of a transmission path is illustrated by the example of carrier transmission, that is, transmitting information by wire or radio involving the modulation of a carrier, as explained above. In the case indicated schematically in Fig. 5, there are two transmission channels in simultaneous use. The information fed into the system from the microphone is passed through a device called a modulator to channel 1 (operating with carrier 1) and transmitted. Similarly, a second signal is transmitted through channel 2 (with carrier 2). The frequency mixture travels along the transmission path (comprising the two channels) to the receiving station, where suitable filters allow the frequencies of channel 1 and channel 2, respectively, to pass, After separation, the speech frequencies are "scooped off" from the carrier frequencies and made audible by means of a telephone or loudspeaker.

The number of channels comprising a carrier transmission system depends on the band width of the channels and the highest carrier frequency, which has to be suited to the frequency response of the transmission path. In some systems the two-way conversation is transmitted through one and the same channel; in others, separate channels are used. Certain systems make use of special tubular (coaxial) cables (Fig. 6a). In such a cable each pair of conductors for communication in opposite directions comprises an outer and an inner cylindrical conductor with a common axis. This arrangement has the advantage of being less affected by capacitive and inductive disturbances than ordinary cables. For the transmission of very high frequencies, it is possible to dispense with the inner conductor. The electromagnetic energy is then propagated along the tubular hollow conductor (known technically as a waveguide) in the form of waves (Fig. 6b). In such transmission the modes of vibration will depend on the geometric features of the waveguide and on the nature of the excitation (shape and disposition of the lead-in electrodes). With the carrier principle of transmission, the multiple utilization of a transmission path is achieved by the superposition of frequency bands with the aid of carrier waves of increasing frequency. This process of transmitting two or more signals over a common path by employing a different frequency band for each signal is termed frequency-division multiplexing.

An alternative possibility is time-division multiplexing, in which the transmission of two or more signals over a common path is achieved by using different time intervals for the different signals (Fig. 7). In telephony the acoustic inertia of the human sense of hearing is utilized: Gaps in transmission of up to 25 milliseconds do not impair the intelligibility of a conversation. A number of "time channels" (corresponding to the "frequency channels" of frequency-division multiplexing) can be accommodated within this time gap. The allocation of the time channels to the telephonic connection between two stations is achieved by means of electronic gate circuits which, using a repetition frequency of 10 kilohertz (for example), connect the speakers for periods of 0.5 microsecond, so that 250 of such connections, lasting a total of only 0.125 millisecond, are established (between each two speakers in communication with each other) within the time interval of 25 milliseconds, so that, in all, about 2000 time channels can be accommodated within this interval.

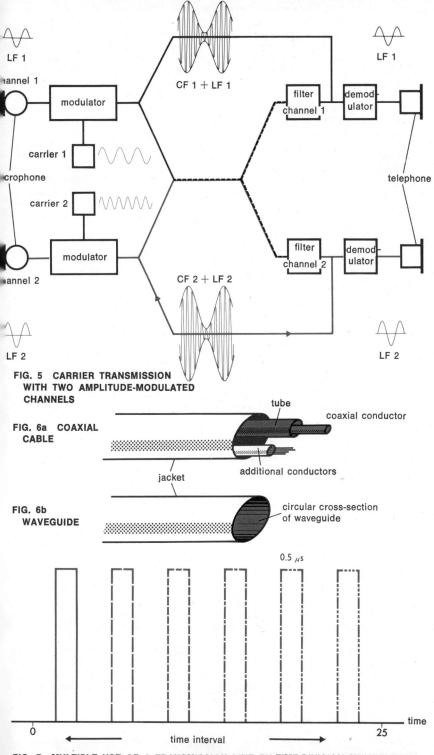

LF 1

channel 1

CF 1 + LF 1

LF 1

modulator

filter
channel 1

demod-
ulator

carrier 1

microphone

telephone

carrier 2

modulator

filter
channel 2

demod-
ulator

channel 2

CF 2 + LF 2

LF 2

LF 2

**FIG. 5  CARRIER TRANSMISSION
WITH TWO AMPLITUDE-MODULATED
CHANNELS**

tube

coaxial conductor

**FIG. 6a  COAXIAL
CABLE**

jacket

additional conductors

**FIG. 6b
WAVEGUIDE**

circular cross-section
of waveguide

0.5 $\mu$s

0

time interval

25

time

**FIG. 7  MULTIPLE USE OF A TRANSMISSION LINE BY TIME-DIVISION MULTIPLEXING**

The rate of the pulse sequence in time-division multiplexing is measured in kilobits/sec. In Figs. 8a and b the two multiplexing principles are compared with each other. Ordinary telephony uses the frequency-division multiplexing method and is designed essentially for analog transmission. The internationally standardized system is based on a band width for a telephony transmission channel of 4 kilohertz (kHz). From this, three groups are formed: the primary group having a width of 48 kHz (12 channels), the secondary group having a width of 240 kHz (60 channels), and the tertiary group having a width of 1200 kHz (300 channels). See Fig. 8a. For reasons of economy it is essential to use this existing communications network also for data transmission. By suitable adaptation a number of data transmission channels can be made available in this network. Time-division multiplexing is used for these; the accompanying table shows how this is fitted into the frequency-division multiplexing groups. From this comparative table, it appears that pulse trains can be transmitted at rates of up to 2000 bits/sec. over a speech channel. Within

| FREQUENCY-DIVISION MULTIPLEXING | Higher Unit | | | |
|---|---|---|---|---|
| unit | speech channel | 48 kHz primary group | 240 kHz secondary group | 1200 kHz tertiary group |
| telegraphy channel 170 Hz (120, 150 Hz) | ×12 to ×24 | | | |
| speech channel, nominal 4 kHz | ×1 | ×12 | | |
| 48 kHz channel | | | ×5 | |
| 240 kHz channel | | | | ×5 |
| **TIME-DIVISION MULTIPLEXING** | 1200 (2400 bit/s) | 38.4 kbit/2 | 153.6 kbit/s | 1228.8 kbit/s |
| 150 bit/s telegraphy channel | ×8 (×16) | | | |
| all-purpose data channel 600 bit/s | ×2 (×4) | | | |
| 1200 or 2400 bit/s | ×1 | ×32 (×16) | | |
| (4.8) 9.6 kbit/s Vocoder channel | | ×4 (×8) | | |
| 38.4 kbit/s rapid digital speech transmission | | ×1 | ×4 | ×32 |

the frequency band of the 48 kHz primary group, it is possible to accommodate 38.4 kilobits/sec., while 153.6 kilobits/sec. can be accommodated in the secondary group, and 1228.8 kilobits/sec. in the tertiary group. These bit transmission rates have been established on the basis of two considerations. In the first place, the pulse repetition frequency (bit transmission rate) can, at most, be of the order of magnitude of the frequency band width of the group channel; secondly, the bit transmission rates must conform to the binary order, that is, it must be possible to represent them as powers of 2.

In using the carrier telephone system, the data to be transmitted first have to be converted into carrier-frequency signals. Conversely, on reception these signals have to be converted back into direct-current pulse trains. This is done by a modulator at the transmitting end and a demodulator at the receiving end, respectively. The combination of these two devices is known as a "modem"

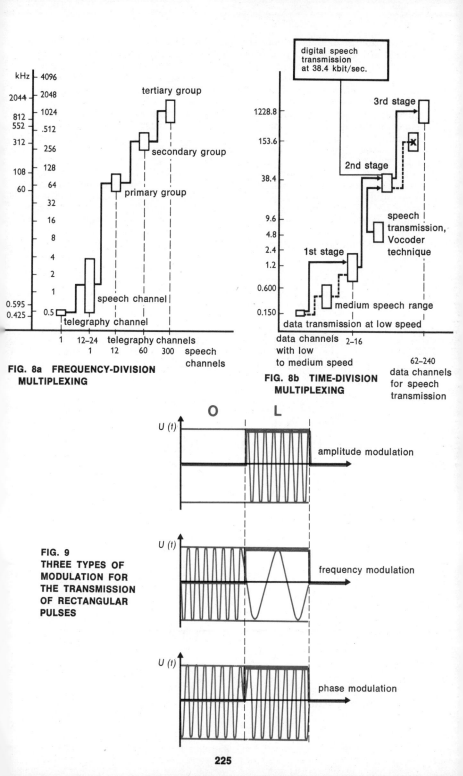

**FIG. 8a FREQUENCY-DIVISION MULTIPLEXING**

**FIG. 8b TIME-DIVISION MULTIPLEXING**

**FIG. 9 THREE TYPES OF MODULATION FOR THE TRANSMISSION OF RECTANGULAR PULSES**

225

(contraction of modulator-demodulator). Data transmission has to be accomplished at a constant bit rate, since constant time spacing of the pulses is an important feature of coding. At present, modems for handling from 200 to 2000 bits/sec. are available — for simplex operation (communication between two stations taking place in one direction at a time), duplex operation (simultaneous operation of correlated transmitting and receiving apparatus at the two ends of a transmission path) and half-duplex operation (duplex operation in either direction, but not in both directions simultaneously). In addition to the telephone system, through which data can be transmitted at a rate of up to 2400 bits/sec., teleprinter lines can be used for the transmission of data at a rate of 50 bits/sec. No modems are used in this case, as the teleprinter system is designed for the transmission of pulse trains. The function of the modem is to convert direct-current signals into carrier-frequency signals, and vice versa. Three different modulation types for the transmission of a rectangular pulse are indicated in Fig. 9 on page 225; in these the binary digits O and L are represented as follows. (1) With amplitude modulation: O is represented by zero voltage, L by an alternating-current pulse; (2) with frequency modulation: O is represented by an alternating-current pulse of higher frequency, L by one of lower frequency; (3) with phase modulation: O and L are represented by alternating-current pulses which are mirror images of each other. Because it is least affected by disturbance, frequency modulation is used in modems.

The block diagram of a modem for 1200 bits/sec. is presented in Fig. 10.

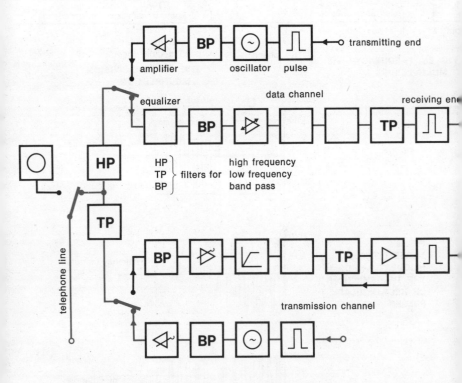

FIG. 10   SWITCH DIAGRAM FOR A MODEM FOR 1200 BIT/SEC.

At the transmitting station, the data signal is first reformed as a pulse in a flip-flop circuit and modulated upon the frequency of an oscillator. The equipment at the receiving station comprises an equalizer, a band-pass filter, an automatic gain control amplifier, a limiter, and a frequency discriminator. The last-mentioned device converts the frequency variation into an amplitude variation, whereby the output pulse is provided in amplitude-modulated form.

During transmission via the public telephone system, the pulses are subjected to distortion and disturbance effects (Fig. 11). These can be minimized by the use of frequency modulation, as already mentioned, but it is, nevertheless, sometimes necessary to take additional precautions. Errors in data transmission arise, more particularly, in consequence of the lack of redundancy (in the information-theoretical sense). The object of coding is to achieve optimum utilization of the transmission channels by reducing redundancy (see page 52), but to do this successfully — without too much loss of signal intelligibility due to disturbance — requires channels that are largely free from disturbing effects. Otherwise a degree of redundancy has to be artificially introduced into the redundancy-free code to convert it into a code permitting the detection of errors. For instance, certain monitoring operations may be applied to check whether the number of L-positions in the correct code words is always an even number (Fig. 12).

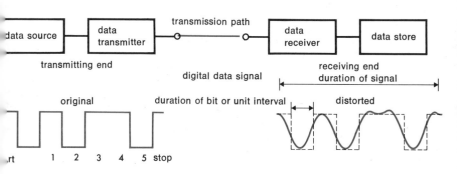

FIG. 11 PULSE DISTORTION IN LONG-DISTANCE DATA TRANSMISSION

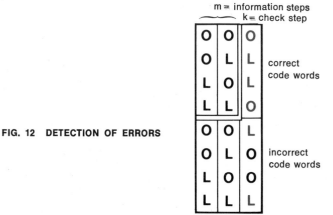

FIG. 12 DETECTION OF ERRORS

# PROCESS COMPUTERS

The concept of "process control" refers to systems whose purpose is to provide automation or continuous operations based more particularly on the use of computers (often analog computers or hybrid computers) for the direct control of production or other physical processes. The input and output of a computer can be linked to a technical or industrial process. The input signals are obtained from measuring devices (detecting elements) which monitor the process. These signals are scrutinized by the computer and compared with the program that controls the process. The output signals from the computer then make the necessary corrections in the process to ensure that it takes place in accordance with the program. Fig. 1 is a schematic diagram of a process computer system for a large power generating plant. The process signals coming from the detecting elements must first be so converted that they can be handled by the computer, that is, they have to be put into digital form in accordance with a special code, if a digital computer is used for controlling the process. The primary signals from the detecting elements are usually either electrical or pneumatic. Electrical detecting elements are, for example, thermocouples, resistance thermometers, light barriers, electronic or electromagnetic relays, and so on.

Transmission of the process signals from the detecting elements over long distances presents no difficulties, so that the computer may be installed in a central position from where it can control the various sub-sections into which a large technical or industrial process may be divided. Transmission of data to and from the computer is usually effected in digital form, that is, as a series of pulses, through suitable data channels. The output signals from the computer must generally be converted back into analog form for utilization by indicating instruments, plotters (devices for the drawing of graphs), servo-motors, controllers, and other monitoring or correcting equipment. Also, by means of data transmission channels, remote control systems can be linked to the central process computer. Typical arrangements relating to the operation and control of a major technical process are illustrated schematically in Figs. 1 and 2 (see page 230).

The completely automated factory—which would, for example, mass-produce stamped, molded, machined, fabricated, and assembled products without a human attendant so much as pressing a button—may still be largely a production engineer's dream, but with existing process computer systems, it is nevertheless possible to achieve a high degree of automation. The function of the human operator is thus reduced to sitting at a console in the control center and observing the monitoring and recording equipment that keeps him informed of the state of the process. Intervention on his part is confined to effecting a change in the program, should that be required, or taking remedial action in the event of technical trouble.

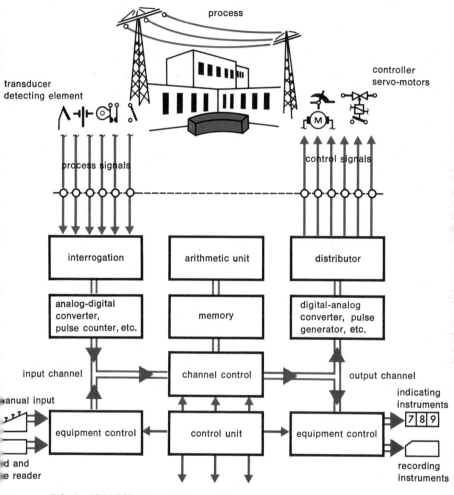

FIG. 1 PROCESS COMPUTER SYSTEM FOR AN AUTOMATICALLY
CONTROLLED POWER GENERATING PLANT

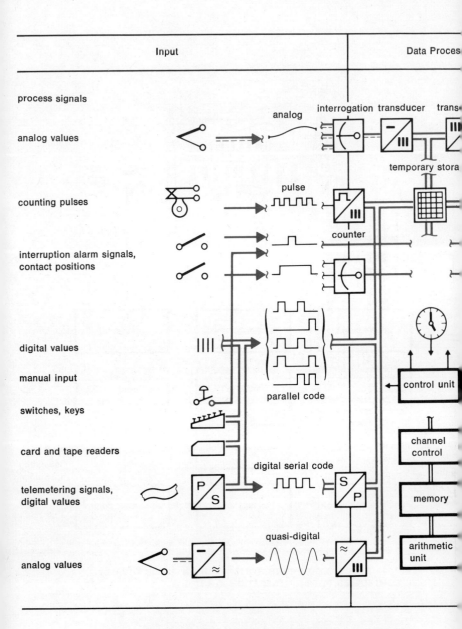

| Input | Data Proces |
|---|---|

process signals

analog values

analog    interrogation transducer    trans

counting pulses

pulse    counter

temporary stora

interruption alarm signals,
contact positions

digital values

manual input

switches, keys

card and tape readers

telemetering signals,
digital values

analog values

parallel code

digital serial code

quasi-digital

control unit

channel
control

memory

arithmetic
unit

**FIG. 2  CONTROL SIGNALS AND FUNCTIONS FOR OPERATING
THE AUTOMATED POWER GENERATING PLANT**

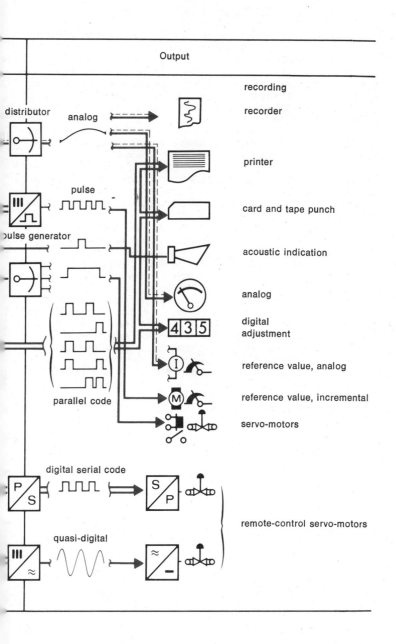

recording

distributor · analog · recorder

pulse

pulse generator · printer

card and tape punch

acoustic indication

analog

digital adjustment

parallel code · reference value, analog

reference value, incremental

servo-motors

digital serial code

quasi-digital

remote-control servo-motors

# DATA BANKS

The term "data bank" describes a comprehensive file of data stored in some suitably accessible form, for example, in a direct access store, that is, a storage device in which the access time to retrieve items of data is constant and retrieval is independent of the location where the items are stored (as opposed to storage on, for example, magnetic tape, which is a so-called serial access store whose items are accessible only in the order in which they occur on the tape). Information stored in a data bank is made available to a large number of users by means of remote terminals.

Technical problems associated with the operation of data banks have largely been solved, but there are still problems of organization. For example, is it preferable to have one large central data bank or several smaller, decentralized (but interconnected) banks? See Figs. 1 and 2. Centralization offers economic advantages, but has the drawback that, in the event of technical trouble with the equipment, a large number of users relying on the data may be seriously inconvenienced. For this reason, among others, the principle of decentralization is gaining widespread acceptance. Technical breakdowns thus remain localized and do not put the whole system out of action. Besides, a number of competing manufacturers of data processing equipment have already established their own computer centers and data banks, which can conveniently be incorporated into a decentralized general system.

Data banks can serve a wide range of reference and information purposes. For example, the information held at the disposal of users may comprise: directories of addresses for publicity and circularizing; economic and commercial statistics; documentation of professional literature; classified information on disease symptoms for medical diagnosis; police records for crime detection purposes; documentation relating to laws, bylaws and other official enactments; information on scientific research in progress; information on technological processes and materials; military information; and so forth.

Data banks can be interconnected nationally and internationally by a network of data transmission lines. Examples of such networks already in existence are those operated by Interpol (the international crime detection organization), international news agencies, weather forecasting services, international banking organizations, air and rail travel booking agencies, and so on. Further developments are emerging in the field of library operation and literature documentation.

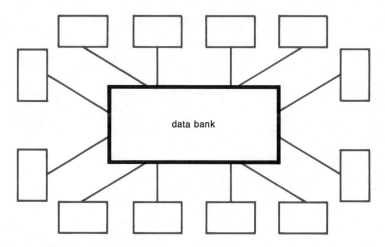

**FIG. 1 CENTRAL DATA BANK ( ☐ = subscriber)**

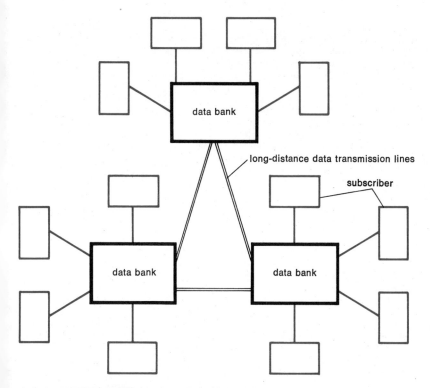

**FIG. 2 DECENTRALIZED DATA BANKS LINKED BY LONG-DISTANCE DATA TRANSMISSION LINES**

# ARTIFICIAL INTELLIGENCE

In the traditional sense of the word, "intelligence" is understood as the ability to assess situations, perform significant logical steps, make decisions, and make use of experience. From this definition it is evident that human intelligence comprises not only rational but also irrational processes. It is indeed possible to simulate the rational part of the intelligence function, but the irrational element remains elusive. Pierre Bertaux has formulated the fundamental difference between human intelligence and the intelligence of the "thinking machine" as follows: "There is hardly any human activity that could not be done by machines — except for one: asking questions." Artificial intelligence can be put into a data processing machine by programming. A program that gives the computer a behavior pattern that can be called "intelligent" is termed a "heuristic" program. In general this denotes a set of computer instructions that simulate the behavior of a human operator when dealing with a problem. More particularly, it is a program that causes the computer to solve a problem by trial and error, the success of each attempt at solution being assessed and used to improve the subsequent attempts until an acceptable solution is reached. Such computer programs have, for example, been developed for playing chess. The heuristic approach is therefore an exploratory procedure based on successive evaluations, as opposed to the algorithmic approach, which deals with a problem in accordance with a fixed procedure comprising a finite number of specific steps. (An "algorithm" is a series of instructions for the step-by-step solution of a particular problem.) "Adaptive heuristic" functioning is an intriguing possibility in the realm of computer development. Conceivably, programs could be devised and equipment designed that would enable the programs to alter and make adjustments to the circuitry of the computer, so that it could adapt itself to changing circumstances and the problems arising in connection with them. The modern computer can, in any case, be regarded as an "intelligence amplifier," that is, a means whereby man can exercise his intellectual capabilities with greater effect, just as power-driven machinery forms an extension and amplification of his muscular capabilities.

Among many possible examples, mention will be made of a heuristic program, developed by T. Evans, which enables a computer to detect similarities and relationships between geometric shapes. Two given diagrams (A and B, see Fig. 1) bear a certain relation to each other. The computer is set the problem of detecting a similar relation between a third diagram (C) and one of five other diagrams ($D_1$ to $D_5$). This problem is actually used in intelligence tests for schoolchildren in the United States. The computer first investigates the similarities and the relation between A and B. For instance, it ascertains that the rectangle $P_2$ is located inside the triangle $P_3$ and that the dot $P_1$ is above the triangle and above the rectangle, and so on. It also investigates whether the similarity changes on rotation of the diagram through 180 degrees. The computer then proceeds to examine how the five other diagrams correspond to C, and it finally picks out the one whose relation to C differs least from the relation of B to A. It thus selects $D_2$ — that is, the pair of diagrams (C, $D_2$) is found to match the given pair (A, B) most closely.

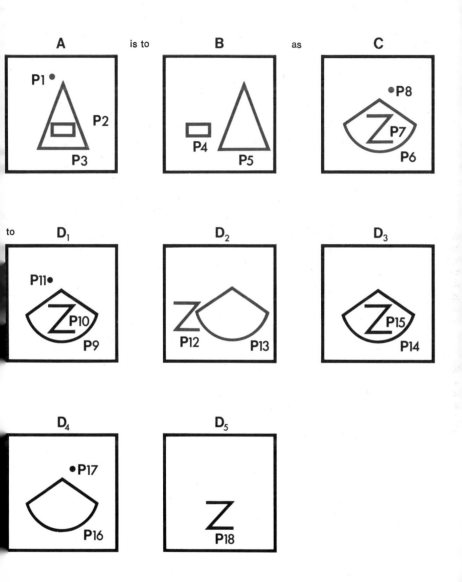

**A** is to **B** as **C**

to **D₁** **D₂** **D₃**

**D₄** **D₅**

FIG. 1   INTELLIGENCE TEST PROGRAM ACCORDING TO T. EVANS

235

# INDEX